A FAMILY OF READERS

THE BOOK LOVER'S GUIDE
TO CHILDREN'S AND YOUNG ADULT LITERATURE

ROGER SUTTON

AND

MARTHA V. PARRAVANO

Editors of *The Horn Book Magazine*

Foreword by
GREGORY MAGUIRE

CANDLEWICK PRESS

Portions of this book previously appeared in *The Horn Book Magazine.*

Text copyright © 2010 by The Horn Book, Inc., Roger Sutton, and Martha V. Parravano

Illustration credits appear on pages 344–345.

First paperback edition 2011

The Library of Congress has cataloged the hardcover edition as follows:

Sutton, Roger.
A family of readers : the book lover's guide to children's and young adult literature /
Roger Sutton and Martha V. Parravano. — 1st ed.
p.   cm.
ISBN 978-0-7636-3280-9 (hardcover)
1. Children's literature — History and criticism.   2. Children — Books and reading.
3. Young adults — Books and reading.   4. Reading — Parent participation.
I. Parravano, Martha V. II. Title.
PN1009.A1S8795 2010
809'.89282 — dc22   2009049104

ISBN 978-0-7636-5755-0 (paperback)

11 12 13 14 15 16 RRC 10 9 8 7 6 5 4 3 2 1

Printed in Crawfordsville, IN, U.S.A.

This book was typset in Chaparral Pro.

Candlewick Press
99 Dover Street
Somerville, Massachusetts 02144

visit us at www.candlewick.com

For our Horn Book family, past and present,
and

For Richard and Buster
R. S.

For my daughters, Emily and Ellie
M. V. P.

Foreword

Gregory Maguire

Some years ago, when the Boston Public Library was considering closing a few branches, I wrote to the *Boston Globe*. To make fresh a point about the value of reading, I mentioned Bill Watterson's popular comic strip, *Calvin and Hobbes*. Remember, I suggested, how many times Calvin is pictured standing in gloomy half-light by the bedside of his parents, who are either lying there groggy, disbelieving, or are bolting upright, horrified. Whenever Calvin is alarming his drowsy parents, glance at the bedside table. Under the lamp. You'll always find a book upside-down on spread pages, half-read. Calvin's parents are *always* in the middle of a book. Is it any wonder that Calvin has the cranial firepower of a Merlin, a Charles Dickens, a Steven Spielberg? He comes from a reading family.

The venerable *Horn Book Magazine* is eighty-six years old. When I first came across it as an undergraduate, the journal was only fifty-two years old (though it spoke with Solomonic confidence born of the convictions of its erudite editor, Paul Heins). As I've grown older, it has grown young — partly because its current editor in chief and executive editor, Roger Sutton and Martha V. Parravano, know that to evaluate contemporary books they are obliged to pay closer attention to contemporary life than earlier editors might have done. The world changes faster than it used to (or is that just me?).

It's grown young as I've aged because children beginning to read are almost always young. A secret benefit of working on the sidelines of children's literature is that access to the newest of children's books is better than Botox at rejuvenation. Watching the dubious reader experience the nitroglycerine jolt of the right book at the right time is one thrill that never grows old.

The Horn Book Magazine is to children's books what the *Blue Book* is to automobile assessments. (Yes, it can be wrong, too: inflated here, distracted there. But only often enough to keep its devoted readers on their toes, kicking the tires of recommended books for themselves.) I bet Calvin's parents flip through *The Horn Book* at their local library, or maybe even have their own subscription. As a parent, I read every issue cover to cover the day it arrives.

Maybe I'm something of an anomaly—but hey, so is Calvin. And I like that company.

Once upon a time, the more authoritarian of *Horn Book* editors—including my dear departed friends Paul and Ethel Heins—would have frowned at my choosing a comic-strip character as a thematic device to introduce a discussion about books and reading. They'd have preferred a fairy-tale favorite: Cinderella, Bluebeard, Rapunzel. Or someone from the classic British fantasies—Alice, Peter Pan, Pooh. They'd have expected (or anyway hoped) that every family would recognize the names of those new-world kids Tom Sawyer, Jo March, Anne of Green Gables, or the Ingalls family of all those little houses in the wilderness.

And since they never neglected to consider what the latest wave of immigrants might be best able to appreciate, they might have suggested I draw on one of those picture-book masterpieces so often known by one name, the way children think of themselves: Madeline. Babar. Eloise. If I *were* to strike out, to dare modernity, I'd be expected to turn to established twentieth-century heroes like Harriet the Spy, the Great Gilly Hopkins, or M.C. Higgins, the Great.

For me to instead employ a pint-size anarchist from the funny pages—what has reading come to? How has the nation's literary life devolved if, in hoping to speak to everyone in the room, I need to rely on a pop-culture figure?

Those earlier enthusiasts for children's books were old-fashioned, yes, but not stodgy. They thought hard and well. After a while, they'd have understood. The worthy missionaries who stocked the libraries we frequented in our childhoods, who talked up new books into classics, these pioneers were not only keen on narrative and cunning on message. They were visually literate, too. Those *Horn Book* editors of the past would recognize that the book on the bedside table of Calvin's parents might more likely be *Charlotte's Web* or *Monster* or *When You Reach Me* than the latest bestseller on the *New York Times* adult list. That open book, caught in mid-story, might well be something that *The Horn Book Magazine* recommends with a starred review. After all, those parents were two-thirds of a family of readers. (Or one-half, if you count Hobbes, and maybe you have to.) Those parents were smart. They knew what they were doing.

Picking up this book, so do you.

TABLE OF CONTENTS

PART TWO: READING WITH THEM

PART THREE: READING ON THEIR OWN

CHAPTER SIX: NONFICTION

PART FOUR: LEAVING THEM ALONE

Introduction
Roger Sutton

Once upon a time, a title like *A Family of Readers* would have called up cozy images of reading by the fireplace — Ma reading aloud, Pa whittling, the children listening respectfully. But today, debates about what qualifies as "reading" are as noisy as the concurrent fights over what can be called a "family." In this book we have no uncertainty: a family is a group of at least two people who care about one another; by reading, we mean books. Right about now you may be sensing that this is a book that features informed opinions from passionate readers, not bland lists of dos, don'ts, and "surefire recommendations." You are right. This is not a book for parents who badly want their children to read but are "too busy" to read for their own pleasure. It's for parents who wish their children would be a wee bit more understanding when Mom or Dad is lost in a book. If the thought of looking up from your dinner — and your book — and seeing heads bowed in pursuance of same is your idea of a good time, you're in the right place.

But your passion for reading isn't necessarily accompanied by a knowledge of children's books, and that's where we come in. In *A Family of Readers*, we seek to provide parents and other interested adults with an essential understanding of books for children and teenagers. Grown-up readers can be a bit like the twins John and Barbara in P. L. Travers's *Mary Poppins*. As babies, the twins happily converse with the sunlight and the wind and the starling who visits through the nursery window until the dark day arrives when they respond to the bird's greeting with gurgles and "Be-lah-belah-belah-belah!" Not only had they forgotten the "language of the sunlight and the stars," but they had forgotten they ever knew it. Adults can be like this with children's books, looking for utility or edification, and completely forgetting what drew them into reading in the first place. Given the chance, kids will read the same way adults do: for themselves. Don't think of books for young people as tools; try instead to treat them as invitations into the reading life.

That life can be a rich place, comprised of the highbrow and the lowdown, the casual and the ambitious, private reading and public sharing. As a parent in that landscape, you'll need to be sometimes traveling companion, sometimes guide, sometimes off in your own part of the forest. A relationship between readers is complicated and cannot be reduced to such "strategies" as mandatory reading aloud, a commendable family activity whose pleasure has been codified into virtue, transforming the nightly bedtime story into a harbinger of everybody's favorite thing: homework. For more than eighty years, *The Horn Book* has been saying that reading is its own reward, for children and adults alike.

A Reading Child

I learned how to read in the first grade. There was no public kindergarten in my town; nor were there early-learning methods of parenting (kindergarten was seen as "progressive," and *parenting* was not yet a verb). I don't remember if my teacher, Miss Weber, drilled us in phonics or whole-word recognition, but I remember with clarity the exercise that earned me my first book. Miss Weber would divide us into pairs and send us in staggered shifts to corners of the classroom to sit on the floor and read aloud from See Sally Run–type primers. (Such books come in for much abuse these days, but I have to say that I loved Macmillan's primer *Ted and Sally*.) When we had completed ten stories in this fashion, Miss Weber would reward us with a new hardcover book. Mine was Betty Baker and Arnold Lobel's *Little Runner of the Longhouse,* a product of Harper's I Can Read glory days. It was a prize: while children don't consciously read to improve themselves, they do appreciate accomplishment.

Little Runner of the Longhouse joined the books that had been part of my preschool landscape at home. Robert Lawson's *They Were Strong and Good* and Elizabeth Guilfoile's *Nobody Listens to Andrew* were the first books I loved. I have no recollection of how either book came into the house; they seemed to have always been there. For children, books are just as much physical objects — like the furniture or the cat — as they are "vessels of meaning." (This is not an identification limited to childhood; think of your dog-eared copy of *Dune*.) The favorite ones, particularly, have a specific physicality apart from their content. I remember the Lawson book mostly physically, as I often scrutinized individual pictures from it at some length. I loved the dark, dramatic lines but completely missed the humor. *Andrew* evokes a different experience, that of knowing a story by heart and of an intense identification with the hero, whose news cannot wait and is truly important: there's a *bear* in his bed.

The important thing is that those books were there for me to find. I'm reminded of the artist Judy Chicago's remark to the assistants with whom she was creating "Womanhouse." The assistants said they would buy a hammer when the need suggested it, but Chicago countered that already having a hammer suggests the need to do something with it. Books work the same way. It's great when a kid fired with enthusiasm for a hobby or a celebrity or an extinct species can read a book that abets and stokes his or her interest. But it's better still to have the potential afforded by reading already in place, both in the reader's fluency and in the shape of lots of things to read. A reader's life will contain annotations to its nature and events in the books that have accompanied it.

By the fourth grade, I was completely into it. I became something of a party trick for my parents after I read *The Scarlet Letter* in emulation of my sister, Anne, who was reading it in high school. One of my earliest book reviews —"I liked best the part where Hester and the minister rolled around in the woods"— always got a big laugh. At school, we had one of those paperback book clubs, where a seductive leaflet would list all the possible purchases for that month. Pondering the choices was an engrossing activity of about a week's duration for me, and I endured the lessons of delayed gratification while waiting for the books to arrive. The teacher handed them out with some ceremony, calling each pupil to her desk and announcing the choices. Did I know what would happen when she proclaimed that I had purchased a book called *Mary Jane*? The book, a story about two black teenagers integrating an all-white school, remained a favorite for many years, but I have never forgiven that teacher for joining in the laughter that greeted her indiscretion.

I have now been working with children and books for thirty years, and I rely perhaps too much on my own history as a lifelong, die-hard bookworm. I can understand the concept of the "reluctant reader," but for me it's akin to saying somebody really doesn't like to eat. Or breathe. I was what the late *Horn Book* editor Ethel Heins called a "reading child." The questions I ask as the current editor of *The Horn Book* are the ones I think necessary for the welfare of today's "reading children": How do we give children the skills and opportunity to read? How do we create books that both interest and respect them? How do we allow children mastery and ownership of their reading? How do we know when to guide, and when to leave a reader alone?

Blowing the Horn

The Horn Book Magazine has a long history of grappling with these questions. Founded in 1924, it grew out of the "suggested purchase" lists compiled by Bertha Mahony Miller as proprietor of Boston's Bookshop for Boys and Girls, established in 1918. The Bookshop was closed in 1936, but the magazine thrived in concert with the rise of children's book publishing and the establishment of children's departments in the nation's public libraries. Throughout *The Horn Book*'s history it has responded both to the events of the moment — new immigrants, the space race (Isaac Asimov was a columnist for many years), the civil rights movement — and to its constant mission, announced in the first issue, to "blow the horn for fine books for boys and girls." *The Horn Book*'s critical standards have always been high (by our lights, anyway; others have called us stuffy and worse!), and our foremost concerns are for literary and pictorial achievement in books for children; the potential popularity or "usefulness" of a given title is secondary.

In this book, executive editor Martha Parravano and I, aided by the work of our editorial colleagues, reviewers, and contributors, hope to bring *The Horn Book*'s point of view to an audience we generally reach only through the librarians and teachers who already know us. It is a book for *readers,* people who need books as much as food or air, and whose idea of the perfect vacation and / or evening meal is to have more time to read. We shall begin with books for the youngest children and proceed on up through pre-readers to new readers, to the evolving independent reader, to the one who reads with friends, to the one who needs to be left alone. In each section we offer an introductory essay, giving our sense of the challenges and opportunities in the literature for a particular age group. We then ask our experts, mainly *Horn Book* reviewers who specialize in particular genres, to weigh in: What are the great children's fantasies? Why are joke books important? Then we invite others, including artists, authors, and designers, to add their views and experiences. In her essay, the New Zealand author Margaret Mahy talks about the "inner echoing library" of children's books that we carry inside us: the contributors to this book have the good fortune of having especially well-stocked shelves to share. Some contributors relate personal moments with a book and child that we hope resonate with you. Others sort out the characteristics that make for a particularly good version of a canonical book or story — such as Mother Goose collections, or "The Three Little Pigs," or the thriller genre. Each chapter ends with a selection of recent books of the pertinent genre; in the very back of this book, you will see lists of all the books recommended here, organized loosely by age group.

A Family of Readers is not meant to be a buying guide; we know readers too well for that. We hope that spending time with us — listening to us, learning from us, even disagreeing with us — will help sharpen your own sense of what makes books work with young people. As we *are* readers, we *respect* readers, and it is in that spirit of companionship and conversation that we present you what we have learned in decades of reading, reviewing, sharing books, and paying attention to the reactions of child readers.

Why do kids read? They read because they are made to, of course, but they also read — via media in a multitude of forms — because they want to find something out, or they want to join their imagination with somebody else's. I will say it again: *They read for the same reasons adults do.*

PART ONE
READING TO THEM

Overview
Martha V. Parravano

R eading to Them" is a useful rubric, but not one to be taken literally. The reading that happens with a child on your lap — or cuddled with you in a chair, or through the slats of a crib, or around a low table in the toddlers' section of a library — is rarely linear. It is a complex give-and-take that falls somewhere along the interactive spectrum, depending on the specific book being read, the age of the child, the relationship of the adult and child, even the time of day. But in general, reading with small children is more sharing than telling, and more activity than lesson.

With a one-year-old baby, you may be the one reading the book aloud, but the baby will probably want to turn the pages herself. With an enthusiastic toddler, reading can be a joyfully communal activity, resulting in an experience that is at once aural (listening as the adult reads), visual (looking at the pictures), vocal (identifying objects, imitating animal sounds, joining in on a text's familiar refrain, asking questions about or commenting on story or art), and kinetic (pointing at pictured objects, mimicking a character, acting out a Mother Goose rhyme). Preschoolers may memorize chunks of text — or whole books — and may want to do the "reading" themselves, with adults or siblings or stuffed animals as audience. (There are many excellent titles that manage to be both satisfying picture book experience and reading primer: from classics such as *Brown Bear, Brown Bear, What Do You See?* and *How Do I Put It On?* to newer titles such as Laura Vaccaro Seeger's *Dog and Bear* and Emily Gravett's *Orange Pear Apple Bear,* to name just a few.)

I think of picture books as stores of transferable potential energy. Rarely, if ever, is the child a total nonparticipant in the "reading to them" equation. A seemingly passive listener may be quietly absorbing story and pictures, storing up enough experience with the book until he is eventually ready to interact more fully. As a three-year-old, my younger daughter was delayed in her speech development and preferred balls and playgrounds to books. I persisted in reading to her, though — lots of Mother Goose, Peggy Rathmann, Byron Barton, Eve Rice, Nancy Tafuri, Lucy Cousins, and Donald Crews. A particular favorite, read night after night, was William Steig's *Doctor De Soto,* in which a mouse dentist and his clever wife outwit a scheming fox. Ellie, basically languageless, never joined in the reading as did her very verbal older sister, but seemed to listen and enjoy. Then late one evening after a very long day, returning from a family vacation, we sat in a crowded DC-10 surrounded by a horde of unrepentantly rowdy high-school hockey players. Ellie sank lower and lower in her seat, trying to get as far away from them as possible. Suddenly she stood up and yelled as loudly as she could, "*No one will see you again, said the fox to himself*" — verbatim, from *Doctor De Soto.* This rather surreal (to the hockey players) statement earned her a few seconds of blessed (and stunned) silence. For me, it reinforced my belief in "reading to them." What pours out of a picture book through repeated readings by an adult reader will eventually be reinvested by the child listener.

There's a simple, benignly empowering part most children can play in the picture-book transaction: turning the pages. If a child is allowed to turn the pages of a picture book himself, whether he is looking at it independently or listening to an adult read, he is in control of the experience. He can choose when to speed up and when to slow down; when to linger on a particularly absorbing spread and when to rush excitedly on to find out what happens on the next page or, conversely, to skip the boring bits. A child turning the pages of a picture book not only learns to exercise power on an age-appropriate scale but also learns about story and pacing and begins to define his own literary and visual likes and dislikes.

Reading to children does not necessarily require traditional picture books. A baby's diet of board books can be supplemented by homemade scrapbooks or family photo albums, or engagingly photographed clothing or toy catalogs, or colorful nature magazines. A five-year-old might want to be read beginning readers and early chapter books as well as picture books. But the reverse is true as well. One needn't ever grow out of picture books — especially now, when more and more picture books are aimed at older elementary-age children. And in this image-ascendant age, visual literacy is arguably becoming at least as important as verbal literacy. The skill of navigating through picture books will translate directly to navigating through, say, graphic novels. In fact, picture books give young readers a basic structural sense of how to tell a story in words and images, and that narrative DNA is all the more important when they leave the thirty-two–page structure. One can think of the picture book as finger exercises on the piano — you return to them even after you've moved on to more complex forms. In any case, it would be a shame to confuse format of book with quality of experience or to deprive a child of the treasures of the picture-book world.

In the ever-shifting continuum of "reading to them" — an evolving range of books, situations, and participants — there remains the ideal of the parent, the child, and the picture book. So much contributes to the unique success of this ideal interaction — even its physical shape. Consider a small child sitting on his mother's lap while she reads him a picture book. The picture book opens to a width that effectively places the child at the center of a closed circle — that of mother's body, arms, and picture book. Or perhaps the child is too big or too independent to sit on a parent's lap — he sits next to her, one person holding the left side of the open picture book, the other the right side. Again, a circle. I don't think it's an accident that so much adult-child book-sharing forms and takes place within a circle, or that so many picture books open to a size that facilitates one. That circle, so private and intimate, is a place apart from the demands and stresses of daily life, a sanctuary in and from which the child can explore the many worlds offered in picture books. Despite all of our society's technological advances, it still just takes one child, one book, and one reader to create this unique space, to work this everyday magic.

Once established, of course, the space grows elastic and expands as the child grows. It stretches to the length and shape of a parent in an armchair reading to a five-year-old in bed, an audiobook entertaining a family on a road trip, a teacher standing before a hushed, enthralled classroom.

But all that comes later. Let's begin with books for the very young.

Chapter One

BOOKS FOR BABIES

A Future of Page Turns
Martha V. Parravano

Babies don't need complex stories, elaborate artwork, or high educational content. Books for babies can be as simple as Tana Hoban's groundbreaking series of wordless black-and-white board books (*Black on White; White on Black*), with their high-contrast images of bibs, pacifiers, stuffed animals, and other homely objects associated with newborns. But though the books themselves may be simple, the interaction is anything but: with board books a baby is honing his visual and listening skills, bonding with the adult reader, and, yes, taking the first steps toward literacy. Every time an adult reads a book with a baby, she is passing on an essential building block of literacy: the page turn. The mechanics of reading—the fact that in order to read a book one has to turn its pages—is a basic skill, but it has to be learned. The page turn—the progression of left to right and front to back (at least in our Western culture)—is the foundation of reading. As an adult reader shares a book with a baby, she is transmitting that essential knowledge, the key to later literacy.

Babies watch with remarkable intentness the components of their universe: faces, their own hands, a mobile. First board books should be a barely differentiated extension of that small universe.

It's not necessary to use books to expand a baby's world—a *reflection* is more than sufficient.

Babies respond to books that promote interaction—animal sounds, vehicle noises, movements, opportunities to name objects or body parts. Pictures in books for babies are not only visual feasts for the baby but prompts for parental commentary. Any book a parent reads to a baby, even a wordless one, will be an opportunity for expressive language, be it a re-creation of animal sounds or the naming of objects or the creation of spontaneous stories to go with the pictures.

Board books are specifically made for babies: with their stiff, sturdy cardboard pages, nontoxic materials, and glossy wipability, they will survive teething, spills, spit-up, and worse—anything a baby can throw at them (sometimes literally). The most successful board-book creators tap into babies' enthusiasms, attention spans, and (occasionally) senses of humor. Helen Oxenbury's series of oversize board books, *All Fall Down, Clap Hands, Say Goodnight*, and *Tickle, Tickle*, features four diverse, active toddlers in an implied day-care setting singing, clapping, falling about, and waving—all with toddler-appropriate energy and warmth. Rosemary Wells's Max books are about the power struggle between a willful baby rabbit and his bossy older sister, Ruby. In *Max's First Word*, Ruby tries to persuade Max to name various innocuous household objects, but "Max's one word was BANG!" Wells connects with her young audience because she is funny, able to shape plot and character with the briefest of texts, and *always* on Max's side.

One distinction to be aware of is between board books conceived originally for the format and those that started life as full-size picture books. Board books are big business for publishers. Consumers love board books, for good reason: compared to picture books, they're less expensive, more durable, and more portable—easier to tuck into a bag already bursting with snacks, extra clothes, toys, games, crayons, and puzzles. But beware: a board-book version of a picture book most probably reflects some compromises made necessary by the format change. While standard picture books have thirty-two pages, board books can have as few as twelve. So board books that are adapted from picture books must either conflate pages (taking the text and art from, say, two spreads of the original picture book and cramming it onto one page) or drop material altogether.

Ann Herbert Scott's *On Mother's Lap* is a classic picture book about sibling rivalry and familial love. It features a generous design based on double-page-spreads; a simple text; and a small, satisfying story. When Michael, a young Inuit boy, has the chance to snuggle with his mother in her rocking chair while his baby sister naps, he is anxious to include all his favorite things — his reindeer blanket, doll, toy boat, and puppy — in the experience. But when Baby wakes up, he balks at including her. "There isn't room," he says jealously. Mother persuades him to give it a try, and Michael finally admits that "it feels good." The book ends with an iconic picture of family warmth and togetherness, with Michael's mother telling him, "It's a funny thing . . . but there is always room on Mother's lap."

The board-book version (at four by six inches) is too small to be a satisfying lap read; it excises two crucial setup illustrations and an entire double-page spread that depicts the conflict (so that, oddly, the board-book version has resolution but no conflict); and it's not meant for babies. It is clearly older brother Michael who is the center of the story, Michael with whom readers are meant to identify. Despite the simplicity of text and layout, this story of a boy dealing with his feelings about a new baby is meant for older siblings, not babies.

A more successful translation from picture book to board book is Anne and Harlow Rockwell's *The Toolbox*. Because the original picture book was aimed at very young children, the pictures (of a saw, a hammer and nails, pliers, and so on) are paramount, set against expanses of white space; the text is extremely brief, almost always one line per page; and the subject matter is of interest to many small children. The board-book version is a complete representation of the original, with no illustrations or transitions omitted, and it's fully two-thirds the size of the original picture book.

The challenge, of course, is how to judge a brand-new board book gleaming up at you from its place on the bookstore shelf. After all, *Goodnight Moon* is just as good in board-book form — better, perhaps, since the board-book version is virtually indestructible. Peggy Rathmann's subversively funny *Good Night, Gorilla* is also a perfect fit as a board book (and its glossier pages make it even easier to spot the runaway balloon on every spread). Janet and Allan Ahlberg's delightful *Each Peach, Pear, Plum,* a must for the nursery, is 99 percent successful (the last page, with all the hidden fairy-tale characters, is perhaps a little cluttered in the smaller size). But as you're standing in the bookstore, it won't be immediately obvious to you which books work and which don't. Publishers don't advertise the fact that they've conflated pages or dropped pictures to make a board-book version of a picture book, and the original picture book is not always available to scrutinize for a page-by-page comparison — even if one had the leisure to do so. In any case, it's not the paring down of pages per se that is so egregious: it's the resultant loss of meaning and story shape. I pity the children (and parents) who know only the butchered versions of some of the best children's picture books — such as unworthy recent board-book editions of *Caps for Sale* and *Mike Mulligan and His Steam Shovel.* They will never know what they're missing.

My best advice is to read a board book as you would any picture book before purchasing it. In that way you can see for yourself whether it holds together as a story, whether it feels like a whole or seems truncated, and whether it's aimed at babies and toddlers or is really better suited to older children.

Choosing original board books — those created specifically for the format — is easier, as long as you don't let yourself get sucked into the latest publishing trend. As publishers have discovered that

From picture book to board book: Peggy Rathmann's *Good Night, Gorilla* makes the transition with great success. (Note how the cover makes an immediate connection between the mischievous gorilla and the child audience—an irresistible invitation to young readers.)

board books make great baby-shower gifts, for instance, we see bookstore shelves filled with titles like *Urban Babies Wear Black*—a hoot for hipster moms but unlikely to appeal to babies, whose interests do not yet extend to art galleries or yoga or, indeed, the concept of urban chic.

Board books seem to be more vulnerable to publishing trends than many other genres and therefore tend to go out of print quickly. (Lesson learned: if you find something your child loves, buy multiple copies!) One of my daughters' favorite books when they were babies was *Let's Make a Noise* by Amy MacDonald and Maureen

Roffey. It was a perfect first board book: pure, simple interaction. "Let's make a noise like a dog (train, cat, truck, sheep, baby)!" It was the enthusiastic and communal encouragement of making the noise that worked so well, as well as the clean, bright, cheerful pictures of the named objects and animals. (An added bonus: the noise the baby makes is "WAAAAH," allowing lots of room for imitation and dramatic expression.)

Two new board books by photographer Margaret Miller are masterpieces of minimalism: each contains just six close-up photographs of babies' faces, with one or two words on facing pages. *I Love Colors* shows a vocal baby wearing a red bow on her head, a serious baby in purple heart-shaped glasses, a happy baby with an orange flower tucked behind one ear, a shy baby peering through a plastic green ring — each photograph tightly focused and absolutely engrossing. *What's on My Head?* is similarly captivating and also quite funny, as the items perching on the subjects' heads — a rubber ducky? — are sometimes unexpected, but always familiar and baby-pleasing.

Baby Happy, Baby Sad by Leslie Patricelli homes in on recognizable baby emotions, tapping into babies' basic realities. With its repeated, limited vocabulary and its humorous, expressive illustrations picturing "Baby HAPPY" (Baby holding a balloon or cavorting au naturel) and "Baby SAD" (Baby gazing up at the loosed balloon or swathed in a confining snowsuit), it is an excellent introduction to the concepts of happiness and sadness — as well as opposites.

Sandra Boynton's must-have *Blue Hat, Green Hat* knows exactly what babies find funny, eliciting laughs even as it explores two concepts of interest (colors and clothes). While the other three animals model the various articles of clothing with deadpan aplomb, the hapless turkey is completely unschooled in how to wear a hat (he stands in it) or how to put on pants (he puts them on his head). The text, brief and straightforward, is infectiously interactive: "Blue hat, green hat, red hat, OOPS!" The word *oops* — short and punchy but with that croonable long *ooooo* — is amazingly fun to say (or shout)

out loud, especially when all concerned know that it's coming at the end of every spread and anticipate it. "Oops!" provides punctuation to the proceedings that will amuse babies and toddlers for reading after rereading. (Boynton's *Moo, Baa, La La La!* — pure fun from the title on — is another crowd pleaser.)

Note the tight focus all these board books purposefully keep — the minimal backgrounds in the illustrations; the hewing to familiar objects and concepts; the brevity of the texts; the physical humor or action; the familiar, comforting emotions. Full-size picture books that babies love follow a similar formula. Books by Byron Barton (*Machines at Work; Dinosaurs, Dinosaurs*) are surefire winners, with their direct, no-nonsense language ("Hey, you guys! Let's get to work!"); simple, eye-catching illustrations, often in primary colors; and perennially fascinating topics (machines, astronauts, construction workers, dinosaurs). Look for tried-and-true children's book creators Tana Hoban, Margaret Wise Brown, Donald Crews, Eric Carle, Anne Rockwell, Vera B. Williams, and Eve Rice and their successors Mem Fox, Emily Gravett, Leslie Patricelli, Kevin Henkes, and Wong Herbert Yee — all of whom seem to have a direct line to small children's likes and dislikes, fears and joys. Satoru Onishi's *Who's Hiding?* is a virtual lineup of animals (eighteen of which stand in an array looking straight out at the reader) in which babies guess which one is facing backward, which one is angry, or which one is missing on a progression of spreads. The distractions are nil; the concepts are age-appropriate; the fascination level is high. Lynn Reiser and Penny Gentieu's picture books *You and Me, Baby* and *My Baby & Me* couldn't be simpler — just clear, wholly engaging photographs of babies from diverse backgrounds interacting with parents and preschool siblings.

For parents interested in giving babies the gift of a love of language, it's never too early to introduce Mother Goose. To read Mother Goose rhymes aloud is to hear the music in language. A good Mother Goose collection is like that magic self-replenishing pot in the folktale: never empty, with something for everyone, for every mood, for every time of day. Shout the rambunctious "Jelly on a plate, / Jelly on a plate, / Wibble, wobble, wibble, wobble, / Jelly on a plate"; growl the swaggering "I'm Dusty Bill / From Vinegar Hill, / Never had a bath / And I never will"; whisper the lullaby of "Come, crow! Go, crow! / Baby's sleeping sound, / And the wild plums grow in the jungle, / Only a penny a pound. / Only a penny a pound, Baba, / Only a penny a pound." (Joanna Rudge Long's "What Makes a Good Mother Goose?" — a more in-depth look at this nursery essential — follows on the next page.)

Babies' reading is no different from that of any other age in one important respect: it can be solitary as well as communal. True, a baby will get to know books first by mouth, and only later by eye and ear, and will need an adult to introduce her to the wonders they contain. But soon that same baby will be reaching out from her parent's lap to turn the book's pages, and then sitting by herself, poring over her book, turning the pages, and "reading" to herself. She will have taken the first steps toward a future of page turns.

What Makes a Good Mother Goose?

Joanna Rudge Long

It is a truth universally acknowledged that every English-speaking child is the better for an early friendship with Mother Goose — "early" meaning from birth, because nothing boosts language development better than those catchy rhymes and rhythms. Scholars and educators alike praise the virtues and resonances of these traditional rhymes. They are essentials of both popular culture and our literary heritage; they stimulate young imaginations; reading, saying, or singing them draws parents and children together in shared delight. Best of all, those beloved, familiar, playful, nonsensical verses are just plain fun.

Mother Goose rhymes have appeared in print for more than two hundred years. Since nineteenth-century illustrator Randolph Caldecott elaborated on verses like "Hey Diddle, Diddle" and "Bye, Baby Bunting" with his ebullient caricatures of English country life, hundreds of illustrators have adapted the rhymes to their own styles and sensibilities. A few of these collections endure; many more have fallen by the wayside, even such treasures as L. Leslie Brooke's 1922 *Ring o' Roses*.

Illustrations for Mother Goose come in several flavors. The most widely accepted are often the sweetest; Kate Greenaway and Jessie Willcox Smith set the tone with their pretty children in the rural, period settings many people associate with nursery rhymes. More stimulating to young imaginations is the kind of rambunctious vigor initiated by Caldecott, carried on by Brooke, and adapted with idiosyncratic verve by such luminaries as Roger Duvoisin, Raymond Briggs, Amy Schwartz, and Michael Foreman — vigor that reflects the outlandish characters and shenanigans in the verse itself. Editions for different audiences have always appeared in different shapes and sizes, from board books featuring single rhymes to the eminent folklorists Peter and Iona Opie's scholarly tomes. Those for the youngest may contain just a few familiar verses, copiously illustrated. Older children can explore fat volumes with hundreds of rhymes, including additional, often omitted verses for well-known rhymes. Smaller volumes may have a particular focus. In *To Market! To Market!,* Peter Spier sets a score of rhymes in the early nineteenth-century market town of New Castle, Delaware. Leonard S. Marcus and Amy Schwartz celebrate the foolish, the disappointed, and various miscreants in a merry take on *Mother Goose's Little Misfortunes.* Robert Sabuda's virtuoso pop-up, *The Movable Mother Goose,* features arresting graphic design as well as extraordinary paper engineering. With *We Are All in the Dumps with Jack and Guy,* Maurice Sendak turns two hitherto unrelated rhymes into a fantasy on urban poverty, social responsibility, and compassion. Versatile Mother Goose provides a rewarding venue for many such creative endeavors.

Each of these books is a world unto itself; to enter one is to go to a place both rich and strange, whether pretty and placid or comically offbeat. Mother Goose is read, reread, chanted, and pored over with a special imaginative intensity.

The collection my children almost wore out was Raymond Briggs's *The Mother Goose Treasury.* Robust, earthy, and sporting more than four hundred verses, Briggs's book features clean, uncluttered pages with lots of spot art; sequenced vignettes for longer dramas; colorful, action-packed full-page art; and a marvelous array of characters — seedy or cranky, feckless or determined, often mischievous, rarely prim.

Now, though there's a plethora of Mother Geese in print, Briggs's isn't among them. It's well known that the swing from the verbal to the visual within the last generation has remodeled not only tastes but the very way children perceive. No longer is it acceptable for color to alternate with black and white; children today expect all color, all the time, and are accustomed to a more generous supply of illustrations. Busy parents are content to settle for a relatively brief collection, perhaps supplemented with picture books spun from single verses.

Fortunately, in this new climate, there are still good choices, big and small, sweet or silly or pungent or all three. Iona Opie's *My Very First Mother Goose* (along with its companion volume, *Here Comes Mother Goose*), illustrated by Rosemary Wells, is a lap-friendly charmer, with large type, ample dimensions, and bright colors. Though some characters are human, more are animals, especially cats, mice, and bunnies. "Little Jumping Joan" is a black, rope-skipping rabbit who doubles as the narrator of "I had a little nut tree" — who better to "skip over water, dance over sea"? Mischievous, anxious, earnestly hardworking, gleeful, or affectionately cuddly, these appealing animal characters will be familiar to readers of Wells's many popular picture books. Also, using them is a tactful way to sidestep the issue of racial balance.

An illustrator of Mother Goose has many such choices, each a chance for creative interpretation. For example, Wells's "brave old duke of York" — a benevolent-looking gent, pajama-clad and portly — watches his *toy* soldiers march up and down a hill built of fat books. (Observant tots may notice that the march ends in a wastebasket; see the illustration on the next page.) The pussycat

Oh, the brave old duke of York,
    He had ten thousand men;
He marched them up to the top of the hill,
    And he marched them down again.
And when they were up, they were up,
And when they were down, they were down,
And when they were only halfway up,
    They were neither up nor down.

who says he "frightened a little mouse under [the queen's] chair" is evidently fibbing — it's the cat who exhibits alarm here, while the mouse, clearly a privileged personage, sticks out her tongue at him. Just about every verse has such nifty details to discover in successive "readings" of the pictures.

With just sixty-eight rhymes, most of them short (or without their final verses), *My Very First Mother Goose* is a fine place to begin. Eventually, however, the well-read child will need a more comprehensive collection. An example is *Mary Engelbreit's Mother Goose*, one hundred rhymes visualized in Engelbreit's old-timey greeting-card style, the round-faced characters reliably cute and pink-cheeked (even the lambs and unicorn). The selections, chosen with the help of critic Leonard S. Marcus, are excellent, as is his introduction, peppered with such sage insights as "It is one of the happy truths about Mother Goose verses that it is absolutely impossible to sound *too* foolish while saying them" and "These days, the first rhymes most children know are those . . . in television commercials. Against this backdrop, wise old Mother Goose holds out a refreshing, life-enhancing alternative: equally irresistible rhymes with nothing to sell."

Two of the best of the more comprehensive volumes still in print came out in the 1980s. With its quaint, innocent-looking figures and childlike drawing style, *Tomie dePaola's Mother Goose* (with 204 rhymes) is immediately appealing. But there's much more going on in dePaola's art than the casual reader may notice at first. His figures — so decorative, so comfortably arrayed in their ample white space — are also subtly expressive; his sophisticated juxtapositions of light, bright colors are unexpectedly harmonious; his elegantly balanced compositions include just enough action and detail to inspire young imaginations to fill out the stories for themselves. Arrangement of the rhymes, from an unusual fifteen stanzas about Mother Goose herself to a series of bedtime entries (closing with two prayers), is coherent. All in all, it's a book to have early and enjoy through childhood and beyond.

For somewhat older children, *The Arnold Lobel Book of Mother Goose* (306 rhymes; formerly titled *The Random House Book of Mother Goose*) is especially rich in variety, story, and visual imagery. Old standards with a full complement of extra verses; variants on the familiar plus much that's unfamiliar; couplets, riddles, limericks, ballads — all are grouped by subject (rain, say, or chickens), or by more tenuous links, and set to good advantage among a wealth of spot art, spreads, and vignettes. A string of small pictures may narrate a single story or multiple rhymes share a setting (the sea, rooms in a house, the moon). Borders sometimes fence the action, but elsewhere it escapes into large, dramatic vistas. Each freely drawn illustration is neatly self-contained, yet all are marshaled into exquisitely designed spreads. Characters are as lively and varied as all humanity, mostly comic or amiable but sometimes unexpectedly dark (a tiny Wee Willie Winkie issues an urgent warning among towering, angular buildings; the cow sweeps over the moon in an awesome celestial phenomenon). Creative touches abound: the crooked man is a cubist portrait; it's mice who like "pease porridge cold . . . nine days old"; London Bridge is a vertiginous, patched-together conglomeration. All in all, this is an ample and robust volume, vibrant with the many human conditions that gave rise to the rhymes in the first place: quirks, incongruities, injustices, nightmares, absurdities, laughter, hopes, dreams.

There's always room for another fresh take on the old favorites. In Leo and Diane Dillon's new *Mother Goose: Numbers on the Loose*, these gifted illustrators bring twenty-four rhymes to life in richly detailed mini-stories of their own invention. Like many a Mother Goose, it's a book for multiple ages: for preschoolers to enjoy the dancing rhymes and rhythms; for primary-age children learning their numbers; and for the older ones, who can appreciate and weave together the many imaginative pictorial details to tell the old stories anew.

So how do we choose among these treasures? As to illustrations, they should create an intriguing world, one to lure a child again and again. For the littlest, it's important to have durable pages, open format, clarity of design, and a preponderance of familiar verses to revisit until, ineluctably, they're learned by heart. These funny, often enigmatic verses beg for visual elaboration — look for illustrators who've made the best of their opportunities. Comparing the illustrations for a favorite rhyme in several collections is a good way to get to know different illustrators, to evaluate their styles, skills, and imaginative strengths, and to discover which ones suit you best.

As to content, a more comprehensive collection can be a grand conglomeration of thumbnail portraits and delicious nonsense, the lyrical and the raucous, sorrow and glee, the witty, the tragic, or — intriguingly — both at once. Tampering with texts is usually a bad thing, though there are exceptions (as those who remember the earlier version of "Eeny, meeny, miny, mo" will acknowledge). If there's much that's unfamiliar, a note on sources shows good faith on the part of the compiler. It's also good to have an introduction, such as Iona Opie provides for *My Very First Mother Goose*. Hers is an inspirational celebration, concluding with a playful alphabet of attributes. And who better than Opie herself to give us these last words, some of them as absurd as Mother Goose herself:

> Mother Goose will show newcomers to this world how astonishing, beautiful, capricious, dancy, eccentric, funny, goluptious, haphazard, intertwingled, joyous, kindly, loving, melodious, naughty, outrageous, pomsidillious, querimonious, romantic, silly, tremendous, unexpected, vertiginous, wonderful, x-citing, yo-heave-ho-ish, and zany it is.

Just so does Mother Goose continue to engage those tiny "newcomers."

TRASHING ELMO

GINEE SEO AND BRUCE BROOKS

When our son Drake was on the way, certain policies and principles regarding his childhood scarcely needed to be spoken — indeed, to mention them aloud would have seemed coarse, even insulting. For example:

WE WILL NOT CENSOR BOOKS AND TOYS.

But because Bruce has been through this business twice before (with Alex, now twenty-four, and Spencer, fifteen), he might have winced a bit at such a declaration. He is aware of something he calls the "Berenstain Loophole," first invoked shortly after Alex's second birthday. On that occasion, one of Alex's pals (with witless parents, obviously) slipped a wrapped package of two Berenstain Bears books in among the other guests' gifts of Hot Wheels racers and Playmobil emergency vehicles. Alas, Bruce — naif that he was — had no idea such . . . *printed matter* existed, so he failed to pounce and destroy until it was too late: Alex got his mom to read him the books several times in the next couple of days.

A disaster unfolded. One of the books related that Sister Bear was afraid of the dark. Her drippy terror played out in lurid imagery, to be solved on the last page by the purchase (suggested, of course, by that nonpareil of homespun wisdom, Mama Bear) of a night-light.

Until this point in his life, Alex was indifferent to the fact that something called the Dark even existed. It had never crossed his mind that the relative luminescence of his room was attached to a value system. Sometimes you could see everything, sometimes you couldn't—you went with what you got. Ah, but chez Berenstain, things were differently ordered, so for two weeks Alex decided that there was a Dark, and maybe he ought to be afraid of it. Bruce was finally subjected to the infamy of following the lead of Mama B.: he bought Alex a night-light.

So, functionally, Ginee-and-Bruce's new rule might read:

WE WILL NOT CENSOR BOOKS OR TOYS
UNLESS THEY ARE TOTAL CRAP.

Alas, this rule does not take into account adoring relatives, babysitters, friends of babysitters, pediatricians, and the nice man at the Rite Aid on Seventh Avenue. Even one's otherwise faultless friends can fall prey to a Thomas the Tank Engine beginner set—and après that, the deluge: the book-with-wheels cannot be far behind. So you do the inevitable (especially when the gift giver is present). You gamely read the thing in question, which may or may not have appendages and emit funny noises. You hope that will do it. But your child appears enchanted. "More?" he inquires, and then you are in for it, doomed to read the thing through at least three more times before suggesting an alternative ("Let's read *Freight Train!*") or a distraction ("Let's have a sugary snack!"). Later, at your leisure, you wrestle: Should I put this back in his book pile, or do the unimaginable and throw it away? A book. In the trash. Like the Nazis and the Branch Davidians.

Here's the thing that every newish parent quickly understands: very young children have inclinations that defy categorization or comprehension. It takes talent to recognize this and speak to it; when those forces are brilliant or at least benign, you end up with books like *Goodnight Moon; Good Night, Gorilla;* and *Blue Hat, Green Hat.* When those forces are greedy and malevolent, you end up with Tinkle Tubsies or non-Henson Elmo or Lord-knows-what beaming character concocted by market research and focus groups, an incubus guaranteed to make serial killers of your kids. This realization, of course, then wreaks havoc on the rash corollary to the second rule, which is:

WE WILL PERSONALLY PURCHASE ONLY THAT WHICH WE COULD IMAGINE MAKING OURSELVES (I.E., WRITING OR EDITING) AT OUR VERY BEST (WE ALL HAVE AN INNER CRAP ARTIST).

But here is the humbling thing: children, especially young children, have strong irrational likes and dislikes, and some of the books they love best are, frankly, a mystery. For example, *Spring Is Here* by Taro Gomi. This was a gift from friends who have a daughter two years older than our son, and it baffled us at first. Don't get us wrong; it's a lovely book, just . . . weird. It's a celebration of the seasons in which a calf metamorphoses into fresh earth, growing grass, and the changing seasonal landscape, only to change back into an older calf at the end of the story. You would not be amiss in thinking it sounds a bit like a short Japanese animated film in board-book form. You would therefore think that it wouldn't be appealing to a developing human unable to say *spring*, let alone *anime* or *Miyazaki*. Yet this quickly became one of Drake's favorite books (and other children's as well; we noticed the book was in its seventh printing).

There is something liberating in all this. It confirms something we all know, which is that "taste" at this — or any — age is an elusive, reaching thing. And that for every non-Henson Elmo book out there (yes, we have one, and yes, he loves it, and Bruce put it in the trash on Tuesday without a moment's pause), there is a Denise Fleming (*Barnyard Banter* — genius!) and a Richard Scarry (*Richard Scarry's Cars and Trucks and Things That Go* — best boy-book ever) and, most wonderful of all, some bizarre yet irresistible new kooky book yet to be discovered to make things right in the universe. And who knows? We, the snarky all-knowing parents, may even learn a thing or two.

So: channel your inner authoritarian and bin everything cutesy and stupid. Trust your ineluctable sense of "taste." But be prepared for some surprises. And for God's sake, stay away from Chuck E. Cheese. That way lies madness.

MORE GREAT BOOKS FOR BABIES

Janet Ahlberg and Allan Ahlberg, *Peek-a-Boo!*
34 pp. This nicely oversize board book with sturdy die-cut pages is the perfect format for the Ahlbergs' classic picture book, which follows a baby through his ordinary but eventful day.

Byron Barton, *Boats; Planes; Trains; Trucks*
32 pp. With simple, direct text and black-outlined, color-blocked pictures, these oversize board books are ideal for young vehicle enthusiasts whose exuberance might otherwise result in ripped pages.

Margaret Chodos-Irvine, *Ella Sarah Gets Dressed*
32 pp. Undeterred by her more decorous family, Ella Sarah insists on wearing a flashy outfit of her choosing. Happily, her friends arrive for tea wearing equally outrageous costumes. In this lap-size board-book version of the Caldecott Honor Book, the illustrations retain their distinctive patterns, colors, and sizes.

Eileen Christelow, *Five Little Monkeys Jumping on the Bed*
32 pp. A popular picture book with a rhyming, repetitive refrain well suited to the audience is nicely reissued — essentially unchanged from the original — as a lap-size board book.

Olivier Dunrea, *Gossie; Gossie & Gertie*
32 pp. Dunrea's captivating stories about two inquisitive goslings make perfect board books. Dunrea is precisely attuned to the toddler world: making friends, losing beloved objects, wanting someone else's beloved objects. The goslings march across the clean white pages in their bright blue and red boots, having tiny adventures and learning about the world as they go.

Mem Fox, illustrations by Judy Horacek, *Where Is the Green Sheep?*
32 pp. This charming tale, in which readers search for an elusive green sheep, works beautifully as a board book. The bouncy, rhyming text will appeal to

very young children, and Horacek's art remains clear and clean and easy to interpret. Right in line with toddlers' sense of playful discovery.

Mem Fox, illustrations by Helen Oxenbury, *Ten Little Fingers and Ten Little Toes*
40 pp. Two babies join a multiethnic playgroup. Fox's lilting verse ("And both of these babies, / as everyone knows, / had ten little fingers / and ten little toes") just has to be read aloud, and Helen Oxenbury's spacious illustrations, featuring her irresistible round-headed tots, will engage even the youngest viewers.

Chihiro Nakagawa, illustrations by Junji Koyose, *Who Made This Cake?*
40 pp. Miniature workers use tiny construction vehicles to make a giant cake. Kids will love searching for the little guy who trips himself up, and truck fans will pore over every action-filled scene.

Satoru Onishi, *Who's Hiding?*
32 pp. Onishi introduces — with humor — eighteen animals, six colors, and the child-appealing visual challenge of camouflage.

Leslie Patricelli, *Higher! Higher!*
32 pp. A smiling dad pushes a little girl on a swing; with each push, she says, "Higher! Higher!" Up she goes, flying to greet a giraffe, a mountain climber, an airplane. Finally, she heads into space, where she meets a little green alien at the apex of his own swing. Cheerful cartoonlike acrylics reinforce the book's preschooler-perfect sensibilities. Also available as a board book.

Phyllis Root, illustrations by David Walker, *Flip, Flap, Fly!*
32 pp. Gently pastoral illustrations and bouncy wordplay introduce animal babies taking their first thrilling "steps." The spaciously composed illustrations are light-filled and blithely anthropomorphic, the babies clearly overjoyed to be doing their thing. Generous doses of onomatopoeia and alliteration add to the fun.

Chapter Two

PICTURE BOOKS

Stores of Transferable Energy

Martha V. Parravano

Five little puppies dug a hole under the fence and went
for a walk in the wide, wide world.
— from *The Poky Little Puppy*, by Janette Sebring Lowrey

There's no such thing as an "average" picture book, any more than
there is such a thing as an "average" child. True, a great majority of
picture books are thirty-two pages long; true, they all work via a
progression of page turns; true, most have a mix of illustrations and
text that tells a story, or sets a mood, or counts objects, or prepares
for bedtime. But a picture book can be twenty-four pages long,
wordless, on the subject of farm animals, and aimed at one-year-
olds. Or it can have forty pages, with a text as long as your average
novella, on a subject as fraught as the Holocaust, and appropriate
for middle-schoolers. The umbrella term *picture book* includes concept books (ABCs, counting, colors, shapes, opposites); folk and
fairy tales, Mother Goose rhymes, songs; intimate family stories
and school stories; bedtime stories; historical fiction; nonfiction;
fantasy; nonsense; bibliotherapy on all subjects from divorce to
death; satires and send-ups. . . . The list goes on — we haven't fallen
off the edge of the known picture-book world yet. In her insightful
book *Reading Like a Writer*, Francine Prose says that the infinite variety of prose styles used by authors "remind[s] us how many rooms

there are in the house of art"; she could easily have been talking about picture books.

Volumes have been written on the art and history of the picture book (see particularly Barbara Bader's seminal *American Picture-books from Noah's Ark to the Beast Within*). But what exactly do parents, faced with shelf upon shelf of skinny spines or (perhaps even worse) loud, glitzy covers, really need to know? Three crucial truths can be stated. One, the picture book is an object, but once opened, it is an *experience,* one that unfolds through time. Two, picture books are intended for *children* (a seemingly obvious statement, but you'd be surprised: current marketplace forces mean that most children's books are sold through large bookstores, and so picture books are often pitched toward the adult buyer rather than the child reader). And three, picture books that work tend to have insight into what makes kids tick at different developmental stages — and many of the best push through those stages to help kids move to the next level of independence.

Every reading parent will be familiar with at least a few classics — the now de rigueur *Goodnight Moon; Make Way for Ducklings; Mike Mulligan and His Steam Shovel; The Very Hungry Caterpillar; Chicka Chicka Boom Boom* — and with favorites from his or her own childhood. But have you ever stopped to consider what a marvel the humble picture book is? Ideally, illustration and text are interdependent, creating a whole in which neither is sufficient without the other (or at least in which one greatly enriches the other). Picture books resemble theater or film more than any other literary format: they rely on the page turn to pace the experience, to unfold the story or build the mood; between one page turn and the next, there must be some tension, or the picture book doesn't function. A true picture book is so much more than a sequence of words and images — the most breathtaking art, the most memorable prose, is static and lifeless without compelling page turns.

On an aesthetic level, a parent can apply his or her own honed skills and tastes to choose picture books for a child. Ask yourself these questions: Whether the pictures are cartoons or reproductions of magnificent oil paintings, are they appropriate for the text? Is the text written in a distinct voice? Is it specific to the situation and/or character (i.e., not generic)? If it is written in verse, does it scan, or land with a thud? Are the pictures and text interdependent, or does the text labor to describe something that's portrayed in detail in the accompanying illustration? Most critically — and this is a criterion that can be applied to any book, for any age, adult or children's — does the book come alive? Is there a recognizable world contained in those thirty-two pages?

You may be overwhelmed by the sheer number of picture books on bookstore and library shelves. To paraphrase a famous stanza from one of the earliest American picture books, Wanda Gág's 1928 *Millions of Cats:* there are hundreds of books! thousands of books! millions and billions and trillions of books! Why so many?

First of all, the picture-book format hasn't changed significantly since *Millions of Cats* or, indeed, since 1878's *The Diverting History of John Gilpin* by Randolph Caldecott — the British illustrator for whom the Caldecott Medal was named — one of the first picture books to feature the fundamental element of interdependent text and pictures. Picture books are typically a size to either spread out on a reader's lap or hold comfortably in small hands. Their established standard length of thirty-two pages is due to the constraints of technology: the presses on which books have traditionally been printed produce "signatures" in multiples of sixteen that are then stitched together and bound (for a clear and fascinating account of the whole process, see Aliki's classic *How a Book Is Made*). This accident of industry and math has become a form, as defining as a sonata, whose rhythm — of dynamic page turns; of rising action, climax, and resolution; of balance of images and text — we have all internalized. (Changes in technology — e-readers, e-books, and so on — may bring changes in form. Whether the established rhythm will hold its power in a digital age — when the length of a work is measured in time rather than space — remains to be seen.)

Small children themselves haven't changed much, either. They still respond, as pioneering children's book editor Louise Seaman Bechtel wrote in *The Horn Book* in 1941, to "rhythm and laughter, the sense of climax, the magic of words." As a child, I loved Gene Zion's *Harry the Dirty Dog* — in which a little dog gets so dirty on his day of adventures that he changes from a white dog with black spots into a black dog with white spots — and my children loved it, too. It continues to appeal to children because of the excitement of Harry's adventures, the strength of Harry's personality, the tension over Harry's identity — will his family recognize him? — and the satisfaction when they do. Sigh. A good story is a good story, whether published in 1956, as *Harry* was, or in 2016. This happy lack of datedness isn't true for all pre-twenty-first-century picture books, of course, and even *Harry* shows its age a bit (with the little girl of the family dressed in a very 1950s-ish frock). But the nature of children and of picture books means that the best books feel just as fresh today as when they were first published.

Another picture book that has stood the test of time is Beatrix Potter's *The Tale of Peter Rabbit* — and it demonstrates another truth about picture books: they can tell large stories in small packages. I have often heard *Peter Rabbit* described as "sweet" or "cute" — Bunnies! Little blue vests! Tidy English gardens! Naughty Peter disobeys his mother and trespasses in Mr. McGregor's garden, where he gorges on produce and makes a narrow escape from the irate farmer; safely home, he is sent to bed with camomile tea instead of blackberries like his more obedient sisters. But Peter Rabbit can also be read as a primal rite-of-passage story, with Peter besting not only Mr. McGregor but also his own father (whom Mr. McGregor caught and "put into a pie"). It's an age-old tale of the small and weak versus the large and powerful — played out in many a legend/folktale/hero tale, from David versus Goliath, to Brer Rabbit versus

Brer Fox, to Luke Skywalker versus Darth Vader. It's an archetypal home-adventure-return story, the basis of the hero monomyth made famous by Joseph Campbell. So, merely cute it's not — and though not all picture books are this deep (or indeed need to be read on that level), the ones you find yourself reading over and over to your child may upon a closer look reveal unsuspected depths: *Where the Wild Things Are* (Maurice Sendak); *Sylvester and the Magic Pebble* (William Steig); *The Snowman* (Raymond Briggs).

The world of the picture book is a child-centered one, where children are the actors, not the acted-upon. When evaluating a picture book, then, ask yourself who's in charge. Picture books, intended to be experiences for a child, work best when they are on the *side* of the child. Children are generally eager to learn about their world, move forward, take steps toward independence. It can be argued that all children's literature is, at its core, about growing up, and picture books in particular mirror that headlong rush.

The very youngest children wake up every day to an adventure. All parents have had the experience of seeing their baby soaking up experiences like a sponge and changing virtually hour by hour. Babies are wowed by just about everything, so books for babies should be all about making connections with their world: What does a cow say? Oh, it says *moo!* What is this a picture of? Yes, that's right, it's a car. *Vroom, vroom!* Their books should have either very little text or a text full of rhythm (see "Books for Babies").

In books for toddlers, there is a shift toward a readiness to explore the world beyond the safe borders of home and parent. A good picture book for a two-year-old may contain a small adventure — but within *very* safe confines. In Nancy Tafuri's *Have You Seen My Duckling?*, a mother duck takes her offspring for a swim, but one adventurous duckling has set off to chase a butterfly. The simple story follows the mother as she asks various denizens of the pond the title question. What makes the book so good is that on every spread the "missing" duckling is always *just* visible: behind a water lily, peeking out from behind a tree. The errant duckling is both the object of the game of hide-and-seek and the embodiment of the reassurance toddlers require. *Pouch!* by David Ezra Stein is perfectly attuned with toddlers' simultaneous need for safety and independence, as baby kangaroo Joey takes his first hop out of his mother's pouch and then, unnerved, dives back in again . . . until he's ready to try again. Each time, Joey ventures forth a little farther before retreating, in the end finding a friend and exploring the world together.

Four-year-olds' worlds have expanded into a larger society: play groups, preschool, and neighborhood. Picture books for this age can contain a lot more tension and can take the protagonist farther from home — as long as they still end up safely and happily resolved. In Shirley Hughes's *Alfie Gives a Hand,* preschooler Alfie attends his friend Bernard's birthday party. Alfie is a bit taken aback to learn that the invitation doesn't include his mother and little sister, Annie Rose, and insists on bringing his security blanket to the party. He hangs on to it doggedly all through the games and lunch in Bernard's backyard. But another friend, Min, is having a miserable time, and Alfie has to choose between letting Min hold his hand and holding on to his blanket. It's a small dilemma, preschool-size, but it's a true one: when he puts the blanket down, Alfie is taking a step toward independence, away from babyhood. At party's (and book's) end, safely heading home with Mum and Annie Rose, Alfie decides that next time he'll leave his blanket at home.

Successful picture books for older children don't assume that the child reader has completed the journey to independence, but they often do provide stories in which the character exhibits a greater degree of same. William Steig's *Brave Irene* is an edge-of-your-seat-exciting, exquisitely told story of a dressmaker mother and her devoted daughter. The theme is love, but the message is one of girl power, as the mother stays home, sick in bed, while young Irene battles darkness and a raging (and brilliantly personified) blizzard all alone to deliver the duchess's gown in time for the ball. In Nancy

Coffelt's *Fred Stays with Me!,* a little girl matter-of-factly describes her two different living situations (her parents are divorced). As the book unfolds, it becomes clear that the one constant in her life is Fred, her dog. But there's trouble: barking (at Mom's) and sock-stealing (at Dad's). When both Mom and Dad declare that "Fred can't stay with me," our narrator stands up for herself. "'Excuse me,' I say. 'Fred doesn't stay with either of you. Fred stays with ME!'" Again, although the girl's level of independence isn't quite total—she works with her parents to come up with plans for Fred's reform—it's realistic and age-appropriate. Tricia Tusa's brilliant and quietly subversive illustrations give the little girl's independence a satisfying visual representation: the parents are never shown in full—we only glimpse them on the edges of illustrations or see their shadows or the backs of their heads.

Not every picture book reflects children's developmental stages. A picture book can simply capture a mood, a moment, or a day (Liz Garton Scanlon and Marla Frazee's *All the World;* Shutta Crum and Carol Thompson's *Thunder-Boomer!*); can be just plain funny or silly (Mo Willems's *Don't Let the Pigeon Drive the Bus!;* Helen Lester and Lynn Munsinger's *Tacky the Penguin*); can be a quiet (Molly Bang's *Ten, Nine, Eight*) or a rowdy (Bob Shea's *Dinosaur vs. Bedtime*) transition to bedtime. But in picture books such as those discussed above, forward motion is key: the book should contain at least the *possibility* of a larger world. When a book actively strives to keep the child locked in childhood relationships and needs, it's not truly a *child's* picture book. A doting parent may enjoy a book about a little bunny whose mission in life is to tell his mommy how much he loves her, but there's nothing there for the child audience. Far more realistic and definitely more on the child's side are picture books in which the parent tells the child that *he* is loved—unconditionally, and despite the child's behavior. Being assured of a parent's unconditional love is of perennial interest to children, who are by nature and necessity the centers of their own universes, and so it is a fine topic for a picture book. And there are a slew of these, from Margaret Wise Brown and Clement Hurd's *The Runaway Bunny* to Barbara M. Joosse and Barbara Lavallee's warm, not-too-sweet *Mama, Do You Love Me?* to David Shannon's hilarious, honest, deeply poignant *No, David!*

The true test of a picture book is, of course, the child. Children's choices are personal, just as adults' are. It all boils down to finding books that speak directly to your child — and then getting more of them. *How* you find the books that fit your child, in this age of vanishing independent bookstores, may require some trial and error. You might want to start with the classics in your library and bookstore and go from there. Was *Curious George* a hit? Mischief abounds in picture books: try Rathmann's *Good Night, Gorilla,* in which a sleepy zookeeper makes the rounds, wishing all the zoo animals good night — not realizing that sneaky Gorilla has stolen his keys and is opening all their cages. Somewhat older readers might enjoy Janice N. Harrington and Shelley Jackson's *The Chicken-Chasing Queen of Lamar County,* in which a young (and unrepentantly naughty) girl just can't help herself from chasing the elusive Miss Hen — until she discovers what Miss Hen has been hiding. Picture books featuring beloved pets (*Where's Spot?; Martha Speaks*) are myriad: one of the best of recent years is Marc Simont's *The Stray Dog,* in which words and pictures work together in tandem to tell a dog story with a very happy ending. And if cars and trucks are the current draw, move from classics such as Anne Rockwell's *Big Wheels* and Byron Barton's *Machines at Work* to Kate and Jim McMullan's *I Stink!* (featuring an unforgettable, in-your-face garbage truck) and William Low's *Machines Go to Work* (with close-ups of favorite hardworking vehicles, a narrative that encourages interaction, and flaps that reveal surprises to boot — toddler heaven).

You will certainly know it when you have found the books that work for your child. You will know by the simple measure of how many times a child must hear it every night ("Again! Again!"), how dog-eared it becomes, how much milk gets spilled on it, and how much it becomes part of your child's frame of reference, her whole way of looking at the world. Picture books do have that power — it's the power of literature. Literature, and readers' strong response to it, knows no age boundaries. I have never forgotten the anecdote I heard years ago about a toddler whose mother found him jumping up and down on his copy of *Goodnight Moon,* trying desperately to find a way into its pages, to find an entrance into the great green room.

Just as the reading of picture books is personal, so is their creation; each picture book creates its own demands for illustration and text. Consider two brilliant picture books, both for young children, that are as disparate as can be, visually and conceptually: Laura Vaccaro Seeger's *First the Egg,* a tour-de-force concept book about order and transformations with a playful twist at the end, and John Burningham's *Mr. Gumpy's Outing,* a story beloved by generations of two-year-olds in which Mr. Gumpy's boat takes on more and more passengers, with predictable — and very funny — results.

Seeger's pages are color-saturated full bleeds in warm browns and golds, cool greens and blues, a bright yellow, and a pink that approaches hot. The impact is immediate, lush, and sensual, as thick visible brushstrokes on canvas draw the hand to the page as well as the eye. The portraits of the animals and the flower are detailed and painterly; because this is a concept book, not a story, the animals are objects to examine, not characters with whom to engage. *Mr. Gumpy,* on the other hand, is not at all painterly — the crosshatched illustrations, set in generous white space, look as if they might have been originally dashed off on a napkin. Two dots for the eyes and two lines for nose and mouth suffice to depict Mr. Gumpy's face and reveal his mood.

The texts are unlike, too. Seeger's text is so minimal, so honed to the essentials, that it eschews verbs completely: "First the egg / then the chicken . . . / first the seed / then the flower . . ." The brevity of the text lets the viewer's attention center on the art and the transformations. Burningham, on the other hand, employs a conversational text: "This is Mr. Gumpy. Mr. Gumpy owned a boat and his house was by a river. One day Mr. Gumpy went out in his boat." Yet how complete and authoritative is this introduction: readers have all they need to enter the story. The simple declarative sentences propel readers forward — just as Mr. Gumpy propels his boat. And there's the humor of the repeated silliness of Mr. Gumpy's name — a foreshadowing of the hilarity to come. As soon as Burningham launches into the action, the text segues into variations on one simple exchange — "Can I come along, Mr. Gumpy?" [asks the rabbit] / "Yes, but don't hop about." The repetition gives toddlers structure and lets the story build tension; the slight variations make each interaction distinct, add flavor, and ratchet up the potential for disaster, as each animal is admonished not to bleat, flap, kick, trample, or — my older daughter's favorite, much echoed — "muck about."

Despite their differences, the two books have crucial elements in common that make them successful. For one thing, each book gives viewers something specific to look at while listening to the text. Both Seeger and Burningham do this spectacularly, focusing on one single kid-appealing item or animal per page or double-page spread until very close to the end of each book. Secondly, each book uses a predictable structure, absolutely necessary for young children, who need that sure footing to negotiate the picture book. Seeger's and Burningham's books stand out because they provide the structure but then put it to work for a more interesting purpose. Seeger stays with her structure from beginning to end, but uses the age-old unanswerable question of which came first, the chicken or the egg, to playfully subvert her careful delineation of order. Some readers will laugh; others might begin asking some rather profound questions. Burningham putt-putts along on his placid river ride and then metaphorically guns the engine, with two double-page spreads

Sometimes you *can* judge a book by its cover. The cover of Laura Vaccaro Seeger's *First the Egg* immediately conveys the book's painterly style; its saturated feel, with thick, bold, palpable brushstrokes; and its playful, open-ended, exploratory nature (what lies beneath that attention-grabbing die-cut egg?). Given the absence of characters — animal or human — on the cover, this is clearly not a storybook. It's a concept book, but one that cannily prepares the reader to expect the unexpected.

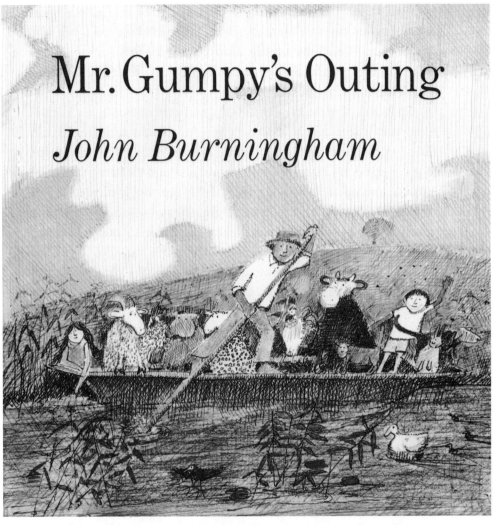

Mr. Gumpy's Outing
John Burningham

Mr. Gumpy's Outing takes an altogether different approach — it's an altogether different book: a story of benign adventure. The casual crosshatching gives the cover a loose, jaunty feel. There are both human and animal characters, some of whom, including the centrally placed Mr. Gumpy, look directly out at the audience (the little boy is even waving). And note how Mr. Gumpy is leaning to the right, inviting the reader to open the book and begin the story . . .

and two pages of lengthy text bringing us in quick succession to the action-packed climax ("for a little while, they all went along happily, but then . . .") and the homey, satisfying, very English resolution (with Mr. Gumpy, the children, and the animals all gathered around a table having afternoon tea).

Speaking of endings — the endings of picture books are important. They can easily be too tidy, too finished, boxing readers in rather than releasing their imaginations or making them eager for more. Seeger and Burningham provide endings that are satisfying, circular, and open-ended. Seeger, with her seemingly flat-out reversal, will bring readers back to the beginning immediately to see why they were so sure about the chicken-egg order in the first place. Burningham follows his adventure with an invitation to "come for a ride another day"— and most children will take him up on the offer sooner rather than later. Great picture books don't stay closed for long.

"AGAIN"

KEVIN HENKES

Before I became a parent (this was back in the 1990s), I would never have believed that a sixteen-month-old could have strong tastes when it comes to choosing books. But my son knew exactly what he liked and disliked. He would stand at the bookshelf and locate his favorite books by their spines. He would go through his stack of board books, tossing the less-than-favorites aside, saying, "No, no, no," until he found what he wanted.

If his mother and I were trying to do something else and he wanted to read, he would follow us around clutching the book of choice, holding it up with outstretched arms. "Book! Book!"

The day came when he learned to say and understand "again." Sometimes he said "again" at the end of a story. Sometimes he said "again" twenty-three times for the same book. Once, I read *School Bus* by Donald Crews for close to an hour without a break.

Luckily, his "again" books were books his parents liked as well. *"More More More," Said the Baby* by Vera B. Williams; *Truck* and *School Bus* by Donald Crews; *Tractor* by Craig Brown; *Little Donkey Close Your Eyes* by Margaret Wise Brown, illustrated by Ashley Wolff; *Of Colors and Things* by Tana Hoban; *Bam Bam Bam* by Eve Merriam, illustrated by Dan Yaccarino; and *Now I'm Big* by Margaret Miller.

All of these books were ripped and bent and chewed and spilled on. All had to be taped and glued, or replaced. Again and again.

The Words
Charlotte Zolotow

Charlotte Zolotow shares her insights as both author
(of such lyrical and beloved picture books as *Mr. Rabbit
and the Lovely Present* and *William's Doll*) and editor
(She succeeded iconic editor Ursula Nordstrom as head
of Harper and Row's children's book department).

The beginning of a picture book comes before the pictures. In
Margaret Wise Brown's beautiful *Goodnight Moon,* it was the magic
of her words, their simplicity and the music in them, that made
Clement Hurd's now-famous visual interpretation possible. Unless
the writer is also an illustrator, the writing always comes first.

Many fine writers can write *about* children but are unable to
write *for* them. Writers such as William Maxwell awaken in adult
readers an understanding of childhood that many of us don't have,
a sensitivity to children that is exquisite. But writing for children is
different. The writers writing about children are looking back. The
writers writing for children are *feeling* back into childhood.

Many adults think of children as an emotionally different species from ourselves. But if there is any difference between the adult's
and the child's feelings, it is in the greater intensity of the child's.
Humor, irony, religion, resignation — anything to give us control
and protect us from the full impact. Kids don't have those defenses
yet. Their emotions are the same as those of adults, except for that
one tremendous difference: children experience anger, loneliness,

joy, love, sorrow, and hatred whole and plain; we experience strong emotions through our adult protection and veneer.

There is no feeling that can't be explored in picture books. Everything from birth to death is the province of those who write them. When we experience an emotion as adults, when the power and the mood returns with the force of childhood, we use writing to reach back to ourselves, to our own childhood, where we still need comfort or understanding. This desire to communicate with someone still alive within us is the source of certain children's picture books.

There are all sorts of picture books. There is a place for them all. There are those with plots and those without plots, stories that are funny and stories that are sad and stories that can be both at once. There are books comprised entirely of a mood that the words, like a piece of poetry, evoke. But in the great variety of books that are picture books, each so different from the others, there is one common gift. Ursula Nordstrom, one of the great children's book editors of our time, called it "retaining a direct line to one's childhood."

Picture books are written from a child's point of view. That is the direct line to childhood Ursula talked about, the off-center way the world looks to children, to whom the world is new and who are trying to make sense out of everything adults take for granted.

The Pictures
Margot Zemach

Margot Zemach gives us a glimpse into the workings of
an artist's mind as she muses over how to illustrate the
folktale "The Three Wishes."

The details in illustrations create a cohesive picture that tells you
more than the story tells. The text says, simply, "a poor woodcutter." But how poor is he, really? And how will I show it? What was it
actually like to be hungry, with one pot of food cooking in the fireplace of a small cottage? Or to live in a world of flickering firelight
and shadows? Or to be part of a family in a folktale, with the whole
family living and sleeping in one room? It behooves the illustrator
to find out through research, and figure out how to re-create the
essence of that life for the viewer.

I could put the woodcutter and his wife in a traditional folksy
cabin, wearing shabby clothes and holes in their shoes, but that's
been done before. Illustrators do that every day. I would like to show
how poor they are in a new way. Hmm. Much of the action takes place
in front of a fireplace, on nine double-page spreads. It had better be
a good fireplace: I'll have to draw it nine times, and people will have
to see it nine times. Aha! Maybe the fireplace can tell us something
about their financial condition. So, I look at a lot of photographs
and old paintings of English country life in the late 1800s. Quite by
chance, I see an old English watercolor of an interior, and there it is:

the fireplace I need! The woodcutter and his wife wear clothing that is heavy and cumbersome, thick and baggy, for warmth and durability. Their cottage is set into the hillside, built of dirt, wood, and stone. It is shadowy inside, and misty outside among the trees.

Later, the pan of cooking sausages will smoke up into the woodcutter's face — even fill the room with smoke. The amount of time the woodcutter has the sausages hanging from his nose will be crucial. It is important to have an extra double-page spread there — to rub in his dilemma. It's no good if on one page the sausages are on his nose and then — bingo! — they're off again, too quickly, on the next page.

As to the great forest they live near: what a chance to extend our understanding of what it would be like to spend one's life in a forest! So we'll add a line to the story to the effect that "all year round, the woodcutter and his wife worked, cutting and chopping and carrying." Now there's the extra richness of seeing them in all seasons. Maybe it's snowing, and I'll show how physically difficult it is for the woodcutter and his wife to work outside in the cold. Also, it gives us a time span in which we can get acquainted and begin to care about these two people.

I think I'll stick in a dog. Because the woodcutter and his wife go hungry, he'd probably be a hungry dog. I'll put the dog in to underline the action. He's always there, reacting. When you've seen the dog for a couple of pages, you'll start looking for the dog throughout the story: "Uh-oh — this or that happens — how will the dog take it?" He gives me more comic possibilities, though he's never mentioned in the text.

On the cover, we first see the woodcutter and his wife, resting in the forest. It's very pastoral. Then, on the half-title page, we see a man and a woman arm in arm, returning from work. We understand something about their simple, simple standard of living and what

their relationship is to each other. "OK," we say, "husband and wife, probably. They seem to be fond of each other." I want it to be an old-fashioned love story — one that is seen in the pictures, though it never appears in the words.

Before the story itself has even started, I've said without words that the woodcutter and his wife are two people who work hard, love each other, are very poor, and live very simply in a cottage by a forest. The stage is set.

How to Read the Pictures:
John Steptoe's *Baby Says*

Kathleen T. Horning

In his tragically short career as a picture-book creator, John Steptoe received attention for his groundbreaking early books (*Stevie; My Special Best Words*) and, later on, for his lavishly detailed folktale retellings (*The Story of Jumping Mouse; Mufaro's Beautiful Daughters*). Published in 1988, a year before Steptoe died at age thirty-eight, *Baby Says* is, compared to his other work, deceptively simple. But surely anyone who has ever shared *Baby Says* with a group of two- or three-year-olds will recognize the ingenuity behind Steptoe's repeated use of three baby words or phrases — *uh, oh; no, no;* and *okay* — which, put into context by realistic pastel illustrations, tell a familiar story of sibling rivalry and harmony. (The entire book contains just seven words: *baby; says; here; uh, oh; okay;* and *no.*)

Baby Says is a true *first* story; appropriately, the illustrations carry much of the narrative. At first glance they appear to be relatively straightforward: as big brother plays with his blocks and a toy airplane, a baby repeatedly throws a teddy bear out of his playpen in an attempt to engage his older brother.

But there is an underlying story being told in the illustrations. Throughout the book, Steptoe uses horizontal lines to connect the two brothers, vertical lines to separate them. On the opening

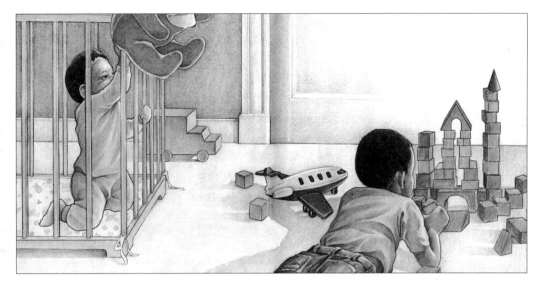

double-page spread, for example, the horizontal lines of the base-board and toy truck and airplane point at big brother, while the bars on the playpen confine the baby and upright building-block towers occupy big brother's attention. Baby brother does everything in his power to destroy the vertical lines by dropping his teddy bear out of his playpen over and over again, a time-tested diversionary tactic. When big brother returns the bear, it results in not just a bond of brotherly love but also a very strong horizontal line that fills the double-page spread (and the playpen bars are barely visible).

Baby's second attempt to get big brother's attention by dropping the bear results in a much more angular return, with the lines of big brother's arm more vertical than horizontal. Baby tries again, this time with a sideways attack that not only gets big brother's atten-tion but also sends a building block flying and releases baby from his playpen and its restricting vertical lines.

Free at last, the baby finds one more vertical empire to topple. If you're reading the pictures just in terms of horizontal versus vertical lines, this picture speaks for itself (despite the fact that it's the wordiest section of text). We've got the original (horizontal) horizon line connecting the two brothers. Babies, when engaged in their chief mode of self-propelled transport, are horizontal anyway. In this case, the baby is given an even stronger horizontal presence, extended as he is by his teddy bear companion. And look at the big brother — he's leaning forward in a way that mirrors the baby's horizontal position, and he's turned his attention to one of the toys that had originally extended their connecting horizon line. So things are looking very hopeful for the baby. But first, there's this vertical structure to be gotten out of the way. In fact, all the horizontal lines point right to it. Of course, the inevitable happens, and the baby topples the tower of blocks. A dramatic wordless spread shows the big brother's reaction to the baby's intrusion.

Interestingly, Steptoe again uses the play between vertical and horizontal lines to depict the big brother's anger. The normally

"Okay, baby.
Okay."

horizontal lines of his eyebrows and mouth point up and down rather than across. To make amends, the baby reaches across the space separating the two brothers to draw them together. Once, as I was reading this aloud to a group of preschoolers, a four-year-old observed, "Look! Their heads make a heart!"

Over the years, I have read *Baby Says* aloud countless times, and one of the things I've observed is that anyone under the age of five identifies with the baby rather than the older brother. This, I think, is another indication of Steptoe's genius — to have made the big brother old enough so that the conflict between them can be playful. He's also old enough that the baby will be recognized by young children as an underdog who gains the upper hand, a favorite theme among the most powerless in our society.

At one preschool story hour at my public library, there was a baby, not quite a year old, being held by her mother. The story hour was for the baby's older sibling; the baby was merely along for the ride. But as I read *Baby Says* to the children, the baby started echoing back the text as I was reading it. "Uh, oh." "Uh, oh." Everyone — the parents, day-care teachers, and other children — all began to listen, waiting for the baby to speak each line after I said it. The baby had suddenly become the book in an odd little play in which the boundary between literature and life had completely disappeared for everyone in the room.

Design Matters

Jon Scieszka

illustrated by Lane Smith

designed by Molly Leach

Design is an essential part of any picture book. It is the first aspect of a book that a reader judges. It is the framework for the text and illustration. It is the subtle weave of words and pictures that allows both to tell one seamless tale.

And because good design is, by its very nature, nearly invisible in the final product, most people have no idea what design contributes to a picture book.

My idea of what design contributes to a picture book pretty much starts and ends with my first sentence. So I asked Molly Leach (designer of *The Stinky Cheese Man* and *Math Curse*) and Lane Smith (illustrator of *The Stinky Cheese Man* and *Math Curse*) exactly what it is that design contributes to a picture book.

The job of a designer, in its most basic form, is to pick the style, size, and color of type, maybe pick the kind of paper and size of the book, and arrange how the type and illustrations are to be displayed on the pages available. But Molly does so much more than that in our books. When she's done, the design tells as much of the story as the text and illustrations do.

Molly designs all kinds of things, from magazines to books to CD covers. She is asked to do elegant, bold, hip, or striking design (to name just a few styles). But the most important thing she does is to find the design appropriate for the piece. *Business Week*'s Mutual Fund Report is not the place for "zany." *The Stinky Cheese Man* was not the place for "stuffy" or "quiet" design.

When I wrote the stories in *The Stinky Cheese Man*, I wrote them with an ear for how they would sound when read aloud. My finished version of "The Really Ugly Duckling" looked like this:

THE REALLY UGLY DUCKLING

Once upon a time there was a mother duck and a father duck who had seven baby ducklings. Six of them were regular-looking ducklings. The seventh was a really ugly duckling.

Everyone used to say, "What a nice-looking bunch of ducklings—all except that one. Boy, he's really ugly."

The really ugly duckling heard these people, but he didn't care. He knew that one day he would probably grow up to be a swan and be bigger and look better than anything in the pond.

Well, as it turned out, he was just a really ugly duckling.

And he grew up to be just a really ugly duck.

The End.

Which might explain why it got rejected by so many publishers. The final line, "And he grew up to be just a really ugly duck" looks a little harsh in its bare typewritten form.

Lane illustrated a goofy little duck. He and Molly designed a page turn so the duckling grows into a bigger, goofier duck on the next page (working almost like a flip book). And then it was Molly who came up with the idea to have whatever words were on the text page expand to fill the space. The final punch-line sentence of the story, the transformation of the illustration, the turn of the page, and the blown-up type — text, illustration, and design — all combine to create one hilarious ending:

THE REALLY UGLY DUCKLING

Once upon a time there was a mother duck and a father duck who had seven baby ducklings. Six of them were regular-looking ducklings. The seventh was a really ugly duckling.
Everyone used to say, "What a nice-looking bunch of ducklings—all except that one. Boy, he's really ugly." The really ugly duckling heard these people, but he didn't care. He knew that one day he would probably grow up to be a swan and be bigger and look better than anything in the pond.

Well, as it turned out, he was just a really ugly duckling. And he grew up to be just a really ugly duck. The End.

Ha. Ha. Ha.

Well, you've at least got to admit it's funnier
than the typewritten version.

Some people have described our books as "wacky" and "zany" and
"anything goes." I wouldn't want to say they're wrong, but I would
like to suggest that they're not exactly right. In order to create the
humor and illusion of wacky / zany / anything goes, there has to
be a reason for *everything* that goes. And this Law of Reasoned
Zaniness applies just as inflexibly to design as it does to writing and
illustrating.

In *The Stinky Cheese Man*, Molly chose, for the entire book, a
classic font (Bodoni) and used it in unusual ways (expanding, shrinking, melting) to emphasize the fact that these were classic fairy tales
told in an unconventional way.

The flexible font size also made it easier for Molly to break the
text at any given point to give the punch lines of the tales more
punch.

The expanding text pushing the boundaries of the page says the book is bursting with
stories.

The Red Hen speaks in red type throughout
(no other character speaks in color) to visually
accentuate her annoying voice.

I thought it would be funny if Jack's never-
ending tale in "Jack's Story" ran right off the
page.

Molly showed me it would look funnier and
more like Jack's voice fading into the distance if
the words got smaller and smaller:

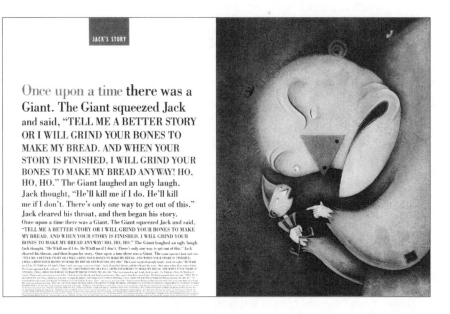

The type and edge of the Stinky Cheese Man illustration melts because he smells so bad:

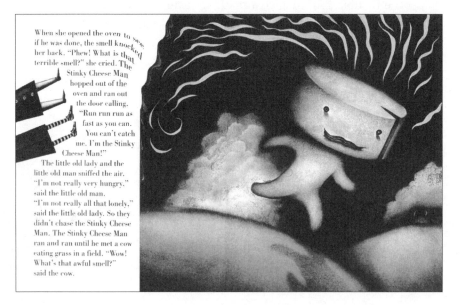

And every tale's "Once upon a time" and "The End" are in color to highlight the fact that these are stock parts of a fairy tale. None of these details is specified by the text. They are design decisions that enhance and amplify each Fairly Stupid Tale.

Design sets the tone for everything.

Don't you suddenly feel like you're reading a wedding announcement? You may not consciously know it, but when you pick up a book, you are reading its layout and typeface and color palette for clues about the story.

Modern kids are even more demanding readers of these design clues than most adults. They have been raised since birth in the ever-more visually intense world of TV, movies, and video. They are more visually literate than generations before them — quicker and better able to read what design has to tell them. They deserve good design.

Math Curse was an entirely different design challenge.

I thought it would be funny to write about a kid's day in which everything turns into a math problem. Lane thought it would be funny to paint the kid actually inside the nightmarish grip of the curse.

We both thought it would be funny to ask Molly to make (8 pages of text and problems) + (19 paintings) + (1 copyright page) + (1 dedication page) = one 32-page book that looked kind of like a math book but not so much like a math book that it would be ugly and scare people away.

Here is what a couple of problematical math text pages could have looked like:

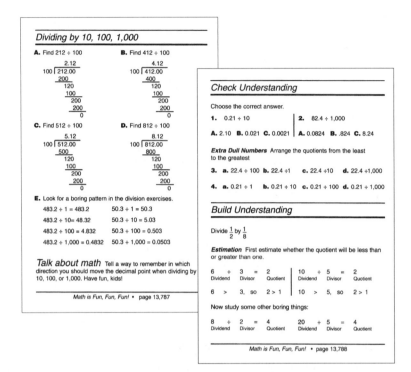

Here is a finished spread from *Math Curse* designed by Molly:

Which of these statements is true?

A. The first design looks ugly.

B. In the second design, Molly boxed problems and broke the text into sections like every ugly math book does, but she used a bold (Franklin Gothic) type clustered in funny tangencies (shifting blocks of copy) to enhance the frantic feel of the illustration.

C. Molly also used bold colors and background tints in geometric shapes to give an overall playful feel.

D. All of the above.

If you answered "D," multiply your Designer SAT score by your shoe size and continue on to the next section.

When Molly, Lane, and I work on a book, I usually write the text and polish it with my editor first. Lane draws preliminary sketches. We decide what to keep, what to cut, how to order things. Then Lane and Molly fiddle with the design and illustration. With the three of us working in close collaboration, Molly, Lane, and I take the opportunity to play off one another's ideas throughout the process. Words can be changed to accommodate design. Design can be juggled to allow a new illustration. Illustrations can be altered to fit a new story twist. We also get to use every last part of the book — price, flap copy, dedication, and copyright — to tell the story.

In conclusion, I would just like to say the only thing that can be said, what you know I'm going to say, what I can't *help* but say: design is an essential part of any picture book.

AN INTERVIEW WITH
Maurice Sendak

ROGER SUTTON: How does it feel to realize that your work — *Where the Wild Things Are* in particular — is so much a part of popular culture?

MAURICE SENDAK: I see that book almost entirely in personal terms: I think about what I was like at that time; I think about Ursula [Nordstrom, see page 42]. I do realize that *Wild Things* has permitted me to do all kinds of books that I probably never would have done had it not been so popular. I think I took good advantage of that popularity to illustrate books that I passionately wanted to do without having to worry if they were commercial or not.

RS: Do you ever feel like it gets in the way?

MS: I know that when *In the Night Kitchen* came out, it was a disappointment to people because it had nothing to do with *Wild Things*. Why couldn't I have just stayed put? The style was different; everything about it was different. The cartoons, the nakedness, everything seemed to be a rebuff of what I had "accomplished." But I had Ursula, who would never have let me do another *Wild Things*.

Never. Never. She never suggested it, to her immense credit. And then the other books were notorious in one way or another, but they've all finally settled in nicely, couched on top of *Wild Things*. When I first discussed *Wild Things, Night Kitchen,* and *Outside Over There* as a "triumvirate," people said, "What's he talking about?" But I always knew there'd be three. It *was* a triumvirate.

RS: It seems as if those three books, in lots of different ways, are a kind of lens people can look through to understand you, your work as a whole.

MS: Everything about me is in those three books. Over the longevity of a man's life and work you get a sense of where his mind is, where his heart is, where his humor is, where his *dread* is. It's the best thing you could ask, that this kind of understanding of an artist doesn't happen posthumously. What more can you ask?

RS: What was it like, then, at midlife, to have published *Outside Over There,* which you acknowledge as your capstone achievement?

MS: *Outside Over There* was the most painful experience of my creative life. It was so hard, it caused me to have a breakdown. I didn't think I could finish it. But at that point in my still-young life, I felt I *had* to solve this book; I *had* to plummet as far down deep into myself as I could. Herman Melville (my patron saint) called it excavation work. *Wild Things* was excavation work, but I got up and out in time, like a miner getting out just before the blast occurs. But I did not anticipate the horror of *Outside Over There*. It is my best work, *Outside Over There*. But I can take no pleasure in it.

RS: What do you think happened?

MS: I went in over my head. I fell off the ladder that goes down

This illustration from *Outside Over There* — in which goblins kidnap Ida's baby sister and leave a changeling ice baby in her place — shows why Sendak describes this book as "the most painful experience" of his creative life.

deep into the unconscious. Melville called it *diving*. You dive deep, and God help you. You might hit your head on something and never come up and nobody would even know you were missing. Or you will find some nugget that was worth the pain in your chest, the blindness, everything, and you'll come up with it and that will be what you went down for. In other words, you either risk it or you sell out. I believe in the nth degree. I believe in going all the way and being ferociously honest, because otherwise it doesn't work; it's contaminated. Why would you bother?

RS: Do you ever question yourself — "Can I go this far? Should I go this far?"

MS: No. I see myself as a fairly weak person. I've gotten better with age. Age has really done well by me. It's calmed the volcanoes down considerably. Age is a form of kindness we do ourselves. But I don't feel like I've been misunderstood. Honestly, I don't feel like my work is that important. I have no brilliant conceptual gift for drawing or any really exceptional gift for writing. My gift is a kind of intuitive sense that I think you would find in a musician — knowing what the music should sound like, knowing where to put your fingers. My talent is in knowing how to make a picture book. Knowing how to pace it, knowing how to time it.

My work is miraculous in that it has kept me alive and kept me employed — constantly, since I've been about fifteen. I have to work; that's who I am. I do it for me — it keeps me living, and it's gotten me over the worst of my personal life into a period of time in which I look around carefully and can say, "It's not so bad now."

I am fortunate in that I still have the privilege of spending so much time in the world of creating picture books, where I need to be. I don't know why I need to be there, but that's the joy of all this. The real mystery is, Why does this make me so happy? Why does this free me of every inhibition? Why does this allow me to be normal?

RS: So the absorption in the creating is the actual reward.

MS: Totally. In that period of time, I am stirred to the top of my last brain cell because I'm working. I am stirred into life by my labor.

Scary Picture Books
Deborah Stevenson

Despite frequent adult fears to the contrary, picture books featuring dark and dire monsters can indeed please small children. True, such books can seem frightening, and they often contain alarming images, disquieting texts, and threatening concepts. In Maurice Sendak's *Where the Wild Things Are,* pointy-toothed monsters pack together and challenge a small boy one-third their size. Their abundant teeth and claws, combined with their roars, bespeak an ability to do harm; they even threaten to eat him up. In Ed Emberley's *Go Away, Big Green Monster!,* a beast of repellent aspect stares out at the young viewer as its lurid features — most notably "a big red mouth with sharp white teeth" — cumulatively appear out of the inky blackness. Both of these books, each in its own way, portray the alarming.

What effects do such books have? Scary books may occasionally frighten some young readers. Many adults can recall a picture or a book that caused them real distress as children. Sendak tells of a woman whose child screamed, apparently not with delight, every time *Wild Things* was read to her. It is quite possible for some young readers or listeners to be moved to alarm by a book, just as they can be moved to joy or excitement or boredom.

But most scary picture books don't attempt, indiscriminately, to terrify youngsters. They also include elements that offer children tools to *control* fear.

Appropriately enough for the genre, picture books most often demonstrate this control not through their texts but through their pictures. Children hear the words of picture books through an adult mediator; picture-book illustrations, on the other hand, they can decode for themselves. The use of visuals often stabilizes an experience for young children, fixes it, secures it, putting boundaries around the playing field of dangerous excitement in a way that makes it acceptable to them.

Look at what the monsters in *Wild Things* do and, more important, how Max reacts. The wild things are fierce in physiognomy, but they never harm anyone: the wild thing on the cover, usually the first one a reader sees, dozes peacefully, and the ones on the title page quail before a fierce and confident Max. While Max's facial expression is somewhat unsure as he sails past the first sea monster, on the next double-page spread he looks on displeased and uncowed as the wild things are at their most ferocious. Sendak's trademark crosshatching, the muted tones of the blues and grays, and the shifts in picture size from page to page emphasize the restraints upon the wildness of boy and thing. The illustrations make it continually clear that this child is more than a match for these wild things. Fierce as those creatures may look, most young viewers have little trouble understanding that Max is not in danger.

Emberley's *Big Green Monster* is an excellent example of the control a picture book can exercise over the emotions it excites. The monster is certainly spiky and alien, but it first appears on the cover of its book in what seems to be a quiet homage to Kilroy — the top half of its head, with eyes, ears, hair, and nose, peeks out over a yellow block that forms the background for the title lettering. The

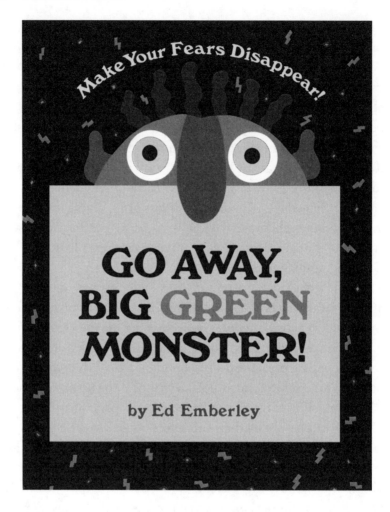

yellow block masks the monster's most fearsome characteristics and gives it a slightly silly air that would probably tide an unsure child past the darker early pages of the book.

The master stroke of Emberley's book, however, lies in its physical structure, which hands the control over to the young picture-book reader. This monster carries with it the seeds of its own undoing; the reader creates the monster, page by page, accumulating new features as the die-cut pages allow pieces of the monster's face to appear out of the darkness. But no sooner does it appear than it starts to disappear, each successive page turning a bold new color and reducing the monster, characteristic by characteristic, until it vanishes. As a four-year-old of my acquaintance pointed out when explaining why the book did not frighten her, "He's not eating any guys." For all its sharp teeth, the monster does nothing but is instead always being done *to*, responding to the beck and call of any child who encounters it.

The most pervasive fear of protective adults seems to be fear itself. (One contemporaneous review of *Wild Things* observed, "We should not like to have it left about where a sensitive child might find it to pore over in the twilight.") Yet learning to *manage* fear is a necessary step forward in any child's life. Parents should decide how much their child is ready for, and when, but so-called scary picture books might be less frightening—and more helpful—than they first seem.

What Makes a Good Alphabet Book?

Lolly Robinson

Trying to figure out what makes a good alphabet book is like trying to determine what makes a good meal for a child. It's a matter of taste as well as developmental maturity. A baby may be partial to mashed peas, a toddler to plain pasta, and a six-year-old might prefer the textural complexity of a peanut-butter-and-jelly sandwich. The child who is still learning to recognize and name letters doesn't want to be overwhelmed, while one who has mastered this trick is looking for a little more action and maybe even a bit of a challenge. Fortunately, there are alphabet books for every age and taste — hundreds, in fact, from the simplest name-the-letter books to those that present puzzles and challenges for older children and even adults. Alphabet books stopped being just for preschoolers and beginning readers long ago.

The first step toward reading is spotting letter shapes and giving them names. Flash cards would get the job done, but where's the fun? It's much more interesting to find letters in the world around you. Stephen T. Johnson and Zoran Milich both provide this chance, showing letters found in cityscapes. Johnson's *Alphabet City* employs spectacularly photorealistic paintings, some of which require a sharp eye to spot the letter. Milich's black-and-white photos in his *The City ABC Book* offer a little more help for beginners by overlaying red to emphasize each letter. Neither book attempts to tie the shapes to words that begin with those letters—we're not ready for that yet. In the now-classic *Chicka Chicka Boom Boom,* Bill Martin Jr. and John Archambault also refrain from tying letters to words, but they add a simple story to the mix, along with rhythm and rhyme. The action-filled plot even brings in the lowercase letters—as the children of the uppercase ones, of course. Lois Ehlert illustrates the raucous goings-on with cutout letters that remain easily recognizable despite some bending and manipulating to add character.

Once all those letters can be named without trouble, children are ready for books that partner each letter with a word. Easy nouns in the *A* for *Apple, B* for *Bear* vein are best—easiest for beginners to decipher in the accompanying illustrations. It's also a good idea for the letter to match its most common spoken sound: *C* for *Cat* works better than *C* for *Cygnet.* If you are ready for a little action, however, Denise Fleming's *Alphabet under Construction* is worth a look. Demonstrating craft-related verbs, a group of mice Airbrushes, Buttons, and Carves a giant alphabet. Books like Woodleigh Hubbard's *C Is for Curious: An ABC of Feelings* pose a problem. Not only are emotions much more difficult to illustrate nonambiguously than nouns, or even verbs, but children's available vocabulary for feelings and emotions is limited. Hubbard is forced to place *xenophobic* and *yucky* side by side. Ouch.

Alphabet books constructed around a theme helpfully provide an extra clue for deciphering the words in question. Jerry Pallotta is the king of this subgenre, with more than twenty titles (*The Beetle Alphabet Book; The Underwater Alphabet Book*) to his name. If you can match the theme to a child's particular interest, then you may have a winner, but his books tend to be wordy and rather earnest. Fortunately, there are plenty of other choices in theme-driven ABC books. Try Lois Ehlert's *Eating the Alphabet*. Showing both common and unusual items from the produce section (Swiss chard, spinach, star fruit), Ehlert's brightly colored collage illustrations make even ugli fruit look appealing.

Recently we've seen a trend toward oversize, action-packed alphabet books presumably geared toward boys — though we could all use a little adrenaline now and then. Chris L. Demarest has two of these: *Alpha Bravo Charlie* with a military theme and the self-explanatory *Firefighters A to Z*. Brian Floca's *The Racecar Alphabet* satisfies the need for speed, and Bob McLeod's *SuperHero ABC* is full of muscles, Lycra, and unexpected humor: "Huge Man is Happy to Help Heroes and never Harms Humans," but "He's not exactly Handsome . . . even His Hands are Hairy!"

For children suffering from alphabet anxiety, a shot of humor can save the day. Plenty of books simply incorporate humor into the art, like Mike Lester's *A Is for Salad*. Lester lets the child feel smarter than the book, with a silly text that gets each letter wrong. The first image shows an alligator eating a salad, hence, "A is for salad." Next, a beaver in a Viking outfit ("B is for Viking"), a cat eating a hot dog ("C is for hot dog") and so on. With great comic timing, Lester breaks his pattern near the end: "X and Y are not important letters. Never use them. And Z is for . . . The End" (showing a zebra's hindquarters).

Ah, yes, we had to come to them sometime: those problematic late letters. An alphabet book is only as good as its weakest link, aka the *X* page. Many a book starts off well only to falter as it grapples with *Q*, *X*, and *Z* — letters worth lots of points in Scrabble but the very devil for alphabet-book creators. Books with themes and plots seem to have the toughest time here, making desperate attempts to plunk a xylophone or X-ray into the story. Some just settle for words that start with an "ex" sound (*eXtreme, eXcellent*). Not only is this cheating — as every child knows — but it can lead to confusion between letters and sounds. One way around this is to present a story in which unusual animals or children's names are used. Joseph Slate and Ashley Wolff do this in their clever *Miss Bindergarten Gets Ready for Kindergarten* and its sequels, with twenty-six animal classmates including Xavier, Yolanda, and Zach. Peter Catalanotto spins this device on its head in *Matthew A.B.C.* All of Mrs. Tuttle's students are (inexplicably) named Matthew, but she has no problem telling them apart: "Matthew A. is extremely affectionate. Matthew B. loves Band-Aids. Matthew C. has friendly cowlicks," and so forth.

Max's ABC by Rosemary Wells is one of the more successful plot-driven alphabet books to come out in recent years. The ants in Max's ant farm escape and go looking for his birthday cake. Unlike many plotted ABC books whose stories swerve off course in an attempt to maintain a strict pattern using each letter within a short space, Wells's text sounds completely unforced. The relevant initial letters are shown in boldface, and some pages have only one alphabet word within several lines of text. The reader becomes so caught up in the conflict between big sister Ruby (trying to clean up and exterminate the ants) and Max (thwarting her every attempt) that it would be easy to forget this is an alphabet book. In the end, " 'Gone forever!' said Ruby. '**X** marks the spots where the ants used to be!' But inside the vacuum bag the ants were enjoying cake and toast. '**Y**um **Y**um **Y**um,' said the ants." Max dumps them out of the bag, and they walk back to the ant farm, exhausted, for some well-deserved sleep: "**ZZZZZ!**"

An excellent alphabet book that's also a terrific bedtime book is Judy Sierra and Melissa Sweet's *The Sleepy Little Alphabet* (see illustration on next page). Happily reminiscent of *Chicka Chicka Boom Boom* in its energy and humor, it features rambunctious little letters who resist their parents' attempts to get them to bed ("*h* tries standing on her head. *i* and *j* jump on the bed") but eventually begin to succumb ("*q* is quiet as a bunny"). Inevitably, it wraps up the alphabet with yawns and zzz's — but ends on an optimistic "See you in the morning, abc's!"

In *The Sleepy Little Alphabet,* illustrator Melissa Sweet manages to infuse her letter characters with personality even as they remain identifiably a lowercase *r* and *s.*

Alphabet books that are used to introduce another language are usually intended for an audience older than the standard two- to five-year-olds. Muriel and Tom Feelings's Swahili alphabet book, *Jambo Means Hello,* works best with children who have mastered the English language alphabet book form. But Laura Rankin's *The Hand-made Alphabet,* showing each letter, an object (asparagus, bubbles, cup), and a hand forming the letter in American Sign Language, is presented so clearly and cleverly that it can work on multiple levels without fear of intimidation.

Illustrators have long been known to have fun with alphabet books' venerated form. The simple rules (twenty-six subjects over thirty-two pages) allow them to enjoy a satisfying creative experience that showcases the picture book as object and art form. Without the distractions of plot and character, each page turn and each pattern that is set up (and sometimes playfully broken) become all-important. It seems odd to list an alphabet book's level as "all ages," but some of the most graphically exciting alphabet books do just that, holding some usefulness for letter learners but greater appeal for older kids. David Pelletier's *The Graphic Alphabet* tackles the daunting task of manipulating each letterform to illustrate a noun or verb beginning with that letter. His *A* crumbles at the top, causing an avalanche; his sideways *B* is a series of dotted lines indicating the path of a bouncing ball. Lisa Campbell Ernst uses sideways letters, too, but hers are the result of the reader turning the book around. *The Turn-Around, Upside-Down Alphabet Book* shows a single letter on each square page with text circling it to describe what the letter looks like from each angle. For example, "E dreams of being" (turn the book ninety degrees clockwise) "an electric plug" (turn another ninety degrees so it is upside down), "a number three" (turn again), "candles on a birthday cake."

So what makes a good alphabet book? It all depends on what you are ready for. From letter learners to fluent readers to puzzle lovers, the menu is large enough to suit every palate.

ACCUMULATED POWER

MARGARET MAHY

When I was a child, books published in the United States were difficult to come by in New Zealand, dominated as it was by its trading relationship with Britain. But by the time I came to read to my daughters, the publishing world had changed. I was able to read them *Blueberries for Sal* (by the American Robert McCloskey) as well as *Peter Rabbit*.

Now, reading to grandchildren, I read newer authors. I read New Zealand writers whose stories make the immediate environment of the listening children replete with imaginative possibility. I also read them *The Stinky Cheese Man, Jumanji,* and *Julius, the Baby of the World* from signed copies acquired at library conferences.

But sometimes, as I read familiar tales to my grandchildren, I weep. One such book, *Honey Bear* by Dixie Willson, was given to me by an aunt in 1939. It is a sweet, rather sentimental story, though mysterious and humorous, too. I read *Honey Bear* to my grandchildren and cry as I read, not because of its sentiment but because of its accumulated power. By now there is more to the story than words, pages, and pictures. The voices of my dead parents come to me out of the story, setting up profound sympathetic resonance in that echoing inner library, both voices mingling with mine as I read, yet again, this little-known book.

It was mysterious then, and it is still mysterious today, and the children I read it to watch my face as I read and stare at my tears — those outer signs of the power of the story working in an individual consciousness — with wonder.

"Have a Carrot"

Cynthia Voigt

I don't know that my children would agree — and I am not consulting them to find out — but high on the list of favorite read-aloud books in the house where I was the mommy was *The Runaway Bunny*. As a mother; as a pillow to the warm, small, nestling body; as reader aloud, that book satisfied. The rhythmic prose, the colorful illustrations, the balanced structure of the story — all of those contributed to our pleasure. For myself, also, there was the thought-provoking content of the book — the mother bunny who was so reassuringly always present. Or was it *smotheringly* always present? Or merely *inescapably*? Was I oversensitive to feel a kind of chill when I read the mother bunny's promise, "I will be the wind and I will blow you where I want you to go"? Was I over-identifying with the child beside me in her/his longing to escape that overflowing, overwhelming Mother? The question the book raises is: What about love?

There are no answers offered, unless in the final line of the story, after the little bunny has remarked, "Shucks. I might as well stay here and be your little bunny." The mother responds — lovingly, patiently, wisely, victoriously, smugly, and above all enigmatically: "Have a carrot."

Have a carrot, I say to my children, and they understand everything I mean. To our children, to their parents, that line constitutes a family cord. It pulls us together, and that is one of the answers about love, isn't it?

What Makes a Good "Three Little Pigs"?

Joanna Rudge Long

Once upon a time, there was an old sow with three little pigs, and as she had not enough to keep them, she sent them out to seek their fortune. The first that went off met a man with a bundle of straw, and said to him: "Please, man, give me that straw to build me a house." Which the man did, and the little pig built a house with it. Presently came along a wolf, and knocked at the door, and said: "Little pig, little pig, let me come in." To which the pig answered: "No, no, by the hair of my chinny chin chin." . . . "Then I'll huff, and I'll puff, and I'll blow your house in."

So begins the classic version of "The Three Little Pigs," a nursery tale that may not prove to be as familiar as you think it is. As the great folklorist Joseph Jacobs told it (in *English Fairy Tales,* 1890), it's just right for small children — lively with action, with repetitive patterns of language and incident and a villain whose fate precisely fits his crime: in the end, the *wolf* is eaten, by his third intended victim.

Citing Halliwell's *Popular Rhymes and Nursery Tales* as *his* source, Jacobs added that the story has few parallels (in contrast to, say, "Cinderella," with its thousand variants). However, Jacobs's pigs have inspired dozens of subsequent versions, with pictures from many excellent illustrators and retellings in as many flavors as an ice-cream shop — traditional or revisionist, comic or didactic, simplified or elaborated, bowdlerized, truncated, popularized, fractured, restructured, or postmodern.

How, then, does the purist's concern — to respect the "original" — apply? Normally, it's nice to find a nod to the new version's source, a note on how it's been adapted, along with the adapter's rationale. But with a story as well known as this one, demanding full disclosure may be unnecessarily pedantic. What we really care about is what goes for any picture book: a good story with good illustrations, to which we might add, in this case, some respectful remnants of the story's original genius, like its pattern, its patter, or its pacing.

But what's it about, really, this story? Most of the characters get eaten! Is it OK to use it with kids?

Yes, of course it is, but deciding which editions are most appropriate depends on how the stories are told and on the nature of the audience. What, for example, do they know of pigs? In times past, a pig was commonly raised for meat on a farm. As Huck Finn observed, "There was generly [sic] hogs in the garden, and people driving them out." This traditional tale comes from that kind of rural culture, where many did need to seek their fortunes, a quest not all would survive. In the 1920s, progressive educators deplored "violent" folklore. Their concern persists; yet twenty-first-century kids, most of whom know nothing of real farm animals (or their necessary ends) routinely zap characters on-screen. Charlotte's death is sad, yet natural; but to have Wilbur suffer his threatened fate would be unbearable: we know him so well. But in "The Three Little Pigs," we don't know the first two pigs at all; they're generically happy-go-lucky. What delights us about the third pig is the way he outwits the wolf. One four-year-old had a typically childlike reaction: "Well! If the wolf ate the first two pigs, and the other pig ate the wolf, he ate the first two pigs, too, didn't he?" Zap!

For that little boy, the story was about the rules of the game — and about winning by guile. For someone else it might be justice, or the relief (or thrill) of escaping the wolf. It all depends on what the listener brings to it. You might say that the story is in the ears of the beholder.

The telling matters, too. Many have adopted this perennial favorite, some by simply giving it new illustrations, some by retelling it so creatively that it takes on quite a different flavor. And some, assuming readers' familiarity with the classic tale, use it as basis for a whole new, mind-bending scenario. Ranging from simple to complex, from earnest to downright hilarious, none of the books described below will appeal to everyone; yet each is excellent in its own way, a worthy choice for the right child.

Paul Galdone's *The Three Little Pigs,* small and lap-friendly, is close to Jacobs's but slightly simplified — a boon for newly independent readers. His deftly sketched piglets are starry-eyed innocents in familiar-looking farmland, his wolf just scary enough to serve the story without provoking nightmares. Cheerful color gives the book a sunny aura and brings out the tale's humor. For the very youngest, this could be the best choice.

Margot Zemach's edition, more sophisticated in both language and art, would suit a somewhat older child, perhaps up to second grade. In old-world peasant garb with caps and patches, her mature-looking pigs set energetically to work, evidently inspired by their weeping mama's advice: "Build good, strong houses, and always watch out for the wolf. Now goodbye, my sons, goodbye." Like the fine storyteller she is, Zemach often rephrases, comfortable in her own voice yet respectful of her source. In her agreeably atmospheric illustrations, the orderly construction and swift obliteration of the straw and stick houses occur amid homely domestic detail. Then, as the scruffy third pig works his wiles on the ingratiating wolf, the pace quickens. Bit by bit, the wolf's gentlemanly façade unravels, until at last he plunges down the chimney, dislodging bricks as he goes.

Barry Moser, Glen Rounds, and James Marshall all retell the tale with notable verve and humor, each in his signature style. Moser's unclad pigs are rough country folk, toothy and bristled. They look like the kind of kids you don't want to meet coming home from school—a plus, given that his gaunt wolf disposes of two in short order. Moser's logic is amusingly sensible: when the wolf fails to blow down the house, he has "no breath left . . . so he [sits] down . . . to think"; the pig uses a block and tackle to get into the apple tree. Such wry flourishes are best appreciated by older children, while adults will particularly admire Moser's masterful composition and watercolor technique.

Also for primary grades and up is Glen Rounds's *Three Little Pigs and the Big Bad Wolf*. Rounds takes the story even further into rural America with roughly sketched pigs trotting on all fours and simply burrowing into heaps of straw and sticks they happen to find. His voice is informal, with such clarifications for modern children as an "empty barrel" instead of a butter churn. Broad, craggy pen lines define Rounds's angular figures, which are elegantly complemented by the bold sans serif type, to handsome graphic effect. Even the skinny, *really* ugly Big Bad Wolf contributes to the book's striking visual harmony.

For pure, lighthearted fun with the essential tale intact, James Marshall's pigs take the cake. The title page sets the tone: one pig paints the title in as many giddy colors as his own wildly patterned trousers, another sleeps, and the nerdy third is reading through a pince-nez. The old sow issues no warnings; it's just, "Now be sure to write, and remember that I love you," and off they go, two pigs scantily clad and one dressed like a banker. Later, he talks like one: "Capital idea, my good fellow!" to the man with the bricks, and "Would three o'clock suit you?" to the wolf he plans to evade. Marshall's narrative bubbles with such diction. His buoyant illustrations are in the same easygoing spirit, from a pig lightly balanced on an airy ridgepole to the dim-looking wolf in red-and-white stripes; from the third pig harvesting turnips ("All you can pick, 10 cents") to his cozy dinner of wolf (served under a lid, the better to hide it from the squeamish).

Marshall's book stands on its own, though it's even more fun as a blithe parody. Jon Scieszka's hilarious *The True Story of the 3 Little Pigs!* (by A. Wolf) assumes prior knowledge of the tale it contradicts: here, the wolf offers his own self-serving account. He was only trying to borrow a cup of sugar to bake his granny a birthday cake, he says, when he sneezed and "that whole darn straw house fell down," leaving the pig inside "dead as a doornail. . . . It seemed like a shame to leave a perfectly good ham dinner lying there." An unreliable narrator? Probably. What's certain is that he's an engaging miscreant, admirably supported by Lane Smith's comical, surreal art. A Dagwood-high cheeseburger with mouse tails and bunny ears protruding from among pickles and patties; the wolf's many, many tiny pearly teeth; a cameo of Granny Wolf abed (recalling "Red Riding Hood") — Smith's illustrations are endlessly droll and inventive.

In *The Three Little Wolves and the Big Bad Pig*, Eugene Trivizas reverses roles for a fable on peacemaking. Working together, the gentle wolves build three houses, each sturdier than the last (brick, concrete, an armed fortress), only to have each in turn demolished by Helen Oxenbury's rogue pig. This scoundrel actually looks a bit less brutish than Moser's pigs; still, his sledgehammer levels the brick house, then escalates to a jackhammer and finally to dynamite that blows the fortress to smithereens. The wolves' fourth house, of flowers, wins the pig over, and he and the wolves settle down happily together. Oxenbury's beguiling wolf cubs and blossom-bedecked landscapes lighten the message somewhat, as does a relatively long text that mentions such innocent pastimes as battledore and shuttlecock.

In his postmodern Caldecott winner, *The Three Pigs*, David Wiesner explores the very idea of story. The wolf blows down the straw house on the first spread (see illustration below), but though the text reads, "and ate the pig up," Wiesner's illustrations have already begun another story, one in which all three pigs escape their page-shaped frames for a different scenario. Those beginning frames are illustrated in a flat, traditional style. As they leave them, the pigs are transformed, like Pinocchio becoming a real boy: they grow sturdier, more rounded and detailed. As they celebrate

their freedom on new, as-yet-unmarked pages, pages from their old story twist, turn, and blow away. One, folded into an airplane, takes them on to another tale: "Hey Diddle, Diddle," illustrated in a sentimental, conventional style. Soon they're leaving that story as well, taking the cat with them, and he, too, becomes more corporeal, like the pigs. Later a dragon, escaping the sword-wielding prince in *his* story, is also transformed. Finally, back on their original pages, the pigs and their two new friends settle down in the brick house, the disappointed wolf still visible through a window.

Wiesner's marvelously comical and just plain beautiful book demonstrates how far a good old story can take an artist inspired by its essential spirit. Joan Bodger once said, "The wonder of these types of stories is that the child knows there's a mystery. . . . Children cannot put it into words — there's no other way to say it except through art or poetry or folk tales — but they pick up on the truth in them." A child who wants the same story again and again is absorbing such a truth. One newly adopted eight-year-old's favorite story is "The Three Little Pigs," which she has explored in many editions. Perhaps "The Three Little Pigs" speaks so eloquently to this young veteran of foster care because it's about finding a secure home. Tales that last for generations have many such resonances; that's why they endure across cultures, circumstances, and centuries.

That's why the old tale speaks to us still.

What Makes a Good Preschool Science Book?

Betty Carter

Several years ago, my then-three-year-old twin grandchildren were going outside. As he always does, Jackson rushed out first. Suddenly he skidded to a stop, squatted down, studied the ground for a moment, and exclaimed, "Wow! Libby, come here!"

Quickly, she joined him and mirrored his actions. "Wow!" she said reverently. "Ants."

"Yeah," whispered Jack. "Ants." A pause: "Wow!"

I love that story and that memory because the kids so naturally expressed the wonder they saw in the world around them. And it made me wonder as well. "How can we encourage that preschool exuberance about science?" Besides ants, there's a pretty exciting amount of nature around us in Texas, including America's only marsupial (the opossum); the ever-present armadillo (which blows itself up like a balloon when swimming in our pool); dinosaur tracks; and breathtaking wildflowers. Yes, we have skunks and coyotes, and snakes, but not even for my grandchildren would I approach any of those outside a zoo, so trips to our two local zoos figured prominently in weekend adventures. Those experiences are important, but, as Rebecca Kai Dotlich reminds us in her picture book

Clarity of information does not mean an artist has to sacrifice wit—in Vicki Cobb's *I See Myself*, Julia Gorton's illustration of the scientific principle of reflection has charm and personality.

What Is Science?, science is about more than plants and animals: "So into the earth / and into the sky, / we question the how, / the where, when, / and why." And where do kids begin to learn how to question? One word: books.

Look carefully at a four-volume series named Science Play written by Vicki Cobb. Both together and individually, these books get right at the process of discovery by asking youngsters to participate in a number of experiments in order to understand scientific principles. Children can discover properties of water (*I Get Wet*); light and refraction (*I See Myself*); gravity (*I Fall Down*); and force (*I Face the Wind*). And they can come to a true understanding of basic scientific principles, a critical piece of knowledge for children. According to Natalie Angier in *The Canon: A Whirligig Tour of the Beautiful Basics of Science,* the intuitive scientific concepts we learn (either correctly or incorrectly) in early childhood remain basic to our understanding (or misunderstanding) of science.

In these four books, Cobb asks adults to reinvent the way they read picture books to children. Rather than start at page one and read right straight through, adults are encouraged to stop about every two pages, work with the children to understand the principle at hand, and then move on to the next point. Here's the pattern: introduce a concept, understand a concept, use that understanding to introduce yet another concept. In a standard introduction for each book, Cobb lays out the process for adult readers and provides them with a list of everyday household items they will need throughout the book. So, what do kids do?

In *I Fall Down,* for example, young listeners are first presented with several everyday references to gravity: "Know what happens when you trip? You fall down! Know what happens when you spill your milk? It drips down!" Similar examples continue as kids are asked to toss an object (such as a ball, a set of keys, a block) up in the air, and then think about what happens. Cobb ends this four-page section with a question: "Does it ever fall up?" Then she introduces the concept of gravity, that it is always pulling things. "Know which way? Down, down, down." At this point she directs them to another experiment: Take a spoonful of molasses or honey, point the spoon toward a container, and watch the slowly moving "goo" dribble into the container. To emphasize this point, the illustrations depict the process and the text runs vertically (down, down, down), explaining, "The goo stretches and gets longer and longer. It looks like a ribbon streaming into the jar. Gravity pulls the molasses from the spoon back into the jar." Got it? Gravity pulls matter down. Next concept: Do all objects fall at the same speed? Several dropping exercises follow (presented as "dropping races" in the spirit of "science *play*"), including those with a tissue or feather, which show how air slows the descent. Read, experiment, understand; read, experiment, understand.

I've read these books to a single child, two children, and groups of youngsters. Each time their responses have been exuberant and playful. During the reading of *I Face the Wind*, it's quite a sight to see a group of four-year-olds running around a room earnestly collecting air in a plastic grocery bag. "I got some," one child will shout. "Me too," says another. That's a moment that recaptures the wonder in science.

Cobb knows her science, and she knows children and their abilities. In *I Face the Wind*, for example, there's one experiment designed to see if air has any weight. Kids are asked to take two balloons, blow one up completely and blow the other up about halfway, knot the ends, tape the balloons on separate corners of a coat hanger, hook the hanger on a pencil, and stand absolutely still to see what happens (Does the side of the hanger with the filled balloon tip down? Does air have weight?). Not only was I a little concerned with the children's physical dexterity, but I also wondered about the "absolutely still" part. No problem with the group I worked with, however — they stood still and grasped the concept.

Will these principles stay with them throughout their lifetimes, as Angier indicates? I don't know, but I do know of an example where one stayed for four years. One day last summer, eight-year-old Jackson, inspired by the movie *Back to the Future*, decided to make a time machine, so he fashioned a contraption that combined a paper airplane and his version of the DeLorean. It worked like an airplane, gliding and crashing, but not slowing down after it hit the ground. What did he need? To collect air. How does one collect air? Why, in a plastic grocery bag stapled onto a time machine. Thank you, Vicki Cobb.

DELICIOUS RHYTHMS, ENDURING WORDS

NAOMI SHIHAB NYE

When a man I met recently told me that his grandfather awakened him as a boy by reciting poetry, giving him a lifelong appetite for delicious rhythms in his ears, I changed my method of waking our son, Madison, up. No more chipper greetings, no more buzzing clocks. Now I sit at his bedside for ten minutes every school day before he needs to rise, reading Carl Sandburg, Langston Hughes, Lucille Clifton, Emily Dickinson, even Wallace Stevens (whom I am finally beginning to understand).

I like imagining what filters down into Madison's deep consciousness. We don't discuss the poems at breakfast, but after a few weeks of my reading them, he began saying, "I really liked those poems today. Could you read them again soon?" or "All day that poem came into my mind."

I feel gratified and strongly suggest to other parents this simple method of helping children "wake up with literature" as well as go to sleep with it. It is our happy task to find as many comfortable ways we can to make enduring words an essential part of all our lives.

MORE GREAT PICTURE BOOKS

Chris Barton, illustrations by Tom Lichtenheld, *Shark vs. Train*
   40 pp. If a shark were pitted against a train, which would win? The answer depends on the contest: the train's belch is louder, but he's no match for the shark when jumping off the high dive. Barton's deadpan text—sparked with dialogue balloons that give the characters both personality and one-liners— is matched by Lichtenheld's spot-on visual humor.

Jonathan Bean, *At Night*
   32 pp. Unable to sleep, a girl follows a breeze to the roof of her apartment building. Muted blues and oranges keep the tone subdued in this bedtime story, perfect reading for a warm night.

Bonny Becker, illustrations by Kady MacDonald Denton, *A Visitor for Bear*
   56 pp. "No visitors allowed." The sign on Bear's door is clear, but one mouse is undeterred. By a friend's persistence, Bear is transformed; text and art handle the shift with aplomb.

Doreen Cronin, illustrations by Harry Bliss, *Diary of a Fly*
   40 pp. Cronin's impeccable comedic timing conveys real-life information in a way that makes the facts memorable. Short sentences and visual jokes make this a great selection for listeners and new readers alike.

Shutta Crum, illustrations by Carol Thompson, *Thunder-Boomer!*
   32 pp. As a fierce thunderstorm blows in, a farm family rushes to bring in the animals. But one of the chickens resists — could it have something to do with a little lost kitten? This satisfying picture book captures the drama of a summer storm even as it rewards readers with a smaller-scale, homey story.

Bob Graham, *April and Esme, Tooth Fairies*
   40 pp. Modern-day tooth fairy sisters convince their parents that they're old enough to collect their very first tooth (Mom: "Send me a text if you

need to"). Youngsters will linger over the detailed illustrations, reminiscent of *The Borrowers*: in the family's cottage, teeth dangle like wind chimes, the bathtub's a milk pitcher, and the sink is a thimble.

Kevin Henkes, *Little White Rabbit*

32 pp. Little White Rabbit hops through idyllic fields and forests, wondering what it would be like to be just about everything. Alternating full-page spreads depict his rich inner life, where he is as green as the high grass, tall as the fir trees, or still as a rock. Bold lines, expressive movement, and a springtime palette of pink, blue, and lush greens delight the eye.

G. Brian Karas, *The Village Garage*

32 pp. At the Village Garage, a diverse crew of municipal workers happily tackle jobs around town through spring, summer, fall, and winter. Few things fascinate young children more than watching workers on the job; visiting *The Village Garage* is almost as good as the real thing.

Helen Lester, illustrations by Lynn Munsinger, *Tacky Goes to Camp*

32 pp. Tacky the Penguin returns for his seventh adventure, his funniest yet. The lovable slob saves the day as the campers discover that their best defense against a ravenous, campsite-raiding bear is a s'more-addled penguin.

Liz Garton Scanlon, illustrations by Marla Frazee, *All the World*

40 pp. After a trip to the beach, a family stops at a farmers' market, visits a park, and waits out a rainstorm in a café before heading home at the day's end. Scanlon's text has a child-friendly simplicity, and the seaside setting showcases not only Frazee's affectionate mix of people but also her stunning, glowing skyscapes.

Bob Shea, *Dinosaur vs. Bedtime*

40 pp. A little red dinosaur takes on the world, from a pile of leaves ("ROAR!") to a plate of spaghetti ("ROAR! CHOMP! CHOMP! ROAR! ROAR!"). An ideal bedtime story for active readers.

MORE GREAT FOLKLORE

Zoë B. Alley, illustrations by R. W. Alley, *There's a Wolf at the Door*
40 pp. Grades K–3. The wolf gets foiled five times over in linked (and humorously fractured) folktales. The wisecracking in the text, echoed by the comic-strip format, is balanced by delicate drawings in pastoral tints. The extra-large format maximizes the fun.

Jim Aylesworth, illustrations by Barbara McClintock, *The Mitten*
32 pp. Grades PS–2. In this new take on the old Ukrainian story, the text exhibits perfect pacing, precisely chosen details, and most of all, participatory repetition: "My toes are cold as ice!/Your mitten looks so cozy,/ and warm toes would feel so nice!" Children will love the humor in the expressive pictures.

Anthony Browne, *Me and You*
32 pp. Grades K–3. In this haunting version of "The Three Bears," have-not Goldilocks, walking her neighborhood's mean streets, gets lost and seeks shelter in the bears' prosperous home. Her story is told in cramped, colorless panels; the bears' story appears on opposite pages, in expansive, cheerful pastels. This innovative retelling will challenge readers' assumptions about the familiar tale.

Ashley Bryan, *Beautiful Blackbird*
40 pp. Grades PS–2. Noted folklorist and artist Bryan presents a life-affirming folktale from Zambia — how birds got their black markings — illustrated with simple scissors-and-brush collage.

Rachel Isadora, *The Fisherman and His Wife*
32 pp. Grades PS–2. Isadora uses collages of paint-striated paper plus scraps of fabric to place the Grimms' well-known tale in an African setting. Dialogue is minimal, suiting the story to listeners and beginning readers. One of several folktales Isadora has reimagined in Africa.

Salley Mavor, *Pocketful of Posies: A Treasury of Nursery Rhymes*
 64 pp. Grades PS and up. Sixty-four nursery rhymes are illustrated with intricate tapestries of wool, felt, embroidery, beads, and every kind of needlework. The textured constructions encourage the eye to linger on every hand-sewn detail as they capture action, emotion, and personality. Every family deserves a fine collection of nursery rhymes, and this is one of the best.

Sam McBratney, illustrations by Russell Ayto, *One Voice, Please: Favorite Read-Aloud Stories*
 167 pp. Grades 4–6. These fifty-six short fables, cautionary tales, and anecdotes tickle both mind and funny bone with unexpected twists of logic. The angular drawings punctuate the pages with their own lighthearted take on wise men, fools, and tricksters.

Jerry Pinkney, *The Lion & the Mouse*
 40 pp. Grades PS–2. Pinkney retells Aesop's fable entirely in his lush pencil-and-watercolor art; the story is all the more eloquent for being wordless. On every page, this beautiful book illuminates both its real setting (the Serengeti) and the world of fable, where a bargain between a regal lion and a doughty mouse can be made, and mutual rescues may happen.

Coleen Salley, illustrations by Janet Stevens, *Epossumondas Saves the Day*
 48 pp. Grades K–3. An irresistible possum and his human auntie and mama reenact the southern folktale "Sody Sallyraytus," which here involves a birthday party, a "great, huge, ugly Louisiana snapping turtle," and a baking-soda–induced explosion—not to mention a distinctive down-home storytelling voice and lively pictures.

Laura Amy Schlitz, illustrations by Max Grafe, *The Bearskinner: A Tale of the Brothers Grimm*
 40 pp. Grades 4–6. With clarity and grace, Schlitz narrates a Grimm tale of an ex-soldier making a bargain with the devil. The full-page illustrations are atmospheric and almost monochromatic, composed of grays and browns with an occasional wash of blue, gleam of gold, or sunset hue.

PART TWO
READING WITH THEM

Overview

Roger Sutton

Family legend has it that one day when I was six, I was sitting at home silently looking at a book when I suddenly looked up and said to all and sundry, "I can read!" Yes, Harper & Row had trademarked that slogan in 1957, but my epiphany was completely my own, as it is for every child upon the discovery that printed words in a row are more than printed words in a row, that printed words *say something*.

That, in fact, printed words say something *worth pursuing*. Easy readers offer children their first crack at seeing — for themselves — how words add up. It's a discovery that goes hand in hand with reading independence: the child, him- or herself, gets to bring the words to life. Books become literally useful. In chapters three and four we look at easy readers and chapter books, those distinct but related genres that don't teach so much as encourage childen to string words into sentences, sentences into paragraphs, paragraphs into chapters, chapters into books. And atop the row of beloved picture books, a new bookshelf comes to life, composed of choices made by an ever more actively independent reader.

Chapter Three
EASY READERS

I Can Read a Whole Book
Roger Sutton

Easy readers build on the foundations (established at home and school) of phonics, word recognition, and aural experience with stories. They allow children to take charge of their own literacy, permitting them to independently enter the world of a whole story with a beginning, middle, and end. A whole book, too, one with a first page, a last page, chapters, and just enough pictures to help you along without making you feel like a baby. When in my thirties I took up running, it was very important to me to be able to run *one mile*. The friend who was coaching me showed me a path and two landmarks, a beginning and an end, with exactly *one mile* between them. Although my first mile probably took me fifteen minutes, the time didn't matter so much as reaching the end. Reading "a whole book" has the same satisfaction for the new reader. And I wish it were a Law of Publishing that all easy readers have page numbers at the bottom of each page. It lets you know in a very concrete way how far you've come and how far you've got to go.

The impetus and format for easy readers came from the old Dick and Jane–style primers, which had been using simple vocabulary, word repetition, and generously leaded and illustrated pages to teach reading since the 1930s. But it was in 1957 that the beginning-reader genre became blessed with genius. Two publishing imprints expressly designed to bring primers into the home began that year, Harper & Row's I Can Read Books, inaugurated by Else Holmelund Minarik and Maurice Sendak's *Little Bear,* and Random House's Beginner Books, with Dr. Seuss's *The Cat in the Hat.*

The books could not be more different. The Seuss is all anarchy, the Minarik / Sendak all comfort. But they both ask the same questions: How will I get on without my parents? What can I do by myself? Am I brave? They each trace the path of a young character from dependency to self-reliance and back, but re-made (a journey you'll remember from *Where the Wild Things Are*), mirroring the experience of learning to read itself. The acquisition of reading skill and fluency is not, and should not, be ever-forward: not every book should be more difficult than the one that's read before. Again: is that the way *you* read?

The Cat in the Hat takes its journey to reading on a road of rhyme, a powerful mnemonic device that Mother Goose knew well. It's a good form for beginning readers, allowing them to use their ears as well as their eyes to figure out what word will come next:

> Then those Things ran about
> With big bumps, jumps and kicks
> And with hops and big thumps
> And all kinds of bad . . .

Only one word can finish off that quatrain, and it's an attractively semi-naughty one, too. Reading has rewards.

The success of Dr. Seuss's books has inspired a raft of imitators, but they mostly miss what makes him so good. Rhyme by itself is not enough, and wedding it to treacly morals or facts about the states is worse. *The Cat in the Hat* demonstrates respect for children by allowing them to face down chaos — whether it's that of a messed-up house or the jumble of letters on a printed page — on their own. It prompts the decoding of words for the sake of fun, not in service of a lesson or didactic point. It is *astonishingly* disrespectful, and in the end invites readers to join in the rebellion when Mother comes home:

> Should we tell her about it?
> Now, what SHOULD we do?
> Well . . .
> What would YOU do
> If your mother asked YOU?

Reading as conspiracy. You gotta love it.

Little Bear is altogether a gentler affair, if far more sophisticated in its understanding of young children and of the components that make up a "real" book — like a table-of-contents page, with four chapters listed. Unlike in *The Cat in the Hat,* Little Bear's mother is much in evidence here, ever-encouraging in her son's attempts to make his own way. In the first chapter, Mother Bear patiently outfits Little Bear to play in the snow, giving him garment after garment until he realizes that his own fur coat is enough. Later, she gently points out that he might not be able to fly to the moon:

> "Maybe," said Little Bear.
> "But I'm going now.
> Just look for me up in the sky."

Wisely, she lets him go: " 'Be back for lunch,' said Mother." Little Bear is both a stand-in for young readers and a figure toward whom they can have some superiority; like Mother, they know Little Bear doesn't really go to the moon. See? Reading *does* make you smarter. Kids spend so much time perplexed by the adult world around them that the opportunity to feel smarter than someone else is a real

LITTLE BEAR GOES TO THE MOON

"I have a new space helmet.

I am going to the moon," said Little Bear to

Mother Bear.

"How?" asked Mother Bear.

36

In *Little Bear*, with text by Else Holmelund Minarik and art by Maurice Sendak, all the narrative content is provided in the words; the mother-and-child portrait adds warmth and humor.

attraction—another classic easy-to-read series that understands this is Peggy Parish's *Amelia Bedelia*, in which the title character takes everything literally: when she's told to trim the Christmas tree, she cuts off the branches. (Not to sound brutal about it, but learning to read is a kind of mastery, and it's no mistake that Amelia Bedelia is a *maid*.)

Such wordplay can be tricky for new readers; some, for example, will simply think that Amelia Bedelia is just being goofy. Shelley Moore Thomas and Jennifer Plecas's *Good Night, Good Knight* introduces one simple homophone, as the good *knight* makes sure that three needy little dragons each have a good *night*. That single tricky bit will be plenty for some readers, but the book also offers something irresistible to all children mature enough to be reading on their own: the opportunity to identify with the grown-up in a story, letting somebody else be the baby for a change.

Where *The Cat in the Hat* uses rhyme to clue readers in to meaning, *Little Bear* uses repetition:

> Little Bear climbed to the top of a little hill,
> And climbed to the top of a little tree,
> A very little tree on the little hill,
> And shut his eyes and jumped.

Notice how the last line both avoids the repeated *littles, trees,* and *hills* and pops with an emphatic rhythm of its own. That's the jump new readers are making, too, moving from what they know to what they don't — eyes open, of course.

Typically, easy readers move away from the adult-child dyad toward a world in which the hero is an independent participant in a world of equals, whether they be siblings, friends (see Arnold Lobel's Frog and Toad series, or Edward and James Marshall's Fox books) or a "companion animal" (surely Cynthia Rylant's Mudge, from her Henry and Mudge books, is too simpatico — and too big — to be just a pet!). As these titles suggest, easy readers often develop into series, for excellent reasons. Kids love seeing what familiar characters get up to next (admit it: so do you), and for new readers, having the characters already in place is one hurdle crossed before a book is even opened.

Fiction is the mainstay of the genre, because it allows children to use the knowledge of story structure gained from listening to help them with a printed text. But there is a smattering of nonfiction. Charlotte Lewis Brown and Phil Wilson's *The Day the Dinosaurs Died* indulges a child's taste for the ghoulish ("Tyrannosaurus rex walked over to the dead Edmontosaurus, and he ripped out a large bite") while offering scientific speculation about how dinosaurs became extinct. Gentler children might prefer one of Lee Bennett Hopkins's many excellent poetry collections, such as *Small Talk: A Book of Short Poems,* with poems like Rebecca Kai Dotlich's "Fossil Finds":

No skin,
no scale,
no ancient moan —
his legacy is strictly
   BONE.

But a kid ready for easy readers is also ready to read everywhere — from his or her old picture books, a sentence or two from whatever Mom or Dad is reading, advertisements, cereal boxes, labels . . . you get the idea. What the easy reader provides is a neatly shaped experience maximized for pleasure and success. It helps you learn the happiness not just of reading, but of finishing.

But you'll notice that publishers don't miss a trick, using the series appeal and the easy-reader design to format books so that they look like easy readers but really aren't. And on a recent visit to a bookstore we noticed that some easy-reader series positively bristle with allegedly educational labels that indicate that *Little Bear,* for example, is a "level one" book for "beginning reading" while *Frog and Toad* is a level two, "reading with help." What's the difference? Got me. The point is that children ready to read on their own are also ready to choose their own books. Let 'em at it.

Unlucky Arithmetic

Thirteen Ways to Raise a Nonreader

DEAN SCHNEIDER AND ROBIN SMITH

1 **Never read** where your children can see you.

2 **Put a TV or computer** in every room. Don't neglect the bedrooms and kitchen.

3 **Correct your child** every time she mispronounces a word.

4 **Schedule activities** every day after school so your child will never be bored.

5 Once your child can read independently, **throw out the picture books.** They're for babies.

6 **Don't play** board games together. Too dull.

7 Give little **rewards** for reading. **Stickers** and plastic toys are nice. **Money** is even better.

8 Don't expect your children to enjoy reading. Kids' books are for **teaching** vocabulary, proper study habits, and good **morals.**

9 Buy only **40-watt bulbs** for your lamps.

10 Under **no** circumstances read your child the same book **over and over.** She heard it once; she should remember it.

11 Never allow your child to listen to **audiobooks;** that's **cheating.**

12 Make sure your kids only read books that are "challenging." **Easy** books are a complete **waste of time.** That goes double for comic books and *Mad* magazine.

13 Absolutely, positively **no reading in bed.**

LOOK

LOIS LOWRY

My oldest child, a daughter, remembers that when she was three, and we lived in Cambridge, Massachusetts, she often walked with me to a nearby grocery store. She tells me that there were letters painted in the street at the corner where we stopped and waited for the light to change. I have no memory of them. But she tells me that I pointed the two *O*s out to her. I told her they were like eyes, she says, and that because of those *O*-eyes she could remember that the word in the street was LOOK.

Then — a miracle! — one evening she glanced at the print in a picture book I was reading to her (who knows which one? We had so many) and happened upon the same word. She saw it on the page, looked up at me, saw that I was reading the print, heard me say the word *look* — and made the magical connection in her mind that propelled her, like a little tow-headed rocket, into reading.

Forty-five years later, I live again near that same street corner. The letters are no longer there, though I believe my daughter that they once were. I never walk past that corner without thinking how private, powerful, and memorable a moment it is, in the life of a child, when the shape of letters takes on meaning and a door of the world opens.

MORE GREAT EASY READERS

Tedd Arnold, ***Hooray for Fly Guy!***
32 pp. Grades PS–2. In this entry in the series that began with *Hi! Fly Guy*, Buzz and his zany pet housefly go out for the football team. Unfortunately for Fly Guy, he's benched — until his special talents are needed on the field. The text's short, accessible sentences, supported by colorful cartoon illustrations, provide silly, confidence-building fun for early readers.

Monika Bang-Campbell, illustrations by Molly Bang, ***Little Rat Makes Music***
48 pp. Grades K–3. In eight short chapters, the small, determined heroine of *Little Rat Sets Sail* and *Little Rat Rides* takes on a new challenge: violin lessons. The matter-of-fact prose allows the flashes of humor in the story to shine even more brightly, and the deep jewel-tone colors provide a rich counterpart to the homey settings.

Judyann Ackerman Grant, illustrations by Sue Truesdell, ***Chicken Said, "Cluck!"***
32 pp. Grades PS–2. A pesky chicken's constant dirt-scratching, captured in humorous illustrations, threatens friends Earl and Pearl's pumpkin-growing project. The book's carefully accumulating structure, repeated refrain, and controlled yet piquant vocabulary are big pluses for brand-new readers.

Grace Lin, ***Ling & Ting: Not Exactly the Same!***
44 pp. Grades K–2. Six chapters tell brief, humorous stories about twin sisters Ling and Ting. People are always telling them that they're exactly the same, but readers will get to know the girls by their unique personalities — and Ting's uneven bangs. The stories are warmly illustrated with Lin's bold color-saturated art.

Kate McMullan, illustrations by R. W. Alley, ***Pearl and Wagner: Two Good Friends***
48 pp. Grades K–3. Whether they are building disastrous science projects or navigating through hurt feelings, Pearl (a conscientious rabbit) and Wagner (a daydreaming mouse) demonstrate the most enduring qualities

of friendship. The illustrations are unusually expressive. Sequels include *Pearl and Wagner: Three Secrets* and *Pearl and Wagner: One Funny Day*.

James Proimos, ***Johnny Mutton, He's So Him!***
42 pp. Grades PS–2. The lovably eccentric sheep (from *The Many Adventures of Johnny Mutton*) again demonstrates the goofy and sweet-natured qualities that are "so him" in five brief, very funny stories related in comic-strip panels. Sequel: *Mutton Soup: More Adventures of Johnny Mutton*.

Erica Silverman, illustrations by Betsy Lewin, ***Cowgirl Kate and Cocoa: Rain or Shine***
48 pp. Grades K–3. Cowgirl Kate and cow horse Cocoa have four rainy-day adventures that highlight the close friendship between girl and horse. The watercolor illustrations emphasize the characters' personalities, while the text is both accessible enough to work as a beginning reader and rich enough to function as a read-aloud story.

Sarah Weeks, illustrations by Jane Manning, ***Pip Squeak***
32 pp. Grades PS–2. Mouse Pip cleans the house in preparation for his friend's visit: "He mops the steps. / He mops the floor. / And when he's done, / he mops some more." The unforced patterned rhyme provides support for just-beginning readers, and there's also a plot and characterization, plus a small concluding surprise. The bright primary colors of the illustrations reinforce the jaunty tone.

Mo Willems, ***Pigs Make Me Sneeze!***
56 pp. Grades PS–2. Gloomy elephant Gerald and his upbeat porcine best friend, Piggie, are provided with easy-to-follow stories, uncluttered illustrations, and pithy dialogue in the popular Elephant & Piggie series. Willems conveys volumes with an expertly placed eyebrow or down-turned mouth; the color-coded speech balloons suggest shared-reading opportunities for pals of any age or disposition. Other titles include *Are You Ready to Play Outside?* and *I Am Invited to a Party!*

Chapter Four

CHAPTER BOOKS

Situations Become Stories
Roger Sutton

The line between easy readers and chapter books is elastic — a salutary reminder that the distinctions between all age- or level-based genres are just so. Marshall's easy reader *Fox and His Friends* has chapters; so does *Moby-Dick*. One of the characteristics of children's literature, from board books to young adult novels, is that readers are always receiving help. Books for young children have pictures because children can understand pictures before they can understand words. Easy readers tend to restrict themselves to short words that children have already learned, or ones that they can figure out based on the ones they know. In their turn, chapter books — by which, let's agree, we mean in this context *first* chapter books — honor a child's ambition to grow. The help offered by the pictures, generous leading, and limited vocabulary of an easy reader becomes another degree less obtrusive (hopefully). Pictures become fewer, and more decorative than helpful. Sentences and chapters become longer. Animal stand-ins become real kids, usually exact contemporaries of the intended readers. Situations become stories, characterization more complex and differentiated, conflict more complicated.

As publishers have become more and more interested in slicing their lists — and targeting their readers — into increasingly narrower markets, chapter books have reached younger and become thinner. Beverly Cleary's Ramona books, for instance, used to be the exact example (and pinnacle) of the genre, but they now speak to the higher end of the range and are usually considered simply as realistic fiction for children. More typical of what we think of today as chapter books would be Stephanie Greene's books about Owen Foote, a boy who goes from second to third grade in the course of the series, growing along with his readers. Each of the six books about Owen is just under a hundred pages, with one or two illustrations per ten-page-or-so chapter.

While chapter divisions are used to make a statement in easy readers, in chapter books they become truly deserving of the name. Easy readers tend to be episodic — you can often read the chapters in any order — but chapter books more often extend a single, and relatively simple, plot over the length of a book. In chapter one of *Owen Foote, Frontiersman,* Owen and his best friend, Joseph, visit the fort they have constructed in a neighbor's backyard. In chapter two, they go back to it and find strangers therein. That's a plot. It's quite brilliantly done by the author, who first brings us into immediate empathy with the hero, then throws some trouble in his direction. Most crucially, Greene has Owen solve the problem without the aid of grown-ups, here represented as obstacles:

> "I know my mom," Owen said. "She'll say we should talk about it. She thinks talking solves everything. And you saw those guys, Joseph. They don't want to talk. They're jerks."

Now, if parents were in charge of this book, Owen would see the error of his ways and talk to his mother, who would offer a sensible, gentle solution to the problem of big boys wrecking your fort. But even though Greene has Owen's mother do just that, Owen and

Joseph know they are on their own to scare the boys away. Which they do. (I'm reminded of the advice YA writer Bruce Brooks once gave about bullies: "Punch them in the nose.")

Owen Foote is just one of several first-rate chapter book series about boy life; other excellent choices are Jessica Scott Kerrin's books about Martin Bridge (including *Martin Bridge: Ready for Takeoff!*), Barbara Seuling's Robert books (including *Robert and the Great Pepperoni*), and Johanna Hurwitz's long-running series about Russell (including *Rip-Roaring Russell*). Books about boys currently seem to command the largest share of this genre, perhaps because there is more anxiety about creating boy readers in a culture that assumes girls will take care of themselves when it comes to reading. It may also be that boys developmentally need more time with chapter books while girls move "up" faster.

But heroines there are, most excellently, the cranky, bossy Judy Moody. Obstreperous children's book heroines can have their "feistiness" overplayed, reminding me of something my colleague Deborah Stevenson once wrote in *The Horn Book*: "*Feisty* and *spunky* are two . . . adjectives reserved for the nonthreatening and the totally unserious [characters] who have the nerve to attempt to be fierce in a world that understands they can be nothing of the kind." But as portrayed in Megan McDonald's ten-and-counting books about Judy and her younger brother, Stink, Judy is as authentically prickly as the bugs she collects. She's outspoken, frequently bad-tempered, and very real. She's a far cry from Barbara Park's ubiquitous Junie B. Jones, a feisty, cutesy, faux-obstreperous baby-talking first-grader whose chapter books are routinely best sellers. (Nobody ever said kids were born with taste.)

Chapter books are a place where kids get to be on their own, both as readers and as characters. And when they *do* need help, they rely as much on other kids as on parents and teachers. Books are currency among readers, creating community. You can swap them and talk about them with your friends. Chapter books create sociability as much as they evoke it; witness the success of Patricia Reilly Giff's Kids of Polk Street School series, two dozen chapter books (beginning with *The Beast in Ms. Rooney's Room*) about life in one particular classroom, which have been ubiquitous among second-graders for almost twenty years. Fantasy, animal stories, and the like are rare in chapter-book fiction: new readers seem to want most to read about kids like themselves in familiar situations.

And, you may correctly infer, they want to read about the same kids over and over again. Children's taste for series books gets a bad rap among adults, whose alleged taste for variety is belied by a glimpse at any best-seller list: *everybody* likes series. But for decades, some series — most notoriously Nancy Drew and the Hardy Boys — were fastidiously kept from the shelves of public libraries even while adult patrons were busy reserving a copy of the latest Hercule Poirot or Perry Mason mystery.

The taste for series books is engendered the first time you heed a toddler's call to "read it again!" It means, "I liked that. More of the same, please." But eventually everybody wants a little variation. We provide that variation to a limited extent in picture books (perhaps so relatively limited because that audience can be bought off with repeated readings of the same book), foster it in easy readers, and make it the mainstay of chapter-book publishing.

It's like having an alternative but constant universe to visit. As an adult reader, I like having Donna Leon's Venice to visit, in the company of her detective Guido Brunetti, for example. I like keeping up with Guido and his wife, Paola, and their kids, finding out about different places in the city, and seeing how he handles the latest mystery thrown his way. The plot is secondary — I'm happy to watch Guido drink espresso — and it serves mostly to tug me from chapter to chapter.

But there are series, and there are *series*. Some are completely formulaic: the characters never change, the plots are stereotyped, the language is bland. Still, this keeps them accessible to a wide range of readers, thus reinforcing the idea that books are something you can share with your friends or use to placate your enemies: The 300-million-copies-selling Goosebumps, for example, gave good readers and struggling readers something in common, because a taste for gore and mayhem is fairly widespread among the young, and as well found an audience among both girls and boys. This series of short paperbacks with simmered-down versions of old horror-movie plots not coincidentally found itself in trouble with would-be censors who were putatively concerned with the series' violence and supernatural themes but, really, did not like the grip the series held on the collective second- and third-grade imagination. These were books kids were buying with their own money. These were books in which the heroes were on their own. Who needs parents?

As both cash cow and focus of censorial wrath, the latest successor to Goosebumps is Dav Pilkey's Captain Underpants series, the first significant inroad from comic-book style to children's fiction. The Captain Underpants books, starting with *The Adventures of Captain Underpants,* are filled with mild potty humor and plenty of pokes at authority, especially in the person of Mr. Krupp, school principal to George and Harold, who discover they can use their Hypno-Ring to turn him into the Don Quixote–like superhero Captain Underpants, named for his outfit. Third-grade slackers George and Harold themselves are direct descendants of James Marshall's Cut-Ups and first cousins to Jon Scieszka's Time Warp Trio. All these characters are variations on a type: goof-off boys who hate to read. And . . . *but try this* is their implicit message.

Interestingly, neither Goosebumps nor Captain Underpants (nor Matthew and Jennifer Holm's Babymouse series, a witty, Jane Austen–like alternative to Captain Underpants's universe) is as dumb as it looks. All three routinely break the "fourth wall" between book and reader, and Captain Underpants and Babymouse require

When the gigantic robots saw that Captain Underpants had escaped, the Harold 2000 launched its rocket arms at our hero.

"Alright!" said Captain Underpants. "But all I'm saying is that—"

"JUST SAY THE WORDS!" screamed George and Harold.

"You know," said Captain Underpants, "you kids have *NO* feel for dramatic tension!" Then he cleared his throat and spoke in a powerful voice. "I SUMMON THE POWER OF UNDERPANTYWORLD!"

Suddenly, Captain Underpants rose triumphantly into the air. He was free at last!

In Dav Pilkey's Captain Underpants books, the faux-dopey line drawings provide a paradoxical sophistication to make chapter-book readers feel like they're growing up. This particular spread is from *Captain Underpants and the Wrath of the Wicked Wedgie Woman.*

flexibility from their readers as the story bounces loopily between words, pictures, and what both leave unsaid as well as between the stories within stories that each of these series (Goosebumps, too) delights in.

As I write, graphic novels are supplanting doorstop-size fantasies as the Next Big Thing in children's literature, but Babymouse and Captain Underpants got there first, and we didn't think of them as graphic novels so much as we did more sophisticated (and hardbound) versions of that hound that has dogged children's literature for a century: that pesky, pervasive, routinely deplored (and at-best tolerated), won't-go-away *comic book*. Chapter books without the respectability.

Comic books were the great equalizer of my generation. We all read them, book lovers and book-averse alike. For the truly awkwardly bookish like me, comics were a place I could find common ground with other boys. As the great gourmet M. F. K. Fisher wrote about educating her young daughter's palate, "I give her a Coke, for social reasons." Like Coke, comic books and series books have the virtue of being everywhere, providing common sustenance, if not nourishment. They're popular because they're popular, serving the social function of being something to like that other people like too.

We begin reading as listeners and move on with assistance — sitting in a lap and following the pictures of a story, helping to turn the pages. Older humans, first in the family and then in school, help us learn to decode the printed word. Easy readers put us on our own, the support still present in the form of an encouraging page design and simple vocabulary. Series books and comic books throw us into the pool with the other kids, and the multitude of series and characters create a body of shared experience. With the persistence of the same characters and plot types across series entries, kids find communities that parallel their own, which itself, through the sharing of books, reinforces and expands the literary possibilities.

The printed word, historically, is unique among the arts because it is designed to be experienced alone — millions may read *The Da Vinci Code,* but by and large they do it one at a time. While books provide many opportunities for shared experience — reading aloud, discussion of books read in common, dramatization — books are best suited for one pair of hands at a time. That's how the story gets into the person, who can choose (or not) a multitude of ways to spread the word.

BOOKS WERE EVERYWHERE

VIRGINIA HAMILTON

Our children grew up with reading, as there were two writers in the house. Home was an exuberant place. Jaime at age three: "Mom, didya know — Iyum da only puhson in nis house who cannot weed?" (He had a New York accent and a slight problem with his *r*'s.) His non-"weeding" didn't last long. Books were everywhere in our house. Every day, Arnold and I shared stuff out loud from newspapers, magazines, books; to each other and to Leigh and Jaime. We devised a strategy: having a set of junior encyclopedias and some favorite picture books and chapter books at couch level in the family room. When the kids got bored watching TV, they would automatically reach for something to read. Something was always there — and it worked!

MORE GREAT CHAPTER BOOKS

Annie Barrows, illustrations by Sophie Blackall, *Ivy and Bean: Bound to Be Bad*

121 pp. Grades 2–4. In this fifth Ivy and Bean book, the two best friends decide to be really, really good — with opposite results. Fast-moving short chapters overflow with a sense of how kids actually talk and play. Text and illustrations are as fine a match as Ivy and Bean themselves.

Stephanie Greene, *Happy Birthday, Sophie Hartley*

128 pp. Grades 2–4. For her special "double-digit" birthday, impulsive, dramatic, middle-child Sophie wants a special present: a baby gorilla. Things get out of hand when her whole third-grade class thinks her parents have consented to the idea. Greene once again showcases her talent for portraying believable characters and family dynamics with humor and insight.

Nikki Grimes, illustrations by R. Gregory Christie, *Almost Zero: A Dyamonde Daniel Book*

115 pp. Grades 1–3. African-American Dyamonde demands that her mother buy her the high-top sneakers she "needs." The next day her clothes disappear, with Mom explaining that she only really *needs* one set of clothes. When a classmate's home is destroyed by fire, Dyamonde realizes the distinction between wanting and needing.

Betty Hicks, illustrations by Adam McCauley, *Basketball Bats* (Gym Shorts)

55 pp. Grades 1–5. It's all about sports in this welcome series featuring fourth-grader Henry and his friends — both boys *and* girls. Plentiful pencil sketches provide humor and ample visual cues for early chapter-book readers. Companion books include *Goof-Off Goalie* and *Swimming with Sharks*.

Kimberly Willis Holt, illustrations by Christine Davenier, *Piper Reed, Navy Brat*

146 pp. Grades 2–5. Being a Navy brat is full of activity and challenges — just the way irrepressible nine-year-old Piper Reed likes it. Holt writes with a

light touch as she captures the details of military life through Piper's personable voice. The pen-and-wash sketches are aptly exuberant. Sequels include *Piper Reed, the Great Gypsy* and *Piper Reed Gets a Job*.

Lenore Look, illustrations by LeUyen Pham, ***Alvin Ho: Allergic to Girls, School, and Other Scary Things***
172 pp. Grades 1–3. Fearful second-grader Alvin Ho doesn't speak in school, though his voice works everywhere else. Generously illustrated short chapters include laugh-out-loud descriptions of Alvin's attempt to grow taller and his brief membership in a not-so-tough neighborhood gang.

Claudia Mills, illustrations by Heather Maione, ***How Oliver Olson Changed the World***
104 pp. Grades 1–4. Oliver's overprotective parents insist on doing everything for him, including homework, and won't hear of letting him attend the third-grade space sleepover. Drawn into opinionated classmate Crystal's orbit while working together on a solar-system diorama, Oliver begins to assert himself. Full-page pencil illustrations add warmth and humor.

Sara Pennypacker, illustrations by Marla Frazee, ***Clementine***
136 pp. Grades 2–4. Third-grader Clementine feels lucky that spectacular ideas (like cutting her friend's hair) are continually "sproinging up" in her brain, but adults don't feel the same way. The first-person narration is fresh and winsome but not too cutesy. The pen-and-ink illustrations bounce along the pages with the same energy as the story. Sequels include *The Talented Clementine* and *Clementine's Letter*.

Lisa Yee, illustrations by Dan Santat, ***Bobby vs. Girls (Accidentally)***
168 pp. Grades 1–4. Those looking for fiction with nonwhite characters in which race is not the focus will welcome nine-year-old Bobby Ellis-Chan. Bobby and Holly had been best friends since babyhood, until fourth grade. The story of how they lose and rediscover their friendship is told with humor, frequent full-page illustrations, and an invitingly spacious layout.

PART THREE

READING ON THEIR OWN

Overview
Roger Sutton

By the time a kid is ready to read on his own, he's ready to . . . read on his own. Your job is, essentially, to let him. So why should you read this section? First, because discussed herein are books no reader should miss. *Harriet the Spy, Holes, Tom's Midnight Garden, Hatchet:* these books are central to the tradition of Children's Literature, which is itself part of the canon of Books, Generally. Some children's books even become landmarks of the latter as well; think of *The Wind in the Willows, The Secret Garden,* or *Anne of Green Gables,* books for children that still influence adult books published decades later. (This of course also goes the other way; witness the effect of *To Kill a Mockingbird* upon subsequent coming-of-age literature for teenagers.) Fantasy fans will already know that Tolkien's Lord of the Rings trilogy began as a children's book (*The Hobbit*) and that most of the touchstones of the genre are found in children's literature.

Second, you should read this section because as a parent it would be good for you to know just how much variety and imaginative reach is out there. Popular series such as (back in the day) Sweet Valley High or today's The Clique can seem ubiquitous, but junior-high chick lit is as various as its adult counterpart, and much of it is actually literate. You might remember the Childhood of Famous Americans series (maybe even passed down by your own parents) but would be stunned to see what historian-biographers such as Russell Freedman, Candace Fleming, Elizabeth Partridge, and Jim Murphy are doing today.

Because independent, private reading varies so much in terms of each reader's personality and affinities, for this section we invited a community of experts — all current or past *Horn Book* reviewers or contributors — to speak to their own particular passions and expertise, acting as native guides, if you will, to the genres they each know best. Just as you may gravitate toward "the mystery lady" at your local library or bookstore for her encyclopedic knowledge of the genre, you can trust these critics to be on home ground in their areas of expertise.

As a reader, you know you don't want to be crowded. We don't suggest monitoring what your nine- to twelve-year-old child is reading beyond a general benevolent interest. By all means, share books: read them aloud or listen together. Talk with your kids about their reading, but do it not as parent to child but as reader to reader. (That means you talk about *your* reading, too.) Go to the library together: allowing your children to see you lost in pursuit of your own reading pleasure is one of the best ways to send them in pursuit of their own. And the library has wealth far beyond what either you or this book can offer. Know that it's there. Know the abundance of books written, published, and kept in print by generations of adults with a staggering respect for young people. Children's literature is another branch of the same tree that so sturdily shelters *you:* books.

Chapter Five

GENRES

Introduction
Roger Sutton

Maybe this has changed since Harry Potter arrived, but for decades reading surveys among children consistently revealed that their favorite genre was mystery. The odd thing, though, is that, beyond formula series, there are relatively few mysteries (as adults understand the term) published for young people, and what those surveys actually showed was that kids enjoy stories with strong plots and elements of surprise or suspense that keep a reader going. As children's librarian Tim Wadham wrote in a *Horn Book* article called "Plot Matters," "Children need to know that something is happening, and what happens next."

Children's literature provides an array of subgenres to serve this essential requirement of interesting things happening to a sympathetic protagonist, and we've chosen four to explore here in greater depth: fantasy, historical fiction, adventure stories, and comedies. Each of these has contributed signal works to the canon—Alan Garner's *The Owl Service*, Elizabeth Speare's *The Witch of Blackbird Pond*, Gary Paulsen's *Hatchet*, Richard Peck's *A Year Down Yonder*, respectively—even while cross-fertilizing like crazy: T. H. White's *The Sword in the Stone* just about manages to be all four.

While fantasy came around in a big way after Harry Potter, we've seen it cycle by before: witness the crazes in adult publishing that surrounded (the pre-movie) *Lord of the Rings, Watership Down,* and H. P. Lovecraft. And it's always been a mainstay of children's fiction as well: C. S. Lewis's Narnia books, *The Wind in the Willows, The Wizard of Oz. The Horn Book* gave a consistent boost to the great English fantasy revival of the 1960s and 1970s, when writers such as William Mayne, Alan Garner, Susan Cooper, and Diana Wynne Jones emerged (and also to its American counterpart, with Natalie Babbitt's *Tuck Everlasting* and Lloyd Alexander's Chronicles of Prydain, to mention just two). Here Deirdre Baker, who teaches children's literature at the University of Toronto and is a frequent reviewer for *The Horn Book,* gives a sense of the breadth and depth of the genre and illustrates just why a child might be drawn to a book that "celebrates boldly the creative power of the artist to imagine things other than they are."

Historical fiction lives in the confluence contained in its name, a place where *getting it right* and *making it real* aren't quite the same thing but need to work together. From the textured and well-researched novels by the likes of Rosemary Sutcliff (pre-modern Britain), Scott O'Dell (historical California), and Mildred Taylor (the Jim Crow South) to the series pleasures of the American Girls books, historical fiction has fans and—more problematically—victims, when it becomes repurposed to the needs of scholastic testing. Betty Carter is a retired professor of library science and junior-high teacher, and a longtime contributor to *The Horn Book.*

As Vicky Smith—librarian, children's book editor for *Kirkus Reviews,* and former *Horn Book* reviewer—writes, the "brush with peril" appeal of the adventure story is obvious even though its reputation is sometimes suspect: while everybody loves "a good story," fewer are proud to admit it (adults, anyway . . .).

When, as a child, Beverly Cleary was taxed by a particularly dreary essay assignment, her mother advised, "Write something funny. People always enjoy reading something that makes them laugh." But it wasn't until Cleary wrote *Dear Mr. Henshaw*, a novel about a lonely boy that was more "serious" than her Klickitat Street books (starring Henry and Beezus and Ramona), that she won the Newbery Medal. Humor has a hard time being taken seriously. As novelist, librarian, and *Horn Book* reviewer Sarah Ellis notes, comedy is social and a great equalizer among children, bringing together boys and girls, eager readers and reluctant ones, to enjoy the joke.

"Your Journey Is Inward, but It Will Seem Outward"

Deirdre F. Baker

Fantasy can and does engage all the themes of other kinds of children's literature — from board books to humor to poetry to hard-hitting young adult novels — but it has one consistent element: "magic." Its "magic" can be expressed in something as obviously fantastical as talking animals or as possibly realistic as someone who hears voices that may or may not be imagined. It can be exercised in a made-up world or in supernatural powers that awaken in a hero in our own world. Time travel, fairy tales, myths, legends, and stories of magical objects popping up in our own familiar world, as well as stories of talking animals, animated toys, and wizard schools, all propose a departure from the laws of nature as we recognize them.

Children with an appetite for fantasy often read it to the exclusion of other kinds of literature, sometimes making parents worry that their reading springs from unhealthy escapism or a fixation on the trivial. Of course, realistic fiction can present at least as much escapist indulgence as fantasy — one need look no further than Gossip Girl and its ilk. But the real argument for reading fantasy is that, at its best, fantasy stretches the imagination, intellect, and emotions in ways that enhance, rather than discourage, children's engagement with real life. True, it can offer consoling escape. J. R. R. Tolkien argues that it can be a way of assuaging profound human longings — to communicate freely with animals, to fly, or to conquer death itself. But it can also make abstract ideas concrete, inviting young readers to consider complex philosophical, theological, and political questions in uniquely accessible ways. Because ideas are central to fantasy, adult / child book discussions on good fantasy can be particularly rewarding. Indeed, it is in fantasy that adult and child readers are most likely to converge: witness the crossover success of J. K. Rowling's Harry Potter series and of Philip Pullman's His Dark Materials trilogy, for example.

In the wake of *Lord of the Rings* and *Harry Potter,* "high fantasy" — stories of heroes on grand epic quests, usually in invented, nonindustrialized worlds — has surged in popularity, but this popularity comes with its own special pitfalls. Some contemporary writers of high fantasy seem to think that wordiness, a self-important tone, and an overdependence on magical creatures, gadgets, and geography (to offer just a few examples) can take the place of well-developed, complex characters, ideas, and plot. They often imitate (poorly) the style of Tolkien. Christopher Paolini's *Eragon* is a particularly egregious example, with its similar names (Aragorn / Eragon; Arwen / Arya), its Tolkien-like dwarf and warrior cultures, and its uninspired prose.

But even reading such run-of-the-mill fantasies can have its benefits if a child can identify their conventional features and question them. (Why do authors so often choose to write about evil wizards who want to take over the world? What does this tell us about what they value or fear?) As well, fantasies that keep readers turning pages on the strengths of their thriller plots and quickly sketched characterizations (for example, Rick Riordan's books about Percy Jackson, based on Greek myths) may spark a reader's interest in more substantial retellings of mythology — just as a love of Tolkien's and C. S. Lewis's fantasies has led many a reader to explore Norse sagas, or *Beowulf*, or medieval Arthurian romances. And any exposure to a well-constructed alternate world (such as in Terry Pratchett's Discworld novels or Philip Reeve's Hungry City Chronicles) allows children to absorb different ways to deal with the pressures and problems of "real life"—one of which is to retreat, now and then, to the gardenlike space in the mind that an alternate world offers.

Epic or "high" fantasy often involves expansive terrain and long journeys, giving children, in imagination at least, a freedom of movement unavailable to most of them in the physical world. In this, fantasy is the quintessential backpacking, trail-riding genre. It also often explores the discovery of new talents and the pleasure of increasing prowess: whether sword fighting or wand waving, these skills symbolize the hard-won abilities that come with physical and intellectual maturation.

Perhaps one of the most enticing satisfactions of a reader's imaginative engagement of an alternate world is that he or she can know pretty much everything there is to know about that world. The world of a fantasy novel is limited by its textual evidence: the story. As a thorough reader, a child can be an authority on an entire world. Fantasy gives kids worlds they can rule over—ones in which they, not their parents or teachers, are experts.

But how does one negotiate the overburdened shelves and pick among the many fantasies, serial and otherwise, that are displayed there? How does one find those that best nourish the imagination; that are most powerfully original; that might draw readers into engaging the hardest, most exciting questions we have to ask about the meaning and nature of human life? Judicious reading is really the answer to these questions—there is no substitute for cracking the cover oneself and looking for a few salient features.

In outstanding fantasy, magic is not just decorative. It is an organic part of setting, plot, characters, and meaning, and works as a metaphor that reveals and deepens all the fantasy's themes. It helps isolate and explore something that is difficult or interesting about being human, and draws attention to the activity of imagination and reason. This is true whether the story involves a magical ability that descends on a person in the otherwise "real" world, or a voyage in time to historical places and periods that really existed, or the hijinks and dragon dueling of a wizard-ridden fantasyland.

Take, for example, the story of a boy wizard: Ursula K. Le Guin's *A Wizard of Earthsea*. Here the hero's mission, the world's geography, the nature of its magic, and the hero's inner development are part of a single coherent vision. Ged, an uneducated boy from a rural island, is lavishly endowed with magical power but is arrogant and ambitious. In a fit of temper, he shows off to a rival at the school of wizardry and lets loose a dangerous shadow creature, which goes on to threaten all Earthsea. Humbled, Ged must track the creature over island and sea and conquer it — which he does by accepting the dark, destructive side of himself.

What a good adventure story! But Le Guin is not just giving children an exciting ride. She makes them think, at every turn, about power and restraint, about how every act and every bit of the world affects the whole. Earthsea is a world of sea and many small islands; each has its own culture, but altogether Earthsea is a single world made one by water. Thus its very geography represents one of Le Guin's most important themes — the interrelatedness of all things. And in this world of sea and boats, the notion of Equilibrium fittingly governs the magic: every wizardly act affects the Equilibrium; the wizard's task is to learn the name of every particle in the world (thus affording it due respect) and to work magic as unobtrusively as possible. This theme reaches its fullness when Ged finally embraces his shadow: accepting the destructive part of himself, he has "made himself whole: a man: who, knowing his whole true self, cannot be used or possessed by any power other than himself, and whose life therefore is lived for life's sake and never in the service of ruin, or pain, or hatred, or the dark." All of Le Guin's ideas — about an ecology that ranges from personal self-knowledge to human cooperation in societies to the global environment — are wrapped up in a story about a headstrong boy who sails wild seas, argues with dragons, and graduates from wizard school. This is the kind of intellectual, moral, and literary nourishment that high fantasy can offer.

Such rich meaning, embodied in one governing metaphor, can also be found in fantasies in which magic enters the real world. In the young adult novel *The Changeover: A Supernatural Romance*, Margaret Mahy uses the idea of the "changeover" from human to witch as a metaphor for changes that are a natural part of maturation. Her heroine, Laura, is just beginning to awaken to her own sexuality and is half fascinated, half nervous at the interest witchy Sorry Carlisle shows in her. When Laura's little brother is possessed by a consuming spirit and she asks Sorry to help her, she is told by his mother and grandmother, two witches, that she must "change over" in order to effect the rescue herself.

Magic, imagination, nature, and sexuality are woven together in Mahy's story. On her heroic quest to "change over," Laura makes an imaginative journey through a forest that is in her own head, furnished with images from her own past. "Your journey is inward, but it will seem outward," Sorry's grandmother tells her, in words that could apply to all fantasy. The forest Laura brings to life in herself represents a magical creative power that will let her win back her brother — but it is echoed in her newly discovered female powers. Sorry's interest in Laura underscores that theme: "She was going to be kissed. On one side of a kiss was childhood, sunshine, innocence, toys and, on the other, people embracing, darkness, passion and the admittance of a person who, no matter how loved, must always have the quality of otherness."

A Wizard of Earthsea and *The Changeover* are good examples of the coherence and cohesiveness with which a fantasy world and its governing magic, or metaphor, can function. Both deepen and broaden readers' understanding of matters that are very real and very human, showing that fanciful invention and impossible creatures are not so removed from the issues realistic fiction addresses. For those who would like to woo their children from the overt trappings of magic, however, fantasy has its own ideal subgenre: time travel. Time-travel stories offer a delicate bridge between fantasy and more realistic fiction, usually historical fiction — as if a visit to the past is not so very different from a visit to a fantasy world. At its best, the magical ability to traverse time suggests that there is a close relationship between imagination, desire, and memory — never more fully, perhaps, than in British author Philippa Pearce's *Tom's Midnight Garden.*

Ten-year-old Tom is frustrated at being quarantined in his relatives' flat in the city, and one midnight, roaming restlessly in the old house where the flat is, he opens the door onto a beautiful garden. When he tries to return the next day, however, he discovers that the door opens onto a parking space; only at night can he visit the garden. There, he eventually befriends Hatty, with whom he spends idyllic hours exploring as the garden presents itself first at one season, then another, without regard for the natural progression of time. Tom soon realizes that Hatty and the garden belong to a time different from his own: by night he and Hatty revel in its freedom; by day he tries to determine when and where Hatty and the garden really are. The intense longing he has for the garden and for Hatty's companionship come to a head as his stay with his relatives nears its end, and he makes plans to stay forever in the past. He hasn't noticed that while he has stayed ten, Hatty herself has grown older: in a moment of poignant distress, Tom is forced to recognize that she is now grown up. The next night, when he opens the door, the garden is nowhere to be seen.

Only in the last moments of the story does Tom begin to understand his visits to the garden. Called up to apologize for waking the building's elderly landlady, he suddenly faces his playmate: "Her bright black eyes were certainly like Hatty's; and now he began to notice, again and again, a gesture, a tone of the voice, a way of laughing that reminded him of the little girl in the garden. . . . Tom suddenly leaned forward and whispered: 'You were Hatty—you *are* Hatty! You're really *Hatty!*'" With intense clarity, Pearce's readers suddenly recognize the child in the adult—that adults do not leave their childhood behind them, but take it with them as they mature. The elderly Hatty's memories of her loveless childhood have made her dream of her youth; Tom's longing for freedom and companionship has drawn him into its past. The garden's erratic seasons and unreliable presence suggest that memory, and even the past itself, are somehow as much a work of shifting imagination and dream as they are of hard fact.

Not all time-travel stories have the depth of *Tom's Midnight Garden;* some are simply devices to teach history, with the extra frill of an astonished contemporary hero who comments on what she or he sees there (see Betty Carter's "When Dinosaurs Watched Black-and-White TV"). However, in Susan Cooper's *King of Shadows,* Ruth Park's *Playing Beatie Bow,* or Kit Pearson's *A Handful of Time,* crossing time makes readers think of how we understand the past, both as we see it in the present and as we reconstruct it through partial evidence and intelligent imagination. It is also a means by which characters come to a new perspective on themselves. Distanced from their own problems, they live parallel stories that help them resolve the emotional crises they face at home. They are changed by realizing what they share with people of the past and also by confronting and accepting a cultural experience alien from their own.

Parodies of traditional fairy tales and adventure stories are another fruitful branch of fantasy. In Gail Carson Levine's fairy-tale fantasy *Ella Enchanted,* Levine offers girls, especially, the means to look critically—and laughingly—at fairy-tale stereotypes and the obstacles they raise for over-believing readers. Ella's fairy "gift" always to be obedient proves to be downright sinister, because it makes her vulnerable to every commanding presence she encounters. With a light, easy tone, Levine gets at something deep at the heart of what is still a struggle for women: the ability to say no. This story and others — such as Terry Pratchett's reworking of the Tam Lin folktale in *The Wee Free Men* and Diana Wynne Jones's flipping of fairy tales' youngest-sister convention in *Howl's Moving Castle* — invite readers to question the status quo. Both in retold fairy tales and in parodic high fantasy, humor makes young readers aware of the fundamental patterns of story, which in turn helps them become more acute readers — not just of story, but of the world.

A voyage to another time can be a device for distancing protagonists from their problems, thus giving them a chance to resolve them in a less threatening environment. Travel between worlds can also work this way, as C. S. Lewis shows in *The Lion, the Witch and the Wardrobe,* as the four Pevensey children exit war-torn Britain, take part in a conflict in a magical land, and return to the real world with the empowering feeling that evil can be vanquished. Similarly, in Neil Gaiman's *Coraline,* travel to an alternate world heightens and focuses the character's anger at her parents and ultimately has the healthy effect of dissolving it. Just as we understand dreams to be stories of what is going on in our subconscious, so can adventures in alternate worlds and times clarify inner conditions.

Whatever the magical element is in any fantasy — a landscape with invented beings, the ability to travel through time and across worlds or to perform magic spells — as readers we understand it to represent something more than itself. Making something fantastic distances it from reality, as if the events and concerns of real life are distilled and concentrated into features more brilliant and intense than their usual selves, set apart for clearer examination. Children enjoy the suspense and action of heroic quests or the desirable notion of flying brooms, casting spells, or communicating freely with animals — but in the best fantasies, all these features point to aspects of our own world and to real human abilities.

Of all forms of literature, fantasy is the one that most openly acknowledges that it is "made up." It celebrates boldly the creative power of the artist to imagine things other than the way they are. Unlike other genres, it has the singular feature of admitting right off the bat that it does not *represent* reality but rather *interprets* it. Fantasy's very departure from reality signals something important to the reader about reading: this is a story that asks to be interpreted and openly demands that we exercise our powers of translation. It is fantasy, in fact, that leads children into some of the most complex questions they can ask about being human. And you can't ask more of reading and books than that.

Waking Dreams
Jane Langton

What if rugs could fly? What if pigs could talk? Every writer of fantasy poses a *what-if* question that is the theme of his book. He can ask it in many ways, and all of these ways are different approaches to the dividing line between truth (the real world) and fantasy (the unreal world). Then, once the fabulous axiom has been cited, the writer must cleave to logic. He must answer the question, "Then what? Given such-and-such a situation, what would really happen?" (It is the *really* that is to be stressed. Realism sharpens fantasy.)

But what is it that makes a fantasy unforgettable? What does it all add up to, the *what ifs* and the *then whats*? After all the invention and the action and the clever devices, *so what*?

I can think of two things that set some books of fantasy apart. The first thing, surely, is a strongly realized personal vision. The writer's obsession comes first, and the books come after. When you open one of them and turn the pages, you are traveling in a place invented by that writer, a piece of fictional territory, a fanciful stomping ground. Many writers have discovered and mapped their own personal geographies, and they are places as real to us now as Iowa or Tibet or the Bronx: Jean de Brunhoff's Celesteville, where Babar is king; the Cherry-Tree Lane of P. L. Travers and

Mary Poppins; Maurice Sendak's land where the Wild Things are; C. S. Lewis's Narnia; the foolish villages of Isaac Bashevis Singer; Milne's Hundred Acre Wood; Antoine de Saint-Exupéry's Asteroid B-612, inhabited by the Little Prince; Tolkien's Middle-earth; Tove Jansson's Moominland; Margery Sharp's Black Castle; the various hilarious provinces of Dr. Seuss. Each of these places is somehow whole and perfect and entire — *real*-ized and altogether there. With the borders of these imaginary territories placed end-to-end, a child's mental dominion can stretch all the way to Homer's Ithaca or Shakespeare's forest of Oberon. A world like this is rich freight to carry around inside any child's head.

The other quality that sets apart some books of children's fantasy is, of course, a second level of meaning — significance, symbolism, allegory; a stab at a moral, a message, a lesson. The meaning may be as bald as the last sentence in one of Aesop's fables ("Slow and steady wins the race") or as unpretentious and delicate as the distillation from the modest adventures of Milne's animals (what it means to be a friend). Meaning is not easy. Sometimes the attempt at it is too vaguely vast, too preachy-teachy, too thin and scant. But when it works, the book gains a value that may outlast the short time span during which young readers are available to us. It may last them all their lives.

There is one more thing that hasn't been said. Perhaps it is the only thing that can truthfully be said of all of these books, and it is the secret of their deathless charm.

They are all dreams. They are waking dreams. They make up to us for the sense of loss we feel when we wake up and find our dreams shrinking out of memory. A literary fantasy gives us a dream back to keep. Surely the reason why we are so inexhaustibly delighted by mice that talk and spells that work is that we want the laws and verities to be different from the ones by which we are trapped during the day. Like Dr. Seuss's foolish king, we want something new to come out of the sky, not just this everlasting sunshine, rain, and snow, even if the new thing turns out to be sticky green Oobleck. And when the writer of a literary fantasy adds a real child to a surreal landscape, a flesh-and-blood Alice in a nonsensical Wonderland, we are given in one package both ends of our daily experience. It is a mixture of waking and dreaming, and *that* has a pungency that satisfies. It feeds a hunger we didn't know we had.

Pauline Baynes's iconic image from C. S. Lewis's *The Lion, the Witch and the Wardrobe* has helped make Narnia "*real*-ized" for generations of young readers.

MORE GREAT FANTASY

Franny Billingsley, *Chime*
 358 pp. Grade 7 and up. Seventeen-year-old Briony can talk to the Old Ones;
 she's convinced she's a witch who has caused harm to others and deserves
 to be hanged. With the help of a young student newly arrived to Swampsea
 from London, Briony begins to reexamine her past. Steeped in the imagery
 of water and sky, this gorgeous fantasy melds ancient lore, false memories,
 real peril, and true love.

Kristin Cashore, *Graceling*
 472 pp. Grade 7 and up. Lady Katsa was born with a hyper-developed talent
 for killing. With creepy villains, romance, and a butt-kicking but emotionally
 vulnerable heroine, this will appeal to fans of girl-power fantasy.

Neil Gaiman, illustrations by Dave McKean, *The Graveyard Book*
 312 pp. Grades 6–8. After fortuitously escaping the murder of his family, a
 toddler is taken in by the ghostly denizens of a local graveyard. Occasional
 art enhances the otherworldly atmosphere. Both bittersweet and action-
 filled.

Grace Lin, *Where the Mountain Meets the Moon*
 282 pp. Grades 4–6. Minli, who lives in poverty at the foot of Fruitless
 Mountain, seeks the Old Man of the Moon, hoping to change her family's
 fortunes. Interspersed retellings of Chinese folktales and luminous full-
 page illustrations, influenced by traditional Chinese art, contribute to this
 fantasy's sense of timelessness.

Kierin Meehan, *Hannah's Winter*
 212 pp. Grades 4–6. Twelve-year-old Hannah stays with the Maekawa family
 in Japan while her mother travels. There Hannah discovers a ghost—a
 young boy who needs her help. Australian author Meehan shrouds her novel
 in a quietly creepy atmosphere that she lightens with unexpected humor. An
 agreeably accessible ghost story.

Terry Pratchett, *Nation*

370 pp. Grades 6–10. In an alternative nineteenth-century universe, a tsunami shipwrecks proper Ermintrude on a tropical island, where she meets Mau, sole survivor of his island Nation. Serious subjects and thought-provoking ethical questions are fully woven into action and character. It's hard to imagine a reader who won't feel welcomed into this *Nation*.

Philip Reeve, *Mortal Engines*

311 pp. Grades 6–10. In this first book in the Hungry City Chronicles, Reeve unveils a futuristic society of predatory wheeled "traction cities" that roam the post-Apocalyptic earth. The technological wizardry will gratify young fantasy and sci-fi lovers, while the intense emotions drive the plot at top speed. The series concludes in the exhilarating *A Darkling Plain*.

Rebecca Stead, *When You Reach Me*

197 pp. Grades 4–6. Sixth-grader Miranda's life is an ordinary round of family and school. But then she starts receiving anonymous notes that seem to foretell the future. The closely observed relationships among the characters make the mystery matter, and the closing revelations are both startling and satisfying.

Shaun Tan, *The Arrival*

128 pp. Grade 5 and up. Seeking a better life for his family, a man travels to a strange, unfamiliar country. It's the triumph of this lavish, somber, wordless graphic novel that readers are kept in sympathetic step with the immigrant hero; we're as out of place as he is.

Kate Thompson, *The New Policeman*

442 pp. Grades 5–9. Time is leaking out of the human world and into the timeless land of Tír na n'Óg of Irish legend, and fifteen-year-old fiddler J.J. determines to solve the mystery. Spellbinding for those who appreciate an original twist on authentic lore. Sequels: *The Last of the High Kings*; *The White Horse Trick*.

When Dinosaurs Watched Black-and-White TV

Betty Carter

In many ways, authors of historical fiction and fantasy have similar tasks: each is involved in world building. For many youngsters, the Middle Ages is as foreign as Middle-earth. And you don't have to go back that far, either: for example, the child narrator of X. J. Kennedy's poem "Remembering Ice" thinking of his grandfather's childhood as the time "when dinosaurs watched black-and-white TV." From the Ottoman Empire to the Tet Offensive, children are most likely looking at blank screens of history, for they have no reference points for such places and events.

These kinds of gaps put a burden on authors, who have three responsibilities in writing historical fiction. First, they have to create a story that catches the attention of readers; second, they must interest these readers in a particular time period; and, third, they must ensure that the story suits the setting. These are the critical points to consider in evaluating historical fiction.

Story

Although we think of historical fiction as a separate genre, in reality multiple subgenres exist under its umbrella. In the books discussed below, for example, you'll find historical mystery (*A Drowned Maiden's Hair*); historical adventure (*The Traitors' Gate*); and historical romance (*How the Hangman Lost His Heart*). If we want our kids to read historical fiction, the best approach is first to consider the types of books they already know and like, and then expand those tastes by recommending similar tales with a historical setting. Few children express preferences for any kind of story set in the past, but they are willing to venture backward in time within the constraints of already beloved genres.

Fine historical novels give readers great characters and great plots. Beginning with the first line of *A Drowned Maiden's Hair*, Laura Amy Schlitz sets up one such character: "On the morning of the best day of her life, Maud Flynn was locked in the outhouse, singing 'The Battle Hymn of the Republic.'" Schlitz makes a promise to readers: keep going, and you'll meet someone interesting, quirky, and definitely worth knowing.

Strong adventure carries Louise Borden's *The Greatest Skating Race: A World War II Story from the Netherlands*. Piet's parents ask their ten-year-old son to usher two children from Holland to Belgium to escape an immediate threat of capture by the Germans. Piet, and his childhood friends Johanna and Joop, must skate over Holland's frozen canals, braving dangers from both the weather and the German soldiers.

Time Period

The second consideration in historical fiction, that of creating an awareness of a time period, means that readers must first know that they're reading about a different time. Obvious title clues can help if youngsters know anything about the period, but their meager knowledge about history limits such signals to a few well-known names and events. Many young readers of Christopher Paul Curtis's *The Watsons Go to Birmingham — 1963*, for example, are shocked at the ending (the bombing of the Sixteenth Street Baptist Church); they are completely unaware of the horrific violence signaled by the city and date in the book's title. So how do writers begin to create that awareness of another time and place?

In *How the Hangman Lost His Heart,* K. M. Grant sets her historical stage nicely. The jacket art, depicting a gallows, signals that this novel probably doesn't take place in contemporary America. Equally important are visual clues about both subject and tone. The noose hangs in the shape of a heart, indicating a touch of romance, and the flowery script used for a few of the words suggests a light tone. The subtitle of chapter one establishes place and time: *"London, August 10, 1746."* And Grant begins courting interest with the first sentence: "When Uncle Frank's head was finally parted from his body, the crowd laughed." Five pages into the book, readers will learn that during the middle of the eighteenth century in London, public executions were a grisly form of entertainment ("Alice had not been able to watch . . . but the sighs and appalled groans of the crowd gave an up-to-the-minute commentary as her beloved uncle was first strung up, then cut down before he was dead, sliced open like a halibut or perhaps a herring, and had his innards removed"). In addition, readers learn that such spectacles were common ("Just a small one today, with only the colonel and one or two others to do") and that the heads of the executed were severed and put on public display. Adroitly Grant hooks her audience by juxtaposing the earthy unpleasantness of the period with a touch of humor. Readers will either continue the tale or move to another, but they will know what they are in for.

Setting

Once a child's interest is piqued, writers face their third responsibility: to continue their narratives while remaining true to the chosen period. One way to capture the spirit of the times is through language. Modern writers typically employ language patterns much leaner than those of a century ago, but by adopting and adapting Dickensian cadences in *The Traitors' Gate,* a novel set in the mid-nineteenth century in which a young boy attempts to unravel the mystery of his father's imprisonment, author Avi helps create a world far removed from this one. "Then too there was a sluggishly moving chaos of wagons, barouches, carts, omnibuses, barrows, hackneys, phaetons, and Hansoms, pulled by London's hundred thousand horses. No wonder the cobblestones fairly sank beneath a sea of dung. No wonder that every breathing thing, every rolling thing, every voice, every cry, call, laugh, and sob, every shoe, boot, and huff made so much din as to produce a relentless rumble that drummed and thrummed into every living London ear — and dead ones too, no doubt." At first these sentence constructions may put a burden on young readers, but the end result is, to borrow a metaphor from Robert Hughes, that they've visited a city with as many twists and turns as the language, a much more authentic experience than visiting the same historical spot with language as straight and direct as the streets of a planned modern suburb.

Individual words matter as much as patterns. A fictional account of Abigail Adams writing to John to "remember the ladies" would ring false if a member of her sewing circle were to prod her with the contemporary "You go, girl."

Authors employ language not only as a way to locate their stories in time and place but also to shape a character's actions, reactions, and responsibilities to reflect the time period. Nathaniel Benchley's *Sam the Minuteman,* a book for beginning readers, introduces young Sam, a boy growing up in 1770s Massachusetts. At the beginning of the Battle of Lexington, Sam's father instructs him: "Get your gun, Sam . . . The British have left Boston and are coming this way." Benchley adds, "So Sam got his gun and followed his father through the darkness to the village green." Although far removed from modern circumstances, ten-year-old Sam's gun ownership is accepted in this setting because Benchley places it in historical context.

But such historical honesty comes with a price. What if kids read books about boys carrying guns or girls sewing samplers? What kind of role models do these stories provide today's children? The most vocal pleas I hear related to historical fiction concern girls, who were assigned largely passive roles in times past. No matter what our dreams for young girls may be today, the historical novelist can't just plop an "empowered" twenty-first-century girl into a nineteenth-century setting willy-nilly, without carefully laying out the reasons why this particular character is rebelling against type. Otherwise, there's little possibility of today's readers understanding why the roles of women were once different and why women fought so hard to become who they are today.

That said, historical fiction almost always features characters we are meant to like sooner or later, and these kinds of heroes and heroines create their own historical inaccuracies. Many real-world children owned slaves, aspired to be Nazis, expected women to be second-class citizens, or hated Indians. They are a part of our history but seldom surface as characters in novels of their times — a caution about the limits of historical fiction.

What I hear as the counterargument to the presence of contemporary youngsters in historical fiction is that we have to "hook" modern readers, to give them stories that start with what they know: their own lives. I would agree, but the universal concerns of humankind appear from the first century to the present one. Good historical fiction incorporates universal themes without sacrificing historical verisimilitude.

In Marthe Jocelyn's *How It Happened in Peach Hill,* set immediately after the First World War, Annie Grey and her mama, Madame Caterina, Spiritual Advisor, perfect the art of the con. Annie's role is to slip into the background to gather gossip that Madame Caterina embellishes in her spiritual readings. As Annie begins to develop her own value system, she begins pulling away from her mother. This kind of conflict between parent and teenager, which is as old as the family unit, certainly provides a contemporary hook for young readers; it's repeated every day in households across the country.

In *My Brother Sam Is Dead,* authors Christopher and James Lincoln Collier use the same conflict between parent and child to alert readers to two widely different viewpoints on the Revolutionary War. Sam and his father argue their respective political views, with Sam electing to serve in the colonial army and his father opposing him: "I will not have subversion, I will not have treason in my house. We are Englishmen, we are subjects of the King." And Sam retorts, "I am not an Englishman, I am an American, and I am going to fight to keep my country free. . . . It's the principle." Change a few words, and this argument could have occurred during the Civil War, both World Wars, the Vietnam conflict, or the war in Iraq. That kind of situation allows young readers an authentic entry into history. The discussion between Sam and his father also alerts readers to the historical setting in a perfectly natural way. Often authors of historical fiction instead fill in that background with awkward asides or artificially interpolated conversations that signal a small history lesson.

No matter how historically accurate a novel may be, it provides but a small glimpse into the panorama of any event. Readers cannot learn *all* about the Revolutionary War by reading *Johnny Tremain;* they can only see how one apprentice might have reacted to the events going on around him. Not only would Johnny Tremain's views be different from those, say, of a privileged son of a colonial governor or a young slave in Virginia, but in re-creating dialogue and situations to tell her own unique story, *Johnny Tremain*'s author was writing fiction, not history.

I began this discussion with the ways in which historical fiction and fantasy are alike. Let me close with one major difference: children tend to prefer fantasy over historical fiction. Why? Because when children read fantasy, we don't quiz them on the setting, we don't ask them to remember particular details, we don't ask them to take away isolated facts to help them in school assignments. In other words, reading fantasy asks little more than immersion in a book and reading for the fun of it. Let those same principles guide us as we encourage the reading of historical fiction.

Writing Backward
Anne Scott MacLeod

I expect we can all agree that historical fiction should be good fiction and good history. If we leap over the first briar patch by calling good fiction an "interesting narrative with well-developed characters," we are still left with the question of what is good history. Alas, there are thorns here, too. The German historian Leopold von Ranke said that writing history was saying "what really happened"—but according to whom? Writers of history select, describe, and explain historical evidence—and thereby interpret. Not only will the loser's version of the war never match the winner's, but historical interpretations of what happened, and why, are subject to endless revision over time. A transforming event of the past—say, the American Revolution—can be understood as a social, economic, or intellectual movement; as avoidable or inevitable; as a tragedy of misunderstanding or a triumph of liberty.

Historical revisionism makes its way into historical fiction, of course, including that written for children, usually in response to changing social climates. Esther Forbes wrote *Johnny Tremain,* her famous novel of the American Revolution, in the early 1940s, when the United States had recently entered the maelstrom of World War II. Forbes's story took the traditional view that the Revolution was a struggle for political freedom, fought, as one of her characters said, so that "a man can stand up." The parallel Forbes saw with a contemporary war against political tyranny was implied but clear. A generation later, the Colliers' *My Brother Sam Is Dead* and Robert Newton Peck's *Hang for Treason* saw the same history through a different lens. Writing in a time of passionate division over a modern war, these authors looked back to the American Revolution and saw not idealism but the coercion, hypocrisy, cruelty, and betrayal that are part of any war, in any country. In the Colliers' story, the success of the Revolution had to be weighed against the suffering it inflicted: "I keep thinking that there might have been another way, beside war, to achieve the same end." Peck looked behind the heroic legend of Ethan Allen and his band of Green Mountain Boys and found more greed for land than hunger for liberty, and renegade tactics as barbarous as any tyrant's. In Peck's telling, Allen's brand of irregular warfare was terrorism, not a noble struggle for liberty.

Revisionist history is still history, still subject to normal standards of demonstrable historical evidence and sound reasoning. While these three novels approach the Revolution from different points of view, they are firmly grounded in documented evidence. Different as they are in emphasis and attitude, all three stay within the bounds of eighteenth-century American social history. None ignores known historical realities to accommodate political ideology.

A good many historical novels for children do. Children's literature, historical as well as contemporary, has been politicized over the past forty years; new social sensibilities have changed the way Americans view the past. Feminist re-readings of history and insistence by minorities on the importance — and the difference — of their experience have made authors and publishers sensitive to how their books portray people often overlooked or patronized in earlier literature. The traditional concentration on boys and men has modified; more minorities are included, and the experience of ordinary people — as opposed to movers and shakers — gets more attention. American historical literature, including children's, takes a less chauvinistic approach to American history than it once did, revising the traditional chronicle of unbroken upward progress.

However, amid the cheers for this enlightenment are occasional murmurs of doubt — and there ought to be more. Too much historical fiction for children is stepping around large slabs of known reality to tell pleasant but historically doubtful stories. Even highly respected authors snip away the less attractive pieces of the past to make their narratives meet current social and political preferences.

Patricia MacLachlan's *Sarah, Plain and Tall* won the Newbery Medal in 1985. It is a simple, warmhearted tale, as popular with children as with adults (which cannot be said of every Newbery winner). The setting is a nineteenth-century farm on the American prairie, though exactly where and when is unspecified. Since there is no mention of farm machinery, and since there is a reference to plowing a new field in the prairie, the period would seem to be the 1870s. Sarah, an unmarried young woman, answers a newspaper ad and travels from Maine to the Midwest to stay with a widowed man and his two children for a month. The understanding is that if all goes well, she and the father will marry. If not, she will return to Maine. She comes alone and stays in the house with no other woman there.

The realities of nineteenth-century social mores are at odds with practically all of this. It was unusual for a woman to travel such distances alone, and much more than unusual for her to stay with a man not related to her without another woman in the house. Had she done so, however, it is unlikely that she could return home afterward with her reputation intact. MacLachlan has said that her story is based on a family experience a couple of generations ago, and I have no reason to question that. Even so, the story as told is highly uncharacteristic of its time and place.

Besides bypassing the usual social strictures of the time, the novel also glides lightly over a basic reality of farm life in the nineteenth century: work. More than work, in fact — *toil,* a word that has all but disappeared from modern vocabularies. Hamlin Garland, who grew up on farms in Wisconsin and Iowa in the 1860s and 1870s, wrote about his experience in *A Son of the Middle Border*. Again and again, Garland describes the constant labor of a farm family's life. A farm asked a great deal of boys and men, yet women's work, Garland said, was even more relentless. "Being a farmer's wife in those days meant laboring outside any regulation of the hours of toil . . . a slavish round with never a full day of leisure, with scarcely an hour of escape from the tugging hands of children and the need of mending and washing clothes . . . from the churn to the stove, from the stove to the bedchamber, and from the bedchamber back to the kitchen, day after day, year after year, rising at daylight or before, and going to her bed only after the evening dishes were washed and the stockings and clothing mended for the night."

While no one expects a child's book to be a litany of toil, work was so central to daily life on a farm that one does expect to see it treated as more than incidental. As Laura Ingalls Wilder tells her Little House stories, the work people did are events in a child's life, as indeed they were; the cheese making and the building of a new door were as memorable for Laura as Pa's fiddling. In *Sarah, Plain and Tall,* work is named but not described; somehow it is manageable enough to give Sarah leisure to lie in the fields admiring nature or making daisy chains for the children. And there is an interchange of jobs between Sarah and the farmer-father that is more New Age than nineteenth century. Papa bakes bread; Sarah helps to reshingle a roof and learns, under Papa's tutelage, to plow. While none of this was impossible, neither was it typical. Division of labor on a farm was a matter of practicality as well as custom. Papa would not often have been in the house enough to tend bread, and Sarah would have plenty to do without taking up plowing.

Avi's *The True Confessions of Charlotte Doyle* was a Newbery

Honor Book in 1991. It's a fine vicarious adventure story. It is also preposterous. The reader is asked to believe that in 1832, a thirteen-year-old girl boards a sailing ship to go from England to America, joins the crew of hard-bitten sailors (all with hearts more or less of gold), performs surpassingly difficult feats of physical strength and daring under the eye of a villainous captain who hates her, and not only survives (sexually unsullied, of course) but becomes captain of the ship. Home at last, she tries out conventional life with her parents for a week or so and finds it restrictive — unsurprisingly — so she climbs out of the window and returns to her old ship as crew. Great fun if you are twelve or thirteen — but fantasy.

Catherine, Called Birdy (a 1995 Newbery Honor Book) by Karen Cushman is a brave excursion into medieval social history through the diary of a fourteen-year-old who questions nearly everything that governed the lives of medieval people in general and of women in particular. Birdy's world is real enough — rough, dirty, and uncomfortable most of the time, even among the privileged classes. Her feisty independence is perhaps believable, as is her objection to being "sold like a parcel" in marriage to add to her father's status or land. However, those were standard considerations in marriage among the landholding classes, for sons as well as daughters, and Birdy's repeated resistance might have drawn much harsher punishment than she got. The fifteenth-century Paston Letters record what happened to a daughter who opposed her mother about a proposed match: "She has since Easter [three months before this letter] been beaten once in the week or twice, sometimes twice in one day, and her head broken in two or three places." As the historian of the Paston papers points out, "The idea that children . . . had any natural rights was almost impossible to a medieval mind. Children were just chattels . . . entirely at the direction and disposal of their fathers."

Cushman sticks to historical reality while Birdy considers and discards the few alternatives to marriage she can think of — running away, becoming a goat-keeper, joining a monastery. But once her heroine agrees to her father's final, awful choice for her, Cushman quickly supplies an exit. The intended husband dies, so Birdy can marry his son, who, fortunately, is heir to the land and thereby meets her father's purposes. The son is, of course, young and educated, where his father was old, ugly, and illiterate. Even granting that life is unpredictable, so fortuitous an escape strains the framework. In fairness, I think Cushman knew this; she just flinched at consigning her likable character to her likely fate.

And therein lies the difficulty I find with these and many other contemporary historical novels. They evade the common realities of the societies they write about. In novels about girls or women, authors want to give their heroines freer choices than their cultures would in fact have offered. To do that, they set aside the social mores of the past as though they were minor afflictions, small obstacles, easy — and painless — for an independent mind to overcome.

To see authors vaulting blithely over the barriers women lived with for so long brings to mind *Anna Karenina*. Anna's is the story these contemporary writers don't want to tell. When she left her husband and child for Vronsky, Anna suffered all the sanctions her society imposed on women who defied its rules. Whether the reader, or for that matter, Tolstoy, finds the rules unfair or the sanctions too harsh is irrelevant. Tolstoy was telling the story of a woman who lived when and where she lived, who made the choices she made, and who was destroyed by the consequences.

Most contemporary writers of historical fiction research the topics and the times they have chosen, and they often provide information about the facts and sources they have used. Yet their narratives play to modern sensibilities. Their protagonists experience their own societies as though they were time travelers, noting racism, sexism, religious bigotry, and outmoded belief as outsiders, not as people of and in their cultures.

Historical-fiction writers who want their protagonists to reflect twentieth-first-century ideologies end by making them exceptions to their cultures, so that in many a historical novel the reader learns nearly nothing — or at least nothing sympathetic — of how the people of a past society saw their world. Characters are divided into right — those who believe as we do — and wrong; that is, those who believe something that we now disavow. Such stories suggest that people of another time either did understand or should have understood the world as we do now, an outlook that quickly devolves into the belief that people are the same everywhere and in every time.

But people of the past were not just us in odd clothing. They were people who saw the world differently; approached human relationships differently; people for whom night and day, heat and cold, seasons and work and play had meanings lost to an industrialized, technological age. Even if human nature is much the same over time, human experience, perhaps especially everyday experience, is not. To wash these differences out of historical fiction is not only a denial of historical truth but a failure of imagination and understanding that diminishes the present as well as the past.

MORE GREAT HISTORICAL FICTION

Laurie Halse Anderson, *Chains*

316 pp. Grades 5–8. Slaves Isabel and Ruth are shipped to New York in May 1776, where Isabel helps foil her Loyalist master's scheme to kill George Washington. Anderson's novel is remarkable for its strong sense of place and nuanced portrait of slavery during the Revolutionary War. Sequel: *Forge*.

M. T. Anderson, *The Astonishing Life of Octavian Nothing, Traitor to the Nation, Volume I: The Pox Party*

359 pp. Grade 9 and up. Young slave Octavian has received, as an experiment, a classical education; in a precise eighteenth-century voice, he narrates the details of his surreal life inside Boston's Novanglian College of Lucidity. Anderson savages the hypocrisy of the nascent United States, creating an alternative narrative of our national mythology. The story continues in *Volume II: The Kingdom on the Waves*.

Audrey Couloumbis and Akila Couloumbis, *War Games: A Novel Based on a True Story*

233 pp. Grades 5–8. Greek brothers Petros, twelve, and Zola, fifteen, are prone to quarrel. The advent of World War II and the invasion of their village by the Germans only fuel the brothers' competition. But when a Nazi colonel moves into their house, the boys realize how serious their games have become. A gripping story and a fine introduction to a complex time.

Christopher Paul Curtis, *Elijah of Buxton*

344 pp. Grades 4–6. Eleven-year-old Elijah is the first child to be born free in Buxton, a refuge for freed slaves established in 1849 in Canada. An arresting, surprising coming-of-age novel, a moving story of reluctant heroism.

Louise Erdrich, *The Porcupine Year*

193 pp. Grades 5–8. In this third book about Omakayas (*The Birchbark House; The Game of Silence*), a renegade uncle robs the family, leaving them close to starvation as winter closes in. Erdrich presents another tale full of rich

details of 1850s Ojibwe life, complicated characters, and all the joys and challenges of a girl becoming a woman.

Jacqueline Kelly, *The Evolution of Calpurnia Tate*
340 pp. Grades 4–6. In 1889 Texas, eleven-year-old Calpurnia and her gruff, intimidating grandfather share an insatiable curiosity about the natural world, culminating in their thrilling discovery of a new plant species. Callie's struggle to identify herself as a scientist amidst very different expectations for her future will resonate with young readers.

Ellen Klages, *The Green Glass Sea*
324 pp. Grades 4–6. In 1943, ten-year-old Dewey's dad is working at Los Alamos with hundreds of other scientists and their families. Klages evokes both the big-sky landscape of the Southwest and a community where "everything is secret," focusing on the society of the children who live there. Sequel: *White Sands, Red Menace.*

Matt Phelan, *The Storm in the Barn*
203 pp. Grades 5–8. This stunning graphic novel brings 1937 Kansas, wracked by drought and hardship, to life, adding a supernatural twist. Exploring an abandoned barn, eleven-year-old Jack encounters a mysterious, threatening figure with a face of rain and a bag that flashes lightning. Phelan's palette of sepias, dusty browns, and charcoal grays perfectly evokes the desolate landscapes of the Dust Bowl.

Rita Williams-Garcia, *One Crazy Summer*
218 pp. Grades 4–6. Eleven-year-old Delphine and her two younger sisters spend the summer of 1968 in Oakland, California, visiting their estranged poet mother. Change is in the air—for the girls and for the country. Williams-Garcia writes vividly about that turbulent summer through the intelligent, honest, vulnerable voice of Delphine.

Banana Peels at Every Step
Sarah Ellis

The art of comedy is a matter of timing and balance. The great comic writer plays the reader like a fish. We are hooked by the plausible and the familiar. We are given false freedom as the line plays out. Finally, at just the right moment, we are flipped out of our element to lie helpless and gasping on the deck. It is all about finesse.

The writer for children, however, is humbled by the fact that, when the laff-o-meter is running, all this artfulness can be completely trumped by a phrase such as *peanut butter belly button*. Middle-grade readers are ready for a broad range of humor—jokey, satirical, slapstick, wacky, and melodramatic—but none of it can stray too far from the banana peel.

Jokes, comedy's smallest components, give young readers micro-narratives, an excellent introduction to the notions of theme and variation, the construction and release of tension, and the power and slipperiness of language. Best of all, jokes are sociable, a link to story's oral roots, demanding collusion between teller and audience. The discovery of the potential of the chicken crossing the road can be a liberating experience for a kid.

In Adam Gopnik's essay collection *Through the Children's Gate*, he describes his young son's discovery of the joke "Waiter, what's a fly doing in my soup?" and all its variants. This discovery leads Gopnik to a reminiscence of his own childhood delight in old-style Jewish comics. He writes, "None of them talked about 'jokes' that you 'told.' Instead they talked about 'bits' that they 'did' — and killed 'them' doing it. That, for me, explained everything, life and art. Life was stuff that happened, art was bits you did."

The joke book section of libraries is often high in circulation and low in respect. It is true that adult joke books have a whiff of desperation about them ("Spark up that sales conference!" "Shine at parties!"), but children's joke books are a different kettle of fish, an early introduction to the notion that, as Gopnik discovered, art is active, something you do. When art succeeds, it is interactive. For the reader who hasn't yet learned to settle in to a page of print, jokes have the huge advantage of being short — and they seem to be particularly appealing to boys, possibly because they are a kind of narrative that can be competitive.

Joke anthologies are one of the few kinds of children's literature in which quality matters less than bulk. A good joke book is a fat joke book. Readers need a big pool to dip into. Lavish color illustrations overwhelm jokes and make them uncomfortable. Jokes like low-quality paper and cartoon illustrations. They like to be stuffed into backpacks and taken to the beach. They positively enjoy broken spines and grease stains. *The Whopping Great Big Bonkers Joke Book: Over 1000 Side-Splitting Jokes* is perfect. "Knock, knock," "Doctor, doctor," and "What do you get if you cross something with something?"—all the standard forms are there. There's an old-fashioned edge to jokes that often makes them a bridge between generations. Astronauts may not be of much interest to contemporary children, but they live on in jokes. "If an athlete gets athlete's foot, what does an astronaut get? Missile toe."

The retro tradition of jokes doesn't give joke books carte blanche to be offensive, however. Jay Leno's *How to Be the Funniest Kid in the Whole Wide World* makes you wonder in what universe he has been living for the last fifty years. It's not actually okay to make jokes about "Eskimos" and fat people anymore, Jay. The general principle of avoiding children's books written by celebrities is in no way threatened by this feeble production.

In the right hands, the impulse toward stand-up can also be harnessed for use in longer fictions. Neal Shusterman's *The Schwa Was Here* is constructed from the Lego of jokes, its surface one long stand-up routine. Hey, did you hear the one about the blind girl and the invisible boy? What about the one about the Italian and the Jew? The hero, Antsy, has a wisecracking, Brooklynese voice and a crazy goal. He wants to turn his friend, Schwa, into a legend. Shusterman knows all the tricks. There's the rule of three, in which if you mention something three times, it becomes funny. There's the delayed punch line, in which you get your reader to almost, but not quite, forget a reference, and then you bring it out with a flourish.

The Schwa Was Here also makes hay with the "ew, yuck!" factor of juvenile humor. Reading it is a bit like driving members of a junior-high boys' soccer team to a distant game. Sooner or later you know it is all going to be covered — bad breath, regurgitation, condiment bottles up the nose, dead rodents, armpits, and the little plastic strainer at the bottom of urinals. There's more here than *Captain Underpants,* however. The bits, the corny old jokes, add up to a thought-provoking, unsentimental, subversive portrait of friendship, rivalry, fame, and heroism.

Nobody is less funny than somebody trying too hard to be funny, and part of Antsy's success as a character is that he is the perfect straight man. For the female equivalent we need look no further than Primrose Squarp, the hero of Polly Horvath's *Everything on a Waffle*. This romp, with its jokes and its judicious dashes of "ew, yuck!" is an outrageous story of small-town life. Horvath pulls out all the stops. She constructs a plot that includes not one orphan but two, both of them disabled. She includes four eccentric spinsters. Her hero loses not one but two bits of her body in accidents. Horvath creates a couple of parents who are lost at sea in a storm and survive on a deserted island for weeks and weeks. She has a character give the following advice on how to deal with school bullies: "Kick the crap out of those stinkers." Then she chooses a real place, Coal Harbour on the coast on British Columbia, takes the elements of its history and community (such as a military base and whaling), and throws them up in the air, letting them fall where they may. There are also recipes. Disgusting recipes. Cherry pie pork chops gives you the idea.

Everything on a Waffle is irreverent, stylish, and cool, a tall tale with a dark edge of satire. Here's Primrose's account of her teachers discussing her "issues," which they hope to alleviate by sending the class guinea pig home with her on weekends:

> "Caring for a small animal instills a sense of ourselves and others," said my teacher.
>
> I didn't see how I could help having a sense of myself and others. But, of course, none of us had any idea what we were talking about. It was just one of those situations where everyone involved feels compelled to say something, anything at all.

Horvath's humor can be somewhat adult, but because her take on the world is so grounded and perceptive, the message to the child reader is not that of exclusion but of respect and invitation: "I know that you've noticed this same weird, absurdist thing." She lays the groundwork for her readers to grow up and read David Lodge and Molly Keane.

In slapstick, comedy can easily tip into disaster, even cruelty. It takes a master hand to keep the balance. Such a master is Jack Gantos. The subject heading for *Joey Pigza Loses Control* would give the reader no hint that this book was funny: "Attention-deficit hyperactivity disorder — fiction." Yet this book has scenes of slapstick that make you laugh till you cry, then wonder if you are really crying for sadness. This is comedy that grows out of an original and entirely winning character. This is the wry territory where you want to send in the clowns.

Joey Pigza is a boy who is at a turning point. "Before I had gone to special ed and got my new meds it would have been impossible for me to sit still and make a list of good things and bad things. I didn't have time for lists. I didn't have time for anything that lasted longer than the snap of my fingers." But Joey's newly discovered ability to pause and think is stolen from him when he goes to visit his father, who believes that "real men can tough it out" and flushes the meds down the toilet. The reader then enters, with Joey, the speeded-up world of ADHD. We are so inside Joey that his good ideas seem like good ideas to us too. Impersonate a mannequin in a department store? Throw darts at the couch cushions? Play some Herb Alpert on your trumpet in church? Get off the bus at every stop and then race to the back doors and get on again? Why not? Joey's hijinks are the familiar stuff of the middle-grade-mayhem novel, except that he is aware that all is not well, and so are we.

This is comedy that grows out of uneasiness. There are banana peels at every step, and we see the disasters looming. It works because Joey and his family are not caricatures. They are real, recognizable people who simply do the things most of us only think about. They are also, in their way, a loving group.

> Grandma had pulled half a cheek full of loose skin all the way back behind her jaw where she had it gathered in a wad and clipped to her ear with a clothespin. "Don't you think I'd look better with a face-lift?" she asked, and breathed through her mouth like a fish out of water. . . .

I didn't know what to say but opened my mouth anyway and said, "You'd better watch out. If you pull the skin too tight it might rip apart like when you pull Play-Doh too hard."

One of the most challenging flavors to pull off in a children's book is wacky. Wacky applied on top of the story like gooey icing becomes quickly tiresome. But wacky built into a story can't be beat. Daniel Pinkwater has wacky in his DNA. Jules Feiffer said of Pinkwater that his "thoughts don't connect like yours or mine." In *Looking for Bobowicz*, Nick, a new resident of Hoboken, joins forces with two new pals, Loretta Fischetti and Bruno Ugg, to solve several mysteries. Mystery one is, Who stole Nick's bike, and how do they get it back? (A subplot involves the theft of a collection of Classic Comics.) Mystery two is, Who is the phantom? Mystery three involves a giant chicken. There is also the hidden cave, a near-death experience (death by sauerkraut), and a wonderful, mad, but effective public librarian called Starr Lackawanna.

What makes Pinkwater unique is that the worlds he creates are 100 percent benign without being one bit bland. The off-the-wall references—to the song "Frozen Yogurt Blues" by Blind Persimmon, the annual Hoboken Bat Hat Festival, the 1930s avant-garde art style of Mama ("like Dada, only nicer")—all add up to a world of joyful pleasure in the varieties of humankind.

During the Bat Hat Festival, all the middle-grade children in Hoboken gather one summer night to throw their hats up into the darkness beyond the streetlight to capture bats. No bats are ever captured. No bats are ever actually seen. What's the point?

> I began to shout too, and then I began to laugh. I noticed that Loretta Fischetti and Bruno Ugg were laughing. Everybody was laughing. After a while I was laughing so hard I couldn't do anything else. I got out of breath and bent over with my

hands on my knees, laughing. Then I sank to the ground and just lay there laughing so hard my eyes filled with tears. My stomach muscles hurt from laughing so hard. Just about everyone else was on the ground too, rolling back and forth and waving arms and legs and laughing until all we could do was sort of sob and giggle.

The fine line between sobbing and giggling is only one of several that comedy walks. In melodrama we walk the delicious line between fear and fun. We know that the blonde damsel tied to the railway tracks is not really going to be smushed by the train, but when we hear that distant whistle, the tension rises nonetheless. For the child reader, melodrama gives a range of reading options, from the naive, straight reading to the more sophisticated, seasoned-with-a-grain-of-salt knowingness.

The craze for the Series of Unfortunate Events by the pseudonymous Lemony Snicket proved that melodrama is alive and well. Snicket grads are well prepared for the Wolves Chronicles of Joan Aiken. Starting with *The Wolves of Willoughby Chase* and ending with *The Witch of Clatteringshaws,* this series was published over the course of more than forty years. The nonstop action takes place in an invented eighteenth century, in which James III and his heirs rule England. Every chapter of every book is a feast of invention. Tidal waves, abandoned waifs, wicked governesses, unmentionable fates, the return of King Arthur, improbable coincidences, ESP, fog, obscure ailments, false teeth made from woolly-mammoth ivory, alternative technologies (an early bicycle called a "dupli-gyro"), and characters who might have wandered in from a Dickens novel combine in roustabout stories breathless in their pace and plotting. The wit lies in the language. Aiken's invented worlds demand invented words, and reading her books is like an intensive immersion in Aikenese. "Queer he keeps his garden so spange when the house is in such a mux." Good comedy does change one's perspective, and

Jon Agee's light touch is much in evidence in this entry in his second book of palindromes, *Sit on a Potato Pan, Otis!*

after a vacation in Aiken's world, many aspects of our own world look a bit rum and fubsy.

From a collection of knock-knock jokes to the sophisticated novels of Joan Aiken, funny books make the same demands of the writer as all fiction. They need imaginative language, a melding of the familiar and the new, a strong narrative pull, a grounding in authentic dilemmas and emotions, a fresh take on the world, characters we care about, and a congenial, welcoming voice. The additional demand that humor makes is that all these elements have to be created with a pastry chef's light hand. A bit of plodding, didacticism, or earnestness is forgivable in an adventure book or a fantasy, but it deflates comedy like a pin in a balloon. When you look for a funny book, look for a soufflé.

Comedian Rowan Atkinson, when asked about the cross-cultural appeal of his alter ego Mr. Bean, said, "Mr. Bean is essentially a child trapped in the body of a man. All cultures identify with children in a similar way, so he has this bizarre global outreach. And ten-year-old boys from different cultures have more in common than thirty-year-olds. As we grow up, we acquire this sensibility that divides us." If we need an excuse for funny books, that's it. It is hard to get on your high horse or look down on somebody else when you're flat on your back laughing, gasping on the deck, hooked, for good and all, by comedy.

"What's So Funny, Mr. Scieszka?"

Jon Scieszka

The voice flew across the room and nailed me to the back of my seat.

"What's so funny, Mr. Scieszka?"

The voice belonged to Sister Margaret Ann. And it had just flown across our fifth-grade religion class at St. Luke's Elementary School to find me in what I had thought was the safety of the back row.

I knew that the correct answer to this question was "Nothing, sister."

"I'm sorry, sister," was also a time-tested and very good reply.

And nine times out of ten, ninety-nine times out of a hundred, I would have used one of those answers. But that day something happened. That day I reached some existential fork in the road.

My friend and back-row co-conspirator, Tim Kavolsik, had just told me the funniest joke I had ever heard. The fact that he had told it while Sister Margaret Ann was droning on about our future options of heaven and hell only made it funnier.

Now I was called out.

I saw the two life paths laid out clearly before me. Down the one path of the quick apology and standard answer lay the good grade for religion class. Down the other path lay the possibility of a very big laugh. A good grade in religion class is always a good thing in Catholic school. No arguing that. But this was a really funny joke, and I knew why it was funny. I was torn between going for the A and going for the laugh. Both were within my grasp.

So when Sister Margaret Ann asked the inevitable follow-up question, "Would you like to share it with the rest of the class?" I chose my life's path.

"Well, there's this guy who wants to be a bell ringer," I began, "but he doesn't have any arms."

Sister Margaret Ann's eyes pop open wider than I have ever seen them. The whole class turns to look at me and at the train wreck about to happen. Even my pal Tim Kovalsik is shaking his head at this point. Nobody in the history of St. Luke's Elementary School has ever volunteered to "share it with the rest of the class." But I feel it. I have to do it. It is my destiny.

"The priest who is looking for a good bell ringer says, 'You can't ring the bells. You don't have any arms.'"

The faces of my fellow fifth-graders are looking a bit wavy and blurry. I suddenly understand the phrase *sea of faces*.

"'I don't need arms,' says the bell-ringing guy. 'Watch this.' And he runs up the bell tower and starts bouncing his face off the bells and making beautiful music."

Half of the class laughs. I'm not sure if it's out of nervousness or pity. But it's a lot of laughs.

Sister Margaret Ann's eyes open, impossibly, wider.

Light floods the classroom. I can't really see anybody now. I can only feel the punch line building. I head toward the light.

"So the bell-ringing guy goes to finish his song with one last smack of his face, but this time he misses the bell and falls right out of the tower. He lands on the ground and is knocked out. A whole crowd of villagers gathers around him."

The whole class has gathered around me. It is a feeling of almost unbelievable power mixed with terror for a confirmed low-profile student like myself.

"'Who is this guy?' the villagers ask."

I feel the whole world pause for just a single beat, like it always does before a good punch line.

"'I don't know his name,' says the priest. 'But his face rings a bell.'"

I don't remember the grade I got in fifth-grade religion class, but I do remember the laugh I got. It was huge. It was the whole class. It was out-of-control hysterical. It was glorious.

So now, from a distance of forty years, I'd like to continue to answer Sister Margaret Ann's question. Because in looking back over my work, trying to make some retrospective sense of my writing for kids, I've realized that each of my books is in some way another piece of the answer to the question, "What's so funny, Mr. Scieszka?"

I'd also like to accept the invitation of Sister Margaret's second question and share with you, the rest of the class, what's so funny.

I believe funny is good. I believe funny is important. And I may just be rationalizing the path I chose back in fifth grade, but I also believe funny isn't given the respect it deserves.

Scholars and historians more learned than I have pondered this problem for ages. Why is tragedy seen as being more substantial than comedy? Why do we believe sadness is a more valid and a deeper emotion than happiness? Why is it that funny stuff never wins the awards? (What was the last funny movie to win an Academy Award? Or, closer to home, in our world of children's books — what was the last funny book to win a Caldecott or Newbery?)

One of my favorite funny writers, a fellow by the name of E. B. White, put it best in the introduction to his *A Subtreasury of American Humor*. "The world likes humor," wrote E. B., "but treats it patronizingly. It decorates its serious artists with laurel, and its wags with Brussels sprouts. It feels that if a thing is funny it can be presumed to be something less than great, because if it were truly great it would be wholly serious."

And it's interesting to note that Mr. White was decorated with a Newbery Honor laurel for his book *Charlotte's Web* but received only Brussels sprouts for his much funnier and much more insightful *Is Sex Necessary?: Or, Why You Feel the Way You Do.*

But don't take my word for it. I'll quote a passage from each book. Then you decide for yourself.

From *Charlotte's Web*, chapter three:

The barn was very large. It was very old. It smelled of hay and it smelled of manure.

From *Is Sex Necessary?*, chapter four:

The sexual revolution began with Man's discovery that he was not attractive to Woman, as such. The lion had his mane, the peacock his gorgeous plumage, but Man found himself in a three-button sack suit. His masculine appearance not only failed to excite Woman, but in many cases it only served to bore her. The result was that Man found it necessary to develop attractive personal traits to offset his dull appearance. He learned to say funny things. He learned to smoke, and blow smoke rings. He learned to earn money. This would have been a solution to his difficulty, but in the course of making himself attractive to Woman by developing himself mentally, he inadvertently became so intelligent an animal that he saw how comical the whole situation was.

Now I ask you — which passage is funnier? Which passage has more insight into the human condition? I rest my case.

We could delve deeper into our collective psyche and debate further the relative merits of comedy and tragedy, but I say we just give E. B. White another quote and get on with the promised business of answering the question, What's so funny, Mr. Scieszka?

Once again, from E. B. White's introduction to his *Subtreasury of American Humor* (and no, that's not the only funny book I have. It just seemed like the quotes from this one would be more literary and seemly than quotes from Jon Stewart's *Naked Pictures of Famous People* or Will Cuppy's *How to Attract the Wombat*):

> Humor can be dissected, as a frog can, but the thing dies in the process and the innards are discouraging to any but the pure scientific mind.

Which is exactly why schools and teachers are not so keen on humor as a legitimate form of writing—it's so difficult to dissect. Teachers love to dig into tragedies and problem fiction, in part because they can be explained and illuminated by discussion.

We can talk about why Charlotte has to die.

We can discuss why Travis has to shoot his beloved dog, Old Yeller.

We can analyze why the boys behave the way they do in *Lord of the Flies*.

We can explain why we cry when Jesse loses his friend Leslie in *Bridge to Terabithia*.

But it's much more difficult to explain or discuss what's so funny about anything. The very nature of humor works against explanation. In many cases, the old adage is true—you either "get it" or you don't.

I can only imagine myself deconstructing my fifth-grade religion class: "Well, sister, the bell ringer is funny because the joke uses the literal meaning of 'ringing a bell' instead of the meaning to 'jog the memory.' And then the image of the guy bonking his face on the bell is . . . well . . . funny. And the other funny part is that you don't understand this until all at once at the end when you hear the punch line."

How's that for killing the humor and dragging its innards out all over the place?

All right. No more joking around. I better get down to business. I'm looking for laurels here, not Brussels sprouts. Let's get started dragging the frog's innards out for examination and answering the question of what's so funny.

Growing up with five brothers and no sisters is funny. I think that's where I first got started on this funny business. In fact, I *know* that's where I got started. Growing up in that group, you either laughed . . . or died.

I was fortunate enough to be the second oldest of the six Scieszka boys. As one of the oldest, I got more parental attention (not always a good thing) but fewer hand-me-downs. I have a card in my scrapbook announcing my birth as "Lou and Shirley Scieszka's new addition to the Tappa-Kegga-Milk Fraternity."

That's kind of funny.

My youngest brother, Jeff (number six), never got a scrapbook. I think my mom was just tired of the whole thing by then. Jeff has a Ziploc bag with some pictures in it. And most of the pictures aren't even of him.

Now that's really funny.

Growing up with younger brothers, I was sometimes asked to watch them. So I did. I watched them dig in the houseplants. I watched them chew on the dog. I watched them play in the toilet.

Kind of funny.

One day when my older brother, Jim, and I were watching the littler ones Jeff and Brian, we were so entertained that we realized we could probably charge other kids to watch, too. We charged the kids from our block a dime each to watch Brian eat cigarette butts.

Very funny.

But the funniest thing I ever did was to teach school. For ten years I taught a little bit of everything, from first-grade homeroom to eighth-grade algebra. And it absolutely changed my life. Because it was there in school that I rediscovered how smart and funny kids are. In school I found my true audience. In school my kids taught me about the importance of play.

Kids are great at playing. That's what they do best. When I was a kid, we had specific clothes we wore to go out and play. We had clothes we called our "play clothes." When we got home from school, we took off our school clothes, put on our play clothes, and went out to play. That was our job. We played.

Teaching in elementary school, and watching kids in action, I came to appreciate how effortlessly kids learn when they play. Babies learn to talk without taking multiple-choice talking tests. Toddlers learn to toddle without writing toddling essays. How do they do it? By playing around.

So from teaching I learned to respect kids as natural learners, supply them with the tools to learn, and then get out of the way. I learned to inspire instead of lecture. I learned to trust play. That philosophy is at the heart of everything I write for kids. I want my readers to laugh, of course. But then I want them to question, to argue, to wonder — What if? I want them to play. I want them to learn for themselves.

MORE GREAT HUMOR

Jon Agee, *Orangutan Tongs: Poems to Tangle Your Tongue*
48 pp. Grades K–3. Inspired by such trusty tongue twisters as "Which wrist-watches are Swiss wristwatches?" the ever-effervescent Agee fashions thirty-four comic verses. The effect is hilarious — especially with Agee's visual extensions of the absurdity in his deft cartoons.

M. T. Anderson, illustrations by Kurt Cyrus, *Jasper Dash and the Flame-Pits of Delaware: A Pals in Peril Tale*
423 pp. Grades 5–8. In this spoof on "foreign adventure" novels, friends Jasper, Katie, and Lily (*Whales on Stilts*) head to the "ancient, eldritch mountains" and mysterious golden temples of . . . Tibet? No, Delaware! Anderson stuffs every scene with exotic details and lampoons everything from organized youth sports to clichéd writing. Absurdist humor at its best.

Deirdre Baker, *Becca at Sea*
165 pp. Grades 4–6. In twelve linked episodes set on her gran's small island off the coast of British Columbia, Becca averts many mishaps and disasters, saving the day with ingenuity, tact, and enough grace to beguile her family and readers alike. A funny and endearing book.

Jack Gantos, *Dead End in Norvelt*
275 pp. Grades 4–6. In Gantos's semi-autobiographical novel set in a community founded by Eleanor Roosevelt, young Jack is grounded for the entire summer for accidentally shooting his father's WWII souvenir rifle, escaping only to help his feisty elderly neighbor write obituaries for all the townspeople who are suddenly dying off. This hyperactive dark comedy will have readers laughing out loud while also considering history, life and death, and the costs of war.

Hilary McKay, *Forever Rose*
291 pp. Grades 4–6. Eleven-year-old Rose is the emotional heart of this fifth and final book about the eccentric Casson family (*Saffy's Angel*, etc.). McKay

delights us once again with her laugh-out-loud disaster scenes and her celebration of the virtue of kindness.

Richard Peck, *A Season of Gifts*
156 pp. Grades 5–8. As irascible, independent, and unorthodox as ever, the unforgettable Grandma Dowdel (of *A Year Down Yonder* and *A Long Way from Chicago*) makes a welcome return in this third novel, set in small-town 1950s Illinois. Pranks and counter-pranks, over-the-top episodes, and colorful characters provide much amusement.

Lincoln Peirce, *Big Nate: In a Class by Himself*
216 pp. Grades 3–6. Sixth-grader Big Nate is convinced that he's destined for greatness—but he seems destined for trouble. There's so much to like here: illustrations or cartoon panels on every page, fast-paced trouble for our hero, and laugh-out-loud commentary on the day-to-day awkwardness of middle of school. Sequel: *Big Nate Strikes Again*.

Ken Roberts, illustrations by Leanne Franson, *The Thumb in the Box*
95 pp. Grades 2–5. With a little ingenuity, eleven-year-old Leon's isolated community (on the coast of British Columbia) turns some unwanted gifts from the government into just the things they need. Leon's breezy, direct narration makes this very funny David-versus-Goliath tale accessible and involving. Sequels: *Thumb on a Diamond; Thumb and the Bad Guys*.

Maryrose Wood, illustrations by Jon Klassen, *The Incorrigible Children of Ashton Place: The Mysterious Howling*
268 pp. Grades 3–6. In this first installment of the series, Miss Penelope Lumley is governess to three children who have been raised by wolves. Let the over-the-top characterizations, ludicrous situations, and tongue-in-cheek humor begin! Like Lemony Snicket, Wood has the gift of both telling her story and sending it up.

Know-How and Guts
Vicky Smith

"You'll love it. He has to eat bugs."
— from *Basher Five-Two*

When I was a working librarian, this was the conclusion to the at-the-shelf booktalk I used to give to fifth-, sixth-, and seventh-grade boys who slouched after their mothers into the library on the prowl for a hundred-page biography of a nonathlete (the boiler-plate assignment in my community when Biography Month rolls around; see "A Story, by Someone Else, More than a Hundred Pages," page 196). The book in question is *Basher Five-Two: The True Story of F-16 Fighter Pilot Captain Scott O'Grady* by Captain O'Grady with the assistance of Michael French. It describes an episode from ancient history: the 1995 downing of an American pilot behind Serbian lines while patrolling NATO's no-fly zone over embattled Bosnia-Herzegovina during the Yugoslav War.

The story has all the hallmarks of a classic adventure memoir: real physical danger, the display of both courage and know-how as the protagonist seeks safety, and a delight in the most minute of details. Readers will learn everything they ever wanted to know about military survival training.

> Before you stick anything strange into your mouth, you are supposed to test it for harmful effects. The first step is to

rub the plant or leaf on the outside of your lip. If your lip becomes irritated, the leaf is no good to eat. If there is no irritation, you rub the leaf on the *inside* of your lip, to see if that causes a reaction. If not, the next step is to put it in your mouth for a few minutes. If there is no burning, itching, or nausea, you can swallow it with some confidence.

By the end of *Basher Five-Two,* the reader will have learned not only how to test a leaf for edibility but also how to make sense of the F-16 console, how to strip flight uniforms of all identifying insignia (and why), how to refuel a fighter jet in midair, and how to communicate with your rescuers when you're trapped behind enemy lines — all very useful stuff. Adventure stories are often the first resort for adults trying to con reluctant readers — usually boys — into reading. The fast pace, the concentration on physicality, and the frequent how-to element of the tales can often seduce children who would rather be out engaging in adventures of their own (or finding them in video games). And it often works: kids who read *Basher Five-Two,* and books like it, manage to fulfill their biography assignments, and they also get to live the adventure for the space of 133 (or whatever) pages. They, like the books' protagonists, learn the skills necessary to survive, and they emerge on the other side of the book as more capable, confident human beings.

But adventure books are not just for reluctant readers. One of my own favorite books when I, a confirmed reader, was a kid was Jean Craighead George's *Julie of the Wolves.* I read it over and over (but after the first reading, I always skipped the dreary middle section that flashes back to before Miyax sets out across the tundra). I learned how to skin a caribou, trap a ptarmigan, make a sled out of water and hide, build an igloo, sew a fur mitten, inveigle myself into the good graces of a pack of wolves, and get them to vomit my supper up for me. Again, all useful stuff.

Like Miyax, I grew to love the wolves and to sorrow for their future in these modern times. But I think that what I mostly got out of that book was the exposure to life-threatening danger, the acquisition of the skills I'd need to survive it, and the encouragement that I would. For an unathletic, loner kid with really thick glasses, it gave me tremendous (if wholly unearned) confidence in my own capabilities: if Miyax could survive on the tundra with nothing but a needle and a couple of knives, then surely I could make it through gym class.

Not all adventure books serve up exactly the same recipe found in *Basher Five-Two* and *Julie of the Wolves,* but they all, to some extent, share in the same basic ethic: protagonist is put in physical danger and survives, thanks to know-how and guts. Most feature fast-paced action and lovingly described detail. All good ones give kids that vicarious thrill that makes them go back for more.

Adventure stories typically hew to one of four basic forms: outdoor adventure (which includes survival tales), war books, thrillers, and picaresque adventures. It's important to remember that nonfiction and fiction share equally at the adventure table, particularly in the first two categories. Memoirs of survival either in the out-of-doors or in wartime can make for gripping reading, with the added fillip that the experiences being described are *real* — and any adult who's ever read to a child knows that one of the most potent curiosities inspired by any book is "Is this true?"

Parents and grandparents whose childhood reading was rooted in the mid-twentieth century may remember that hoary old staple of the outdoor adventure, the boy-and-his-dog story, perhaps best typified by Jim Kjelgaard's *Big Red* and its successors. Danny, his dog, and his gun enjoy what seems now to be a wilderness idyll, tromping through the woods around the cabin Danny shares with his father, a trapper, and facing off against Old Majesty the bear. The clash of cultures features as a subplot, as Danny becomes drawn into the rarefied world of dog shows, but what I, and doubtless most other readers, remember are the scenes in the Wintapi woods, as

Danny uses his woodsman's expertise and Red his guts to protect their trapline against Old Majesty.

Although the boy-and-his-dog formula has faded in popularity, it has not totally disappeared. Meja Mwangi's tremendous 2005 novel *The Mzungu Boy* takes place in Kenya, during the Mau-Mau uprising of the 1950s, and tells the tale of young Kariuki, who, with the unlikely company of his white landlord's grandson, Nigel, tears around the countryside with Jimi the dog in pursuit of the boar Old Moses.

If Jean Craighead George could be described as the grandmother of the modern survival story, Gary Paulsen, of *Hatchet* fame, is its granddaddy; in fact, *Hatchet* is often the benchmark used when describing other survival tales, and his memoir *Guts* consists of anecdotes that formed the basis of his survival fiction. Thanks to *Hatchet,* generations of readers know not to eat just any old berry if they suddenly find themselves alone in the wilderness. Paulsen has no shortage of successors: Will Hobbs and Roland Smith, among others, consistently deliver rugged outdoor action.

Another successor, Terry Hokenson, begins his novel *The Winter Road* in *Hatchet*-fashion, with a plane crash, but it is very much its own creation. Willa, the unlucky pilot, unlike Brian, knows how to take care of herself in the wilderness. Also unlike Brian, however, she has crashed her plane in far northern Ontario in the middle of winter, when "warm" is defined as "zero degrees" and snow is both friend and enemy as she struggles to make her way to safety. *The Winter Road* is worth mentioning, as its female protagonist represents a significant minority within the genre. Perhaps as a nod to the aforementioned received wisdom that most reluctant readers are boys, and adventure stories often serve to draw those boys in, by and large these books feature leading men, not leading women.

An enthralling true adventure is Jennifer Armstrong's *Shipwreck at the Bottom of the World: The Extraordinary True Story of Shackleton and the Endurance*. In 1914, polar explorer Ernest Shackleton set out to lead a party across Antarctica, but his ship, the *Endurance,* never made it to shore. With the *Endurance* frozen in the ice that surrounds the continent, Shackleton kept his men alive for a year and a half, first camping on the ice and then, after a perilous open-water crossing, on the tiny, uninhabited Elephant Island—before making yet another nearly impossible voyage to South Georgia Island and its whaling station to fetch help. It's a mind-boggling tale of hubris and courage, and it will have readers wrapping themselves in extra blankets as they suffer with the members of the Imperial Trans-Antarctic Expedition.

War is a terrible human tragedy, but it is also the source of some of the world's greatest stories—look at *Henry V.* The best war stories for kids walk the fine line between acknowledging the alluring rush of adrenaline produced by battle and keeping the real costs of war present in the narrative.

In *Code Talker,* Joseph Bruchac tells the fascinating story of Ned Begay, one of the Navajo Marines who were key to American military success in the Pacific Theater in WWII. Simply the facts of how the Navajo code worked—those minute details again—make the book worth reading, but also the always-welcome feeling of being let in on a closely kept secret lures the reader into the story: "While [the code] remained classified, not one of us ever told about the code, not even to our families. We kept it secret throughout the war and long after." Ned's first-person account balances vivid combat scenes with retrospective reflection in which readers are treated to the great staples of war stories: the analysis of tactics and a specialized vocabulary. Ned's commanding officer tells his men that they will not be landing on Guam at the most strategic place because that's "just where the enemy expects us." One page later, Ned's out of his landing craft and running across the beach: "It was easier for me to run now because all us code talkers had the new lighter portable radio units. But it was not just because the new unit on my back was lighter that I ran so much faster. I no longer had forty pounds of TBX radio to hide behind and I needed to get to cover as fast as I could."

The immediate impact of Ned's equipment change on his personal safety is exactly the concrete detail aficionados of war stories crave. Tom Lalicki's nonfiction *Grierson's Raid: A Daring Cavalry Strike through the Heart of the Confederacy* tells the astonishing story of an 1863 raid through Mississippi by some 1,700 Union cavalry and artillery soldiers, who for sixteen days wreaked havoc under the very nose of Confederate command, evading capture and providing a distraction to enable Union troops to muster for an assault on Vicksburg. As in *Code Talker,* one of the strongest elements of Lalicki's storytelling is its dwelling on the tactical details that made this seemingly impossible adventure a success. The narrative combines contemporary newspaper accounts with the voices of the participants themselves to make for absolutely riveting reading.

But not all war adventures take readers into combat. *In My Hands: Memories of a Holocaust Rescuer* by Irene Gut Opdyke with Jennifer Armstrong is the mesmerizing account of a young Polish nursing student's own struggle to survive her country's successive occupation by the Russian and German armies and her decision to hide twelve Jews in the basement of a Nazi officer's house. No Holocaust story is easy, and this one is no exception, bracketed as it is by its teller's sexual degradation, first at the hands of Russian soldiers who rape her and then in the bed of her Nazi employer, who, when he discovers the fugitives in his basement, forces her into concubinage to purchase his silence. Does this make Opdyke's story "inappropriate" for young readers? Human beings are regrettably prone to brutality; by allowing kids to encounter it first in adventure reading, we can give them tools to survive and combat it that are just as important as Scott O'Grady's ejection seat and parachute.

To speak of the Holocaust within the context of children's adventure stories is to risk accusations of poor taste, to say the least. But for those kids who seek extreme adversity in their reading,

Holocaust stories are often a perfect match — with the added bonus that in enduring the unspeakable horrors along with real-life survivors, these readers may gain an additional appreciation of and respect for the history that has gone before.

If war stories, real and imagined, have a certain tooth-clenching aspect at the extremity of the dangers endured, thrillers turn up the tension a notch and take it down at the same time. The exaggerated nature of a thriller insulates readers from the peril but also provides a pleasing dose of adrenaline to carry them through the story. These days, the thriller genre for kids is dominated by series offerings, most notably the Alex Rider adventures by Anthony Horowitz. Their debt to James Bond is acknowledged openly in detail after detail, including young Alex's mocking nickname at his MI6 training camp: Double O Nothing. The action includes car chases, frantic trips through flooded tunnels, and a memorable episode that finds Alex trapped in a giant fish tank with a Portuguese man-of-war. The Alex Rider adventures are such harmless, outsize fun that they're being copied right and left, in one case by James Patterson's Maximum Ride novels; in another, by Charles Higson's Young Bond books. Catherine Jinks's *Evil Genius* and its sequel, *Genius Squad,* is a rather more nuanced example of the genre; it pits teen super-genius Cadel against the criminal mastermind who has nurtured him. (For more on thrillers for teen readers, see Nancy Werlin's essay on page 302.)

I label the last category of adventure story "picaresque." *Britannica* defines the term as "relating the adventures of a rogue or low-born adventurer . . . as he drifts from place to place and from one social milieu to another in his effort to survive." One key difference between the classic eighteenth-century picaresque novel and the contemporary children's picaresque is that rarely is the protagonist a rogue, though often he or she *is* lowborn. Almost always the protagonist is at a huge disadvantage in life because of age, size, lack of means, or some other issue.

While hardly lowborn, the young Charles Darwin was largely directionless when he convinced his father to let him try his hand at being a naturalist. Ruth Ashby's nonfiction account, *Young Charles Darwin and the Voyage of the Beagle*, charts his experiences as a world explorer, during which he encountered any number of indigenous peoples and customs and survived both a volcanic eruption and an earthquake. The backstory to the scientist's world-changing thought makes for great adventure reading.

Christopher Paul Curtis's *Bud, Not Buddy*, on the other hand, is classic picaresque, rogue and all: Bud Caldwell, in making his way across Depression-ravaged Michigan, encounters such disparate social types as librarians, the homeless, a Pullman porter, jazz musicians, and the occasional white person. His frequently adduced "Rules and Things for Having a Funner Life and Making a Better Liar Out of Yourself" contains the kind of survival tips that kids need to know: "If You Got to Tell a Lie, Make Sure It's Simple and Easy to Remember" (#3).

At first glance, there seems to be little in common between a book like *Bud, Not Buddy* and *Basher Five-Two*. The former is an at times sidesplitting tale of an orphan questing for a home; the latter, the gritty true story of a soldier doing his job. Both, however, provide child readers with a brush with peril, with a model of competence under adversity, and with strategies to triumph over that adversity. Bud Caldwell lies; Scott O'Grady eats bugs. For child readers, avid and reluctant alike, the chance to identify with a protagonist who risks and succeeds is an emotional necessity, and adventure books — of whatever stripe — can provide it.

THE INCREDIBLE JOURNEY

BETSY BYARS

When I was a child, I loved animal stories. It seemed back then that the dog or the cat or the horse started out as words on a page but quickly became flesh and blood and moved directly into my heart. At some point the words were dissolved by my tears, and I would make out the rest of the passage by blotting my tears on my sleeve.

One of the great animal stories of all time is *The Incredible Journey* by Sheila Burnford. The book was first published in 1961, but nothing about it seems dated. The land the animals travel over, beautifully described, is a part of Canada that probably has not changed. Neither have the emotions the story evokes.

Three animals — Bodger, an old English bull terrier; Luath, a Labrador retriever; and Tao, a Siamese cat — undertake a two-hundred-mile journey to reach their family. None of the animals could have survived the journey alone, but by mutual caring and help, they succeed.

I reread the book this summer, and near the end, the Hunter family stands at the edge of the woods. They think the dogs and cat are lost and they'll never see them again. Then young Elizabeth hears something. Her father, not daring to believe, gives a whistle. A joyous answering bark rings through the hills, and Luath and Tao come into the clearing. By the time old Bodger makes his appearance, his ragged banner of a tail streaming out behind him, I am once again blotting my tears on my sleeve.

MORE GREAT ADVENTURE BOOKS

Paolo Bacigalupi, *Ship Breaker*

326 pp. Grade 7 and up. In a dystopian future America, Nailer lives on the drowned coast of New Orleans, eking out a desperate living as a lowly "ship breaker" stripping wrecked tankers for salvage. When he comes upon a shipwrecked girl, Nailer risks all to help her. The novel is both a vivid depiction of a bleak society and an edge-of-your-seat thriller.

Frank Cottrell Boyce, *Cosmic*

313 pp. Grades 4–6. Twelve-year-old Liam, tall for his age, is often mistaken for an adult, a fact that he uses to his advantage when he finds himself among a group of children sent on a secret space mission. When things go wrong, the kids' quick thinking averts a disaster. Likable characters, lots of humor, and the far-fetched situation make this a page-turner.

Suzanne Collins, *The Hunger Games*

374 pp. Grades 6–8. Katniss volunteers to represent her district in the Hunger Games, a compulsory, government-sponsored reality-TV show from which only one of twenty-four teenage contestants will emerge alive. The twists and turns are addictive in this compulsively readable blend of science fiction, romance, and social commentary. Sequels: *Catching Fire*; *Mockingjay*.

Siobhan Dowd, *The London Eye Mystery*

323 pp. Grades 4–7. When twelve-year-old narrator Ted's cousin disappears, he and his sister join forces to solve the conundrum. Ted has Asperger's syndrome, and his hardwired honesty and never-ending struggle to make sense of the world make him an especially sympathetic character. The mystery itself includes well-embedded clues readers can follow.

Jeanne DuPrau, *The City of Ember*

275 pp. Grades 4–6. The city of Ember has no natural light, and the blackouts of its antiquated electrical grid are coming more and more frequently.

Doon, a curious twelve-year-old, and his spirited schoolmate, Lina, determine to save the city. The writing is spare and suspenseful; fans will savor the entire series, which culminates in *The Diamond of Darkhold*.

Kenneth Oppel, **Airborn**
355 pp. Grades 6–8. Matt Cruse, a cabin boy on the airship *Aurora*, helps rescue hot-air balloonist Benjamin Molloy. Set in an alternate Edwardian-styled past and featuring an enthusiastic narrator, this is a fast-paced adventure. Sequels: *Skybreaker*; *Starclimber*.

Rick Riordan, **The Lightning Thief**
375 pp. Grades 6–10. Percy Jackson, living with ADHD, finds meaning behind his difficulties at last — he's really a half-blood offspring of Poseidon. The book is packed with allusions to Greek mythology as well as rip-snorting action sequences. The first book in the Percy Jackson and the Olympians series, which closes with *The Last Olympian*.

Trenton Lee Stewart, illustrations by Carson Ellis, **The Mysterious Benedict Society**
487 pp. Grades 3–6. Orphan Reynie Muldoon becomes a member of a crack team tasked to infiltrate the evil-intentioned Learning Institute for the Very Enlightened. With its lively style, fresh character portrayals, and well-timed revelations, this story flies along. Sequels: *The Mysterious Benedict Society and the Perilous Journey*; *The Mysterious Benedict Society and the Prisoner's Dilemma*.

Scott Westerfeld, illustrations by Keith Thompson, **Leviathan**
438 pp. Grades 6–10. As World War I breaks out, Prince Aleksandar escapes the enemies of his father, the assassinated archduke; meanwhile, Deryn Sharp, disguised as a boy, is aboard the British airbeast *Leviathan*. The excitement escalates when the two sides meet — the German Clankers with their traditional machinery and the English Darwinists with their biotechnology — in this mix of alternative history and sci-fi steampunk.

Chapter Six

NONFICTION

Introduction
Roger Sutton

Everybody reads more nonfiction than they notice, but it has been the perennial stepchild of children's literature, with the lion's share of prizes and attention going to novels and picture storybooks. In her 2008 Newbery acceptance speech for *Good Masters! Sweet Ladies!* Laura Amy Schlitz confessed that "like most librarians, I secretly favor fiction over nonfiction. Facts are necessary, facts are useful, facts are fascinating. But stories enrich our lives." Yet the powers of storytelling are readily found among writers of nonfiction — a constant theme in the essays that follow; at the same time, they insist that storytelling is just one of many ways to effectively convey information and an author's passion for his or her subject. Marc Aronson, himself an author of social and political histories for young people, writes here about how to rescue readers from both the tyranny of fiction and the paint-by-numbers approach of so much nonfiction published for children.

On the topic of biography, Betty Carter writes that "for many children, biographies may well be their first introduction to point of view," and her essay on this staple of the school report demonstrates the far richer possibilities for how biographies can speak to young readers.

Back in the early 1960s, when Isaac Asimov was a columnist for *The Horn Book,* he gave us a salutary reminder of the value of scientific thinking: "We want the bright youngster to be interested in the world about him, and I have no patience with those who think of 'nature' as a saccharine subject consisting chiefly of daisies and bobolinks." Our present science specialist, Danielle Ford, is associate professor in the school of education at the University of Delaware and brings a similar briskness to considering what to look for in a science book for young people.

And poetry. Poetry! (Yes, thanks to a quirk in the Dewey decimal system, poetry is classified as nonfiction in your local library.) Through over-teaching and ill-advised homework ("write a haiku about your grandfather"), kids learn to loathe it. Two poets offer some wisdom: Alice Schertle advises us on the intrinsic rewards of close attention to "concentrated language," while Naomi Shihab Nye recommends we use it to make life saner.

Cinderella Without the Fairy Godmother

Marc Aronson

Nonfiction for middle-grade and teen readers requires parents to adjust their expectations, as if they were in a foreign country and getting used to the language and customs. You may well have trouble finding the equivalent of the nonfiction books you enjoy or recall having loved as a child. In compensation, you will find it easy to select books that are carefully designed and illustrated, that have lots of engaging information, or that enter into some aspect of history in a very personal voice.

Here's my guess about why nonfiction for younger readers is so different from books for adults. From the expansion of national literacy in the late nineteenth century through the 1970s, middle-class Americans shared an assumed nonfiction knowledge base. The great nineteenth-century magazines like *The Century, Scribner's,* and *Harper's* were published for those readers. Then, in the twentieth century, adults bought books for their homes to display that learning.

Even if no one in the family actually ever read Winston Churchill's four books on *A History of the English-Speaking Peoples,* or the eleven volumes in which Will and Ariel Durant recounted *The Story of Civilization,* you nonetheless owned them. (Fortunately, the Durants' books came in red-and-white dust jackets, so they stood out on your shelves, where they announced your familiarity with the great ideas and heroes of the past.) *Life* and *Look, Time* and *Newsweek,* the three TV networks — all assumed a standard base of, say, eighth-grade-level knowledge of history and science.

The attitude in schools, libraries, and children's publishing was that young readers would be eager to catch up, to learn about the Childhood of Famous Americans (for example) or Microbe Hunters so that they would be on their way to being informed adults. The first book to win the Newbery Medal, Hendrik Willem Van Loon's *The Story of Mankind,* was actually an adult book, but it was so readable it offered young people an entry into that universe of shared knowledge. Nonfiction reading was a kind of ladder into citizenship, one adults believed their children wanted to climb, and books were offered as handholds along the way. The last stand of this sense of shared knowledge may well have been James Michener's sweeping historical epics — he filled in what readers did not know, but he did so using fiction.

The intellectual rebellions of the 1960s, followed by the Culture Wars that lasted through the rest of the century, arrived just as cable splintered television into endless niches. We were each encouraged to learn our own branch of identity-based history, or to select which version of hard, New Age, or Intelligent Design science appealed to us. Much good came of this opening up, but there was no one book, or set of books, that every cultured family was assumed to own. We got the History Channel instead of History. For adults, this meant that nonfiction reading became a choice — one more option for adding a touch of interest to your life. While nonfiction increasingly became identified with adult pleasure reading, just the opposite happened in schools.

The sixties challenged what it meant to be a citizen, what kind of person deserved to be seen as famous, and even the use of the term *mankind;* they also celebrated Youth Culture. From the Beatles to Woodstock (and on to Facebook and iTunes today), we as a society came to believe that young people would be interested in themselves, their own world, their own music, the social networks of their peers. This view has taken particular hold in schools. Teachers assume that reading for pleasure means reading about yourself, or a fantasy version of yourself. In turn, nonfiction became the province of schoolwork.

Nonfiction books occupy two distinct and equally unhappy places in elementary and middle schools. All too often, teachers from pre-K through second grade view nonfiction as facts, and facts as a necessary evil, linked to other forms of cod-liver oil such as outlines, citations, multiplication tables, and common denominators. One study published in 2000 of elementary education in more than twenty schools found that teachers devoted just 3.6 minutes a day to nonfiction books (in schools located in poor neighborhoods, this declined to 1.9 minutes a day). Then — starting in third grade — the ominous shadow of state-mandated testing falls. At this point teachers see the need to focus on nonfiction, since their students are going to have to demonstrate reading comprehension and write expository-writing essays with a statement, three supporting facts, and a conclusion. Nonfiction becomes a big part of the classroom — but entirely as a tool, a form of test prep.

Speaking in broad, but not too broad, generalities, those in charge of your child's early education view fiction as reading for pleasure and nonfiction as reading for assignments. And while that changes as your child ages, those early years set a tone that shapes publishing, libraries, and the whole field of nonfiction for young readers. There are a great many nonfiction books in libraries, but the overwhelming majority of them are designed to be useful for classes. This creates two problems for you and your child — how do you pick through the clutter of assignment books, and how do you find those few nonfiction books that have been crafted for your child's pure reading pleasure?

For assignments, pick books that seem well researched as well as eye-catching, or pair them—a visual cornucopia with a more narrative text that gives you a sense of its sources. Take out a bunch of books on a topic and do a bit of compare-and-contrast, to catch the subtle but telling differences.

Frustrated at the selections available at libraries, you may head off to your local bookstore. If you are lucky enough to be near a good independent children's store, you may skip the rest of this essay. The owner or staff knows kids, knows nonfiction, and will help you. If you rely on chains, you face the second dispiriting realization: nonfiction books are everywhere, and none of them are what you want. You will see the same overpublished niches (see "What Makes a Good Dinosaur Book?"); photo-driven kid versions of coffee-table books; nonfiction movie tie-ins (most recently, pirates, pirates, pirates); a growing section of books of facts, from Guinness to the spate of retro boy books; a clearly ignored shelf of unappealing biographies; and a bit of special interest (African American, Jewish, Women-Who-Have-Made-a-Difference, sports, science experiments). If you wander over to the YA section, you will see acres of self-help books aimed at girls trained in how to read about relationships, body changes, health, dating, and fashion by popular magazines. Your child's interest in a nonfiction book to *read* is as fully ignored in this clutter as it was by the school library's devotion to assignments.

The glaring absence in nonfiction for younger readers is precisely the kind of narrative nonfiction adults have embraced. The assumption behind those books is that a browsing reader who previously knew nothing about, say, Longitude, or Cod, or Year X that changed the world, or How the Irish Saved Civilization can be seduced by an author whose prose is supple, whose story is interesting, and whose ideas are stimulating. The overriding assumption in nonfic-

Elizabeth Partridge's award-winning biography *John Lennon: All I Want Is the Truth* is a perfect example of the key role design plays in nonfiction for younger readers. The size of the book recalls one of the Beatles' record albums; the design, pacing, and visuals tell you as much as the words.

tion for younger readers is that it must be on a familiar subject tied to an existing curriculum, or from a list of tried-and-true topics — storms, diseases, Greece, Rome, knights, Vikings, sports figures, heroic women. At present, that is just the reality of the field. You are far more likely to find that kind of browsing interest in historical fiction (see "When Dinosaurs Watched Black-and-White TV," page 138) than in nonfiction.

Mark Kurlansky, who, along with Dava Sobel (*Longitude*), really changed the field for adult nonfiction, crafted a fine picture-book version of *Cod* (*The Cod's Tale*), and a not-quite-as-successful one of *Salt* (*The Story of Salt*). But what makes his picture book work is that it is a true picture book; it is not trying to present a simplified version of adult narration. Jim Murphy's multi-award-winning *An*

American Plague for older readers is probably the closest thing to the achievement of adult authors: he has rendered an obscure topic (a yellow fever plague in Philadelphia in 1793) fascinating purely through the power of his writing—and clever use of book design.

Note that Kurlansky's book is a picture book, and even Murphy's relies, in part, on design. What the world of children's books has lost in missing out on the explosion in narrative nonfiction, it at least partially gets back in its attention to illustration and design. Indeed, the last informational book to win the Newbery Medal was Russell Freedman's 1987 photobiography of Abraham Lincoln, with a text that couldn't be separated from the pictures.

Almost every nonfiction book for younger readers has pictures in it, and so it speaks in two voices: in words and in images. As you begin searching for nonfiction, look for both: for good writing and also for art that works well with the text. Many claim that young people today are more visual—I think that argument can be over-stated. But there is a real craftsmanship in the use of art in the best children's nonfiction that you will soon come to recognize. This craftsmanship is also present in teenage nonfiction, where the graphic-novel memoir (which adults know from books such as *Maus* and *Persepolis*) holds real promise. From Judd Winick's *Pedro and Me* to Gene Luen Yang's *American Born Chinese*, this is a format that manages to be accessible and challenging at the same time.

Basic question: what is it about nonfiction your child likes? If he (and I *do* know that there are also many *shes*) really does like facts, he is in luck. Librarians recognize the appeal of the omnium gath-erum of stuff, tables, catalogs, record books (see "Stats," page 261). But not all teachers are willing to count these kinds of compilations as reading. This is a case where you may need to speak up for your child—the challenge here is not in finding the books, or getting your child to read them, but getting his school to value the books that he reads.

But what if your child enjoys nonfiction because he or she likes to think? That is, if your child enjoys knowing about the world not only to collect information, but also to ask questions and formulate theories? Biography aside, children's publishing does better on this score for science than it does for the humanities. And there are a few math books, such as Hans Magnus Enzensberger's *The Number Devil*, that capture the dizzying vistas mathematical thinking can open up. We are also starting to see memoirs, from Ji-Li Jiang's *Red Scarf Girl* to Jack Gantos's *Hole in My Life* and Peter Sís's *The Wall*, that, like Anne Frank's diary, give nonfiction lovers an entry into complex subjects through a very personal voice.

My best suggestion is that you make clear to your librarian or independent bookseller what your child likes, and ask her to be on the alert for the exceptional book. Children's books do experiment more than adult books, so whether it is in the personal and highly emotive power of a book such as Tom Feelings's wordless *The Middle Passage*, or the dazzling (but now endlessly imitated) design innovations of the Dorling Kindersley Eyewitness books, or the 'Ology books, which are fiction that is one step away from nonfiction (a step they may soon cross), the field is constantly tossing up new surprises. Come to nonfiction knowing what not to expect, and you may find unexpected pleasures.

THE MISSING PARTS

DEBORAH HOPKINSON

In fourth grade, what I liked best about American history was the size of my textbook. It was big. Big enough to hide whatever other book I happened to be reading. And since I was always reading, this was a good thing.

History in school never engaged me completely. But eventually it did make me curious about all the missing parts. For one thing, where were the women? Surely Clara Barton and Harriet Tubman weren't the only females in America's past. And what about everyone else: African Americans, Asian Americans, Latinos, children? What were the rest of us doing all that time, anyway?

Although I took a number of history courses as an undergraduate and graduate student, I never really learned *how* to study history. It's one thing to memorize "Kansas-Nebraska Act, 1854" and quite another to explore what people felt, said, and did about it.

Now, as a writer, I've found myself searching for all those missing people and stories I wanted to know about in fourth grade. When I visit schools, I ask children how they do research and how they learn about the past. They tell me they use books, computers, and encyclopedias. But invariably, no matter where I am, I have to really dig before a student will suggest that one way to research is to visit a place and see it with your own eyes.

I try to focus on this firsthand aspect of research when I tell them about my books. I show photographs of places I've been and people I've met, even the listening equipment I've used to hear oral history interviews. I tell them, for instance, how Ella Sheppard and the Jubilee Singers gave concerts all over the world to raise money for their school, now Fisk University. Then I show a photograph of Jubilee Hall, the beautiful building they funded, and students gasp in amazement.

I find it harder, though, to speak to a large group about how all this research makes me *feel*. How I get chills when I walk up the worn steps of Jubilee Hall, how the spirit of another person seems to reach across time through their words and touch mine. Or how people seem to stare out of photographs, daring me to come stand beside them. It's also difficult to speak in public about how, when the research is done and I'm ready to write, I often just close my eyes and try to "go there."

I can get part of the way on my own. It's not, after all, hard to imagine standing in a Gettysburg field on a hot July day. The sky a bright blue, or perhaps hazy in the heat. Robins chirping. The sharp cry of a blue jay. The hot smell of grass.

But it's never quite enough. I'd love a way in to all those missing parts. I know exactly what I'd say to someone from the past. I would simply say, "Tell me, what is it like here? What is it really like?"

MORE GREAT NONFICTION

Marc Aronson and Marina Budhos, *Sugar Changed the World: A Story of Magic, Spice, Slavery, Freedom, and Science*
  160 pp. Grades 5–9. Two authors who found sugar stories in their own family histories trace how one product first created the hell of Atlantic slavery and then played a key role in the drive to free all people from enslavement.

Don Brown, *All Stations! Distress!: April 15, 1912, The Day the* Titanic *Sank*
  64 pp. Grades 2–5. Brown recounts the complicated, compact last moments of the *Titanic*'s only voyage. The glory of the book is in Brown's moody watercolors done with a brush dipped in stardust and frozen mist; they reach a terrifying crescendo as the ship upends before the final dive.

Andrew Chaikin with Victoria Kohl, illustrations by Alan Bean, *Mission Control, This Is Apollo: The Story of the First Voyages to the Moon*
  114 pp. Grades 4–6. In this outstanding history of the piloted *Apollo* missions, Chaikin conveys the excitement, tragedy, humor, and quest for knowledge that drove the golden age of the U.S. space program. In addition to historical photographs and technical diagrams, Alan Bean, an *Apollo* astronaut turned artist, lends his impressionistic paintings of the missions.

Jan Greenberg and Sandra Jordan, illustrations by Brian Floca, *Ballet for Martha: Making Appalachian Spring*
  48 pp. Grade 4–6. A remarkable collaboration between choreographer Martha Graham, composer Aaron Copland, and artist Isamu Noguchi resulted in the iconic ballet *Appalachian Spring*. Concise sentences and fluid, energetic illustrations echo Graham's spare approach to dance.

David Macaulay, *Built to Last*
  272 pp. Grade 5 to adult. In this omnibus edition, David Macaulay revisits and substantially revises three of his classic architectural histories, *Cathedral*, *Castle*, and *Mosque*. With newly drafted and colored illustrations,

Macaulay gives a clear and dramatic sense of how these buildings were built, and what they meant.

Kadir Nelson, *We Are the Ship: The Story of Negro League Baseball*
88 pp. Grades 4–6. Imagine listening to Willie Mays and Ernie Banks swapping tales. That easygoing, conversational storytelling is what Nelson achieves in this pitch-perfect history of Negro League baseball. The grand slam, though, is the art: in Nelson's spectacular oil paintings, the from-the-ground perspectives make the players look larger than life.

Elizabeth Partridge, *Marching for Freedom: Walk Together, Children, and Don't You Grow Weary*
72 pp. Grade 5 and up. In this tightly focused, dramatic historical narrative, Partridge writes about the 1965 civil rights march from Selma to Montgomery from the viewpoint of children and teenagers who participated. The black-and-white photographs add unusual visual force and immediacy.

Tanya Lee Stone, *Almost Astronauts: 13 Women Who Dared to Dream*
134 pp. Grade 7 and up. The story of the ultimately unsuccessful effort to get women into NASA's Mercury astronaut training program is meticulously researched and thrillingly told. First- and second-hand sources, interviews, and outstanding historical photographs reveal the personal and physical risks taken by the women in pursuit of their dreams.

David Weitzman, *Pharaoh's Boat*
48 pp. Grades 4–6. This handsome book on the construction (and, over four thousand years later, the *re*construction) of the boat Pharaoh Cheops rode into the afterlife focuses on intricacies of design and creation. Clear schematic drawings of the boat's parts and assemblage are captivating.

A Story, by Someone Else, More than a Hundred Pages

Betty Carter

Ask your child what a biography is, and I suspect you will get an answer somewhat like this: "A biography is the story of someone's life." Wait a few seconds, and you might get: "It's written by somebody else." And, if you're talking to a middle-schooler who's handled the obligatory biography book report several times over, you will also hear, "And it has to have more than a hundred pages." Since these responses indicate a child's thinking, and since each contains a grain of either theoretical or practical truth, let's start there.

Story

The key word in "the story of someone's life" is *story*. An enormous number of biographies lack the elements of story and instead merely list an individual's accomplishments. Such books offer no more information than would an encyclopedia, a source that may provide much-needed background, a quick spot for fact checking, or a chronological overview of someone's life. But no story.

Stories contain beginnings, middles, and ends, and many popular biographies of living sports heroes or media celebrities necessarily have no end—an unfinished life is most likely not yet defined.

Certainly there are exceptions, such as the 2007 picture-book biography *Young Pelé: Soccer's First Star* by Lesa Cline-Ransome. Pelé has already made his mark on sports history, and, barring any future disclosures related to his soccer career, Cline-Ransome's story of Pelé's childhood not only has the requisite beginning, middle, and end, but also has purpose and worth. Such accounts are quite different from the biographies of individuals "in the moment," which often appear to be expanded (and frequently unauthorized versions of) reports in popular magazines — reports that remain static as lives change. Think of biographies of sports or music stars, whose fame can be transitory, or of presidents George W. Bush before September 11 or Bill Clinton before Monica Lewinsky. There is simply not enough perspective on these rushed-to-press lives to give the biographies endings beyond unproven optimism: "whatever the future may hold for Britney Spears . . ."

Are such works — instant biographies, school-report-driven books — bad for children? I like to think of them as metaphorical doctors with incomplete creeds of *only* (as opposed to *first*) do no harm. Yes, youngsters are practicing their reading skills, moving their eyes across pages, and encountering words and sentences. Some are collecting facts of interest; others are engaging in wish fulfillment. But these books, and a number of popular magazines that deliver similar short biographical profiles, do not provide the potential for independent thinking that stronger biographies offer. In other words, like the aforementioned physicians, they bring temporary solace through the visit, but little else.

As story, though, biography often provides an early bridge between fiction and nonfiction reading. Teachers typically devote more time and attention to the story narratives in fiction than they do to the multiple prose patterns of nonfiction, and across the country children's test scores show that they are much more practiced with the former than the latter. Youngsters have two hurdles to overcome when reading a book: content and structure. The structural familiarity with story helps children handle unfamiliar content found in biographies that deal with lives, times, and concepts different from their own.

Some time ago I was listening to my granddaughter, Libby, then a second-grader, read *Marvelous Mattie* by Emily Arnold McCully. This picture-book biography covers Margaret E. Knight's attempts in 1871 to obtain a patent on a device that folds paper bags used in grocery stores, but Charles F. Annan, who had stolen Mattie's idea, challenged her for the rights to her invention. To my knowledge, Libby had never read a biography before, and two major obstacles stood in her way of understanding this one: the unfamiliar past and the notion of intellectual property. As I looked at Libby's school notebook, adorned with the words "Girlz Rule" in bright pink letters, it was clear that the biography's setting — the age of industrialization, which didn't honor the work and ideas of women — did not fit into her view of the world. But here's where structure saved her. Mattie's story, which follows a poor but clever heroine as she uses her wit and determination to triumph over a greedy and powerful foe, was as familiar as "Jack and the Beanstalk," "Puss in Boots," or "Cinderella." Libby's awareness of long ago and far away, again so familiar in fairy tales, helped her with the nineteenth-century time period. Then only one unknown, the concept of a patent, remained. And with just one strange concept to deal with, she got it.

This familiar story structure allowed Libby not only to understand new content but also to use that knowledge to negotiate the additional information offered in a concluding author's note. She is now ready for the road to other kinds of reading, perhaps historical fiction, perhaps other works on industrial America, perhaps nonfiction. Whether or not she continues down any of these literary paths is her choice, but she's developing the rudimentary skills that will allow her to do so if she wishes.

Books such as *Marvelous Mattie* may contain a story structure closely resembling historical fiction, but they also offer new kinds of reading experiences. In Mattie's case, the one incident covered in her biography sets the stage for other accomplishments briefly outlined in the author's note, encouraging readers to dig deeper into either the subject or the times. This kind of inquiry is different from the musings readers may have about the characters they meet in fiction. Readers of fiction resolve their questions largely through their imaginations. Questions about someone's life, on the other hand, require less fanciful answers. These questions direct readers back to the life itself, to the individual's actual successes and failures, and to various historical records. Rather than going from an imaginary character to further imagined outcomes, readers can move from a real life, through research questions, to new knowledge. In other words, they may begin to become critical thinkers.

By Someone Else

The second statement that children make about biography, that "it is written by someone else," separates biography from autobiography. But the power of biography extends far beyond this simple format distinction. The best biographies, those that have the most potential for demanding critical thinking, not only are written by someone else but also let children know what someone else thinks about the subject. For many children, biographies may well be their first introduction to point of view.

Take Leonardo da Vinci. Middle-schoolers will most probably associate Leonardo with art — the Mona Lisa; "The Last Supper" (they've seen, heard of, or read *The Da Vinci Code*); or the iconic Vitruvian Man. In her biography of Leonardo, however, Kathleen Krull emphasizes his contributions to science. She focuses on Leonardo as a pioneer who observed, recorded, and hypothesized about the natural world, a pattern that leads directly to the inductive reasoning in the scientific method (described thoroughly in another Krull biography, *Isaac Newton*). Similarly, James Cross Giblin, in *Good*

Brother, Bad Brother, raises the biographical curtain on his subject John Wilkes Booth not as an assassin but as an actor. This is not another book about Lincoln or the political turmoil of the times; instead, Giblin emphasizes brothers John Wilkes Booth and Edwin Booth's theatrical talents and positions their careers and the mid-nineteenth-century arts at the center of his own literary stage. In both cases, Krull and Giblin give a unique slant on their subjects — a slant that may be initially unfamiliar to young readers, but one that shows them that authors deliberately choose a particular point of view and defend that point in their writing. Becoming aware of a writer's stance is another important step children take in becoming critical readers. Books open up this possibility, one not typically available on websites or in encyclopedia articles.

Sometimes biographies can challenge what children think they know in ways that other works can't. While my granddaughter was reading *Marvelous Mattie,* my grandson, Jackson, was hot on the trail of information about Galileo. He had just seen the movie *Night at the Museum,* in which Galileo comes to life every night holding a telescope. Jackson decided his biography report would be about the man who "invented the telescope." He checked the Internet but told me, "I don't know why they didn't say anything about Galileo inventing the telescope." The idea that Galileo had *not* invented the telescope wasn't in Jackson's universe of thinking, and he figured he was just looking at the wrong sources. I suggested that he read *Starry Messenger* by Peter Sís, since his assignment was, in part, to *read* a biography, and perhaps he would find the answer there. He did, and he did. Halfway through his reading, Jackson brought the book to me and with his finger traced the path the development of the telescope had taken through Europe, realizing that Galileo had not invented the telescope but rather improved it. Yes, a book on the history of the telescope would have produced a similar understanding but might not have allowed Jackson to recognize Galileo's place in history, which was what he wanted to know. His next question was: "So what did this guy do, anyway?"

This process of taking information about a person and evaluating its veracity is a skill that individuals use throughout their lives, beginning with playground gossip, moving through high school's cliques, and culminating in assessing political figures, operating in the workplace, raising families, and sustaining partnerships and friendships. Reading biographies will certainly not ensure success in all these areas, but it does provide opportunities for youngsters to discover multiple points of view about some individuals and evaluate single points of view about others.

Interestingly enough, these critical-thinking skills are often negated by our desire to use biographies to provide kids with positive role models. Yes, it would be wonderful for our children to grow up and be as courageous as Dr. Martin Luther King, as dedicated as Rachel Carson, or as astute as Thomas Jefferson. But none of these heroes or heroines developed those qualities by reading books populated solely by role models!

More than a Hundred Pages

The last statement children make about biographies, the reference to the hundred-page rule, is so instituted and entrenched in educational settings that one editor suggested, perhaps in jest, that his publisher create a series of biographies of exactly one hundred pages. But this restriction is no laughing matter.

Notice that books such as *Marvelous Mattie* (at thirty-two pages) and *Young Pelé* (forty pages) cover only portions of their subjects' lives instead of an entire cradle-to-grave story. Biographers typically look for a telling incident that not only holds potential appeal for children but also illuminates the subject. And they do so in few pages, recognizing that unfamiliar contents are best understood in small doses, sometimes in books of thirty-two or sixty-four pages. Often, to ease the reading burden, original illustrations or archival photographs supplement the written word. Illustrations in biography reveal physical characteristics of different subjects, unfamiliar settings, and points that either need emphasis or can best be shown through photographs or original art. A picture isn't always worth a thousand words, but sometimes illustrations help children *read* those thousand words. In any case, to expurgate biographies under a hundred pages from a child's reading life would eliminate some of the finest biographies of this century.

Russell Freedman's *The Voice That Challenged a Nation: Marian Anderson and the Struggle for Equal Rights* clocks in, without back matter, at ninety-two pages, and so fails to meet the arbitrary page count. Every word, image, and page turn is carefully chosen as Freedman traces Anderson's life and career, along with explanations of Jim Crow and the beginnings of the civil rights movement. He orchestrates the tension between society's praise of Anderson the singer and disdain for Anderson's race until the book's climax, a crescendo that places Marian on the steps of the Lincoln Memorial. Readers turn the page, and there is Anderson, her strength, determination, and power captured perfectly in a full-page photograph that takes your breath away. The addition of eight more pages might have made the book work for a book report but would have diminished Freedman's mastery of his craft.

At forty pages, Peter Sís's *The Tree of Life: A Book Depicting the Life of Charles Darwin, Naturalist, Geologist & Thinker* wouldn't even be a contender for assigned-biography reading. Yet what Sís has done with this book is remarkable. He asks readers to become Darwin, to observe, think, and learn. The man, with all his demons, his methodical approach to science, and his detractors, fills every page within a book that constantly changes the narrative pattern and demands close attention to both text and illustrations.

The final endpapers consist of twenty-three squares of great thinkers and great ideas. The twenty-fourth one portrays an outline of a child, presumably the reader with his or her ideas yet to be formed. These ideas won't come through a single biography, or a single book, or a single idea, but rather through a lifetime of reading and thinking. Biography is part of that life. Someone else writes it. And it's not necessarily a hundred pages.

AN INTERVIEW WITH

RUSSELL FREEDMAN

ROGER SUTTON: When you're writing about someone — Eleanor Roosevelt, for example — how do you balance the facts of what she did and why she did it, either according to her own point of view or a recorded point of view, and your own speculation?

RUSSELL FREEDMAN: Well, I try not to speculate. I try to find clues in the documented record — from the subject's own testimony, from the testimony of other people. When you're writing a biography, you're trying to understand your subject in the same way that you try to understand one of your friends, and that effort at understanding is always very imperfect. I mean, can you really understand anyone? Can you understand yourself? It's difficult to nail down motivations exactly, so you try to go by the record — what Eleanor Roosevelt says about why she did what she did, what other people say, what the actual behavior was. I try to avoid personal speculation because I think it can contaminate the historical record. Scholars who are doing original research in their chosen field may be uncovering all sorts of new information and may come up with some astounding new take on what happened and why it happened—that's a good time to speculate. I do original research, too—I interviewed some of Eleanor Roosevelt's grandchildren, for example, and read many of her letters and newspaper columns. That's essential. But digging up new information and speculating on it isn't your primary purpose when you're writing a biography intended for young readers, unless you find compelling evidence that departs from the accepted wisdom. A biography for young people calls for the demanding art of distillation, the art of storytelling, and your responsibility is to stick as closely as possible to the documented record.

RS: Is history what happened or the record of what happened?

RF: Let's say that history is what happened. The record of what happened is how each individual happens to see those events. They've already been filtered. When the historian or biographer takes over, history is no longer exactly what happened, because there has been a process of selection going on; it's impossible to write about anyone, any event, in any period of time, without in some way imposing, even unconsciously, your own standards, your own values. You simply can't avoid that. The historian strives for objectivity, does the best he or she can, but the result inevitably reflects the life experience and the values of the person writing the book. Abraham Lincoln lived twenty-four hours a day for fifty-six years. How much of that time has come down to us in the record? A tiny percentage. Now, of all of the material we have about Lincoln, what percentage of that can a biographer actually include in a book, and most especially in a book for kids? So not only do you have a partial record, a very incomplete record of a life, but by the time you finish deciding what to include and what to leave out, it's even more incomplete. In fact, that's where I would say that speculation takes place, in the process of selectivity. Deciding what to include and what to leave out is like picking stocks. You're trying to guess what will pay the best dividend in terms of helping evoke a world and create a character. And every biographer makes different choices. Every book I've ever read about Eleanor Roosevelt is about a somewhat different person. And that's even more true about Lincoln.

RS: A recent picture-book biography of Lincoln states that the Emancipation Proclamation declared all slaves free, when, of course, it freed only the slaves under Southern control. How do you decide when simplification becomes distortion?

RF: Anyone writing a picture-book biography of Lincoln has a different set of responsibilities from someone writing a biography for sixth-graders, say, or from a Lincoln scholar writing an academic book on Lincoln. Each of these writers has a different audience and different goals. That's obvious. A picture-book biography can't deal with the same complexities and nuances as a 150-page biography for older kids. You can't use the picture-book format if you want to go into all those complications, and yet, you still want to capture a sense of a life being lived. In some respects, I suppose, a picture-book biography is actually harder to write.

With the audience I write for, I want to make sure that the reader is eagerly turning every page. I want each of my books to be an absorbing reading experience, an authentic piece of literature. The worst thing that can happen is for a book to have a chilling effect on the reader, to have a kid pick it up and look at a bunch of footnotes and think, No, I'm not going to read this; it's too intimidating. Or even worse — if I thought that I was writing books just so that kids could write classroom reports, I'd quit. I'm not interested in doing that. I want to write books that a ten-year-old or a teenager or maybe their grandmother will pick up and sit up all night reading, and then can't wait until they go on to a longer book about the same subject.

RS: If we look at fiction for children, at least 90 percent is about children, at least as the central character. In a biography, how do you avoid giving undue emphasis to what might be child-appealing aspects at the expense of adult achievements?

RF: In the case of Eleanor Roosevelt, it was easy. Her childhood is fascinating, because it was so horrible. It gave her so much to overcome. With material like that, you can hook the reader right away, and by the time Eleanor is out on her own, the reader doesn't want to stop. I mean, why do kids read biographies? Why does anyone read them? I think it's because we're all trying to learn how to live our lives. We want to see how other people have lived and how they have overcome tough problems. A kid reading a novel might want a protagonist his own age or a little older, but a youngster reading a biography has a different motivation, I think. That reader wants to see how the subject of the biography got along in life. If you can establish the conflicts, the problems, the hurdles, at the beginning — in the case of Eleanor it's easy; and with Lincoln, too, the log cabin, the dirt floor, reading by the fireplace — then I think you can carry the reader through.

The letters I get from kids are almost never about the childhood of the subject. They're about something that Eleanor or Lincoln or Crazy Horse did as an adult. That's what they want to know. Plenty of kids are fascinated by biographies, thank heavens. I get letters from two kinds of readers. History buffs, who love to read history and biography for fun, and then kids who want to be writers but who rarely come out and say so in their letters. You can tell by the questions they ask — How did you get your first book published? How long do you spend on a book? — that sort of thing. So I guess those are the readers that I'm writing for — kids who enjoy that kind of book, because they're interested in history, in other people's lives, in what has happened in the world and in what's going to happen. I believe that they're the ones who are going to be the movers and shakers.

RS: How would you articulate the difference between writing history and biography for an adult audience versus that for a child audience?

RF: A biography for kids has to be lean and approachable. You don't have eight hundred pages to work with. Blanche Wiesen Cook's two volumes (so far) on Eleanor Roosevelt amount to some twelve hundred pages, and they only go as far as 1936, I believe, when Eleanor hadn't fully hit her stride yet. Those books serve an important purpose. They involve original research, they strive to be definitive, and they will become sources for all future historians and biographers. But a biography for young readers, if it's successful, is a feat of imaginative storytelling that is informed by the historical record. As I said before, it has to be a distillation. You're writing for a reader who hopefully will be motivated to go on to a longer and more comprehensive work. A children's biography doesn't have to be comprehensive, and it doesn't have to be definitive. It does have to be accurate, to the extent that's possible. And most of all, it has to be a piece of literature, a compelling read. I want the reader to discover the joy of reading.

MORE GREAT BIOGRAPHIES

Candace Fleming, *The Lincolns: A Scrapbook Look at Abraham and Mary*
181 pp. Grades 4–6. Chock-full of reproductions of primary sources, both textual and visual, and an abundance of interesting anecdotes, this readable, accessible dual biography is equally inviting for reference, browsing, or pleasure reading.

Jan Greenberg and Sandra Jordan, *Christo and Jeanne-Claude: Through the Gates and Beyond*
50 pp. Grades 5–8. In Central Park during the winter of 2005, the artists Christo and Jeanne-Claude unveiled an art installation, *The Gates,* more than twenty-five years in the making. The book encourages children to expand their visions of what art is and to better understand the devotion and labor that allow an artistic dream to materialize into a work of art.

Deborah Heiligman, *Charles and Emma: The Darwins' Leap of Faith*
278 pp. Grades 6–10. With great empathy, puckish humor, and a lively narrative, Heiligman examines the life and legacy of Charles Darwin through the unique lens of his domestic life.

Phillip Hoose, *Claudette Colvin: Twice Toward Justice*
125 pp. Grades 5–8. Nine months before Rosa Parks, fifteen-year-old Claudette Colvin refused to give up her seat on a Montgomery, Alabama, bus. Hoose fashions a compelling narrative that balances the momentous events of the civil rights movement with the personal crises of a courageous young woman.

Barbara Kerley, illustrations by Edwin Fotheringham, *What to Do About Alice?: How Alice Roosevelt Broke the Rules, Charmed the World, and Drove Her Father Teddy Crazy!*
48 pp. Grades K–3. Spunky and headstrong, Alice Roosevelt Longworth "was hungry to go places . . . do things." With a palette emphasizing Alice Blue, her

signature color, the illustrations match Alice's energy with zigzag streaks, slanting figures, and circular spot art.

Kathleen Krull, illustrations by Boris Kulikov, *Albert Einstein* (Giants of Science)
143 pp. Grades 4–6. In this engrossing and accessible biography, Krull lingers just long enough over Einstein's childhood to give readers time to connect with him; she also does an admirable job of explaining his theories. Occasional pen-and-ink illustrations capture Einstein's curiosity and imagination — and his unforgettable finger-in-a-light-socket hairstyle.

Vaunda Micheaux Nelson, illustrations by R. Gregory Christie, *Bad News for Outlaws: The Remarkable Life of Bass Reeves, Deputy U.S. Marshal*
40 pp. Grades 2–5. Bass Reeves, born a slave, captured more than three thousand outlaws as a deputy U.S. marshal. This captivating biography, told in colorful language, grabs readers with an 1854 gunfight, then flashes back to Reeve's early life. Sharply textured paintings offer detailed portraits of Reeves, his black hat conveying unmistakable authority.

Elizabeth Partridge, *John Lennon: All I Want Is the Truth*
220 pp. Grade 9 and up. In her biography of the musical genius Lennon, Partridge contextualizes the Beatles' story with enough background information, both politically and musically, to illuminate the chaotic world behind the top-ten charts. Black-and-white photos on nearly every page project a visual commentary that adds substantively to an accessible text.

Steve Sheinkin, *The Notorious Benedict Arnold: A True Story of Adventure, Heroism, & Treachery*
344 pp. Grades 6–10. An ultrareadable, accessible biography of the infamous Revolutionary War traitor places Arnold's story in its political, social, and military context while maintaining the pace of a great adventure. Gruesome descriptions of winter marches through the northern woods balance a nuanced depiction of Arnold's character as bold, arrogant, and overweeningly ambitious.

More than Just the Facts
Danielle J. Ford

Should a science book be judged primarily on the basis of accuracy? According to most sources, children's science books ought to be error-free in text and illustration, and representative of the prevailing theories and ideas of the discipline covered.

This is not a stunning revelation. Science books are about science; science is full of facts about the natural world; and children shouldn't be misled by inaccuracies, right? To some extent I would agree; however, the complexity of the (human-defined) realm of scientific practice isn't easily captured in a fact-centered text. Distilling science to isolated facts leaves out other, equally important qualities of science. Some of these crucial characteristics can be conveyed through books that include portrayals of actual scientists and their practices, discussion of the originality of certain scientific questions, and examples of the relevance of science to children's lives.

This is not to say that I dismiss concerns for accuracy — quite the contrary. Books that play fast and loose with factual information, or are written in a manner that oversimplifies ideas to the point of inaccuracy, do not serve readers well. I am especially sensitive to language and images that play into misconceptions commonly held by children. For example, a diagram with colored layers representing different rocks or layers of earth may look pretty straightforward, but in the minds of children, the layers tend to become paint stripes or literal rock colors.

What other qualities do I look for? One of the most valuable contributions a book can make is introducing children to the community and practices of science. A focus on facts alone might reward inherent interest in the subject, but it can be only a partial view of how science actually functions. Science is a dynamic social activity, where a "fact" is more a product of popular consensus than a truth to be uncovered. How those facts become stable is an important component of understanding the context in which knowledge is produced and of understanding the people who are dedicated to investigating scientific questions. Books that include portraits of scientists along with content information help to demystify the work of science — the excellent Scientists in the Field series comes immediately to mind. These books show how scientists actually work, which results not just in more accurate portrayals of science but also in more human images of scientists. In Donna M. Jackson's *Extreme Scientists,* for instance, microbiologist Hazel Barton explores caves in a tank top and sports a tattoo — she looks like a real person, not the stereotypical image of a pocket-protected, nerdy scientist.

These types of books give readers a realistic view of the work of science. They're an important counter to "hands-on" experiment books that often misrepresent science in order to make it doable by children. Experiment books often go for cool or gross or exciting results, which draw focus away from the science and onto the activities themselves — not bad, but not science. At other times, the "experiment" is matched so unimaginatively to a scientific principle that students are reduced to conducting time-consuming multi-step experiments that give no-brainer results. The gravest sin, though, is the inclusion of an answer or explanation with each experiment. Why on earth go through an elaborate activity when you already

Books such as Pamela S. Turner's *The Frog Scientist* — an entry in the admirable Scientists in the Field series — help dispel the stereotypical image of scientists as pocket-protected nerds.

know the outcome? Thankfully, books like Enslow's Science Projects series include some thoughtful, open-ended activities that are actually worth the effort students will put into them. I am also intrigued by Simon & Schuster's Let's Try It Out series. These books, written by Seymour Simon and Nicole Fauteux, use experiments as starting points for discussion about science concepts, not as the Answer to All Our Questions.

Good experiments that are well explained can link science practice to children's lives, empowering kids to actively participate in the evaluation of scientific ideas — a key component of scientific literacy. Positioning the reader in an active rather than passive stance toward scientific information is an important step. An author who poses open-ended questions, guides readers in the scrutiny of scientific data, and encourages readers to draw their own conclusions rather than neatly tying up all loose ends rates favorably with me. In the long run, this is what we want for children — to be informed, skeptical interpreters of the scientific information found in newspapers, on television, or on the Internet.

Another measure of quality is the extent to which a science book complements existing books on a given topic. If a child reads several books on a topic, any error in one of the books can be countered with information from additional sources. (Of course, there can also be too much of a good thing. Certain topics are definitely overrepresented in children's science books: endangered baby-animal survival stories, dinosaurs, and natural disasters — to name just a few. While many high-quality books appear on these subjects, they often come at the expense of other, less popular topics. So a good book on a unique or underrepresented theme deserves recognition.)

What are some other criteria? The clarity of the explanations is very important — a scientifically accurate book presented in obscure or jargon-filled language can render a book ineffective. There is an art to explaining science to children, and some authors are able to skillfully balance child-friendly language with scientific rigor. It is helpful to be able to relate to a child in his or her own terms, as Seymour Simon does in *Gorillas,* for example, when he compares the weight of an adult gorilla to that of "ten second-grade children."

Illustration is another important issue. While a good design and excellent illustrations can enhance a book's appeal, they must also be scrutinized for alignment with scientific content and the conventions of scientific representation. A book that includes only decorative photographs or illustrations has missed the opportunity to introduce readers to accepted scientific standards for diagrams and figures—important means of conveying information in scientific communities. In evaluating illustrations I look at accuracy, their match to the text, and the degree to which their captioning helps define their importance to science and scientists. Some artistic license is fine, but not if it overshadows the science. In order to appeal to children, some illustrators stray too far into anthropomorphism, which can compromise the science. In Marilyn Singer's *Tough Beginnings: How Baby Animals Survive*, Anna Vojtech's illustrations of young animals are very appealing but unrealistically cheerful-looking. Other books mesh art and science perfectly, such as Sophie Webb's *My Season with Penguins: An Antarctic Journal*. Webb's sketches of penguin antics offer important scientific data on animal behavior yet still convey the artist's sense of humor and her affection for the animals.

Cultural inclusiveness is more pertinent than you might think. It is important to encourage all children to consider science as relevant to their lives, in hopes of inspiring some of them to continue on in science and perhaps expand the boundaries of what we consider to be acceptable scientific thinking. While we do see ethnic and gender inclusiveness in collective science biographies, for example, equally important is respect for the contributions of multiple viewpoints in scientific investigations. Sy Montgomery's *The Man-Eating Tigers of Sundarbans* is a particularly good example of cultural inclusivity in science. To examine the mystery of why these tigers like to eat people, Montgomery draws on the contributions of scientists and local wildlife experts, religious and cultural myths, and the experiences of everyday people as important sources of evidence. Traditional science cannot solve the puzzle without these other, equally valid, ways of thinking.

Finally, conveying a love of science and nature is a valuable component of any science book. The pleasure of experiencing nature as a scientist would is challenging to convey. When an author manages to accomplish this, it's a true contribution to readers, providing important insight into the reasons why scientists do what they do.

So what makes a good science book? For me, it's a book that makes science come alive through explicit treatment of the practices of science; generous links to the people who participate in scientific investigations; consideration of rich, rewarding, and relevant scientific topics; and an engaging, clear, and personal voice. A good book models for children the nature of scientific thinking, provides opportunities for them to engage in this thinking, and uses text, images, and graphics to best convey scientific information. Above all, a good science book is imbued with passion for science and nature, and invites readers to engage with, imagine, and experience science in ways they may never have thought of before.

Three Tests

Diana Lutz

When I size up children's science books, I apply three tests. I ask if there is an authentic connection to science and scientists. Has the author tagged along with a scientist, talked to a scientist, read primary science journals, or tried her hand at science? I ask if there is a story. Is there a beginning, a middle, and an end, and are these parts not interchangeable? And I ask if the book manages to suggest in some way — I don't really care how, so long as it does — why most scientists love being scientists and wouldn't be anything else, given the chance. In other words, I want it all. I want good science, and I want good literature. I want writers to straddle the old dichotomy between nonfiction (truth) and fiction (story). I value good writing at least as much as correct facts. I want a book written with enthusiasm and love, qualities whose absence deadens most science writing. In the end I'm far more worried about children finding the whole scientific enterprise boring than I am about them getting a fact or two wrong. Facts are cheap, but enthusiasm is rare.

What Makes a Good Dinosaur Book?

Danielle J. Ford

Step into the science section of any library or bookstore (you know — the section way in the back) and you are guaranteed to find plenty of dinosaur books. Few science topics get the star treatment lavished on these creatures. You'll likely find grisly stories of death and destruction, heartwarming tales of cuddly young dinosaurs, and a host of encyclopedias listing the Latin names for multitudes of dinosaur species. Dig deeper, and there might be fossil field guides, ride-alongs with modern-day paleontologists, and historical accounts of their predecessors. But of all the books published on this one topic, what makes a good dinosaur book?

First of all, walk past the books up front in the picture-book section — the ones that feature talking, thinking, feeling dinosaurs as models for children's development. As cringe-inducing (Barney) or likable (the appealing dinos in Jane Yolen and Mark Teague's popular How Do Dinosaurs . . . ? series) as they may be, these books feature dinosaurs as child stand-ins, not as objects of scientific inquiry. However, heading back to the nonfiction section does not guarantee informational accuracy, either. Some science-y dinosaur books use artistic license in their portrayals of dinosaurs by presenting them as peaceful and calm, or focusing only on behavioral traits that align with the ones we humans value.

So a good dinosaur book tells it like it is. Dinosaurs were not nice *or* mean; they were animals. They cooperated with other animals when there were advantages to doing so, and they beat one another up when there were advantages to doing so. Different species had different levels of aggression. There were no moral dilemmas involved in dinosaurs' decisions to defend their mates from rivals or to kill their weaker offspring to ensure survival of the stronger.

A good dinosaur book is careful to represent dinosaurs in shapes and colors that are as accurate as the evidence can support. Cartoon-like dinosaurs in soft pastels with big round eyes and hints of smiles on their faces mislead readers. While it's true that scientists don't have a whole lot to go on in terms of what dinosaurs looked like, it's probably safe to say they weren't mint green, mauve, or baby blue.

A good dinosaur book doesn't contradict scientific evidence but instead brings something new to it, such as Steve Jenkins's *Prehistoric, Actual Size* (see next page), in which true-to-scale representations help readers to conceptualize how big or small these creatures were. If you don't have a museum handy, this book is a great substitute. Robert Sabuda and Matthew Reinhart's wonderful Encyclopedia Prehistorica series also is a leap forward in visualizing dinosaurs and their contemporaries. The three-dimensional paper representations allow readers to turn, touch, and scrutinize dinosaurs in ways not possible before. And although the colors used are bright, they are not outside the norms found in nature.

Among dinosaur books is a subgenre that is the polar opposite of the pink, cuddly, friendly dinosaur books: the doomsday, death-and-destruction books. I'll admit I much prefer these. Although they have the potential to be too scary for some readers, they are more realistic, if sometimes overly dramatic. Who can resist the real-life events at the end of the Cretaceous period — an asteroid crashing into Earth, a fiery sky of doom followed by ash clouds, no

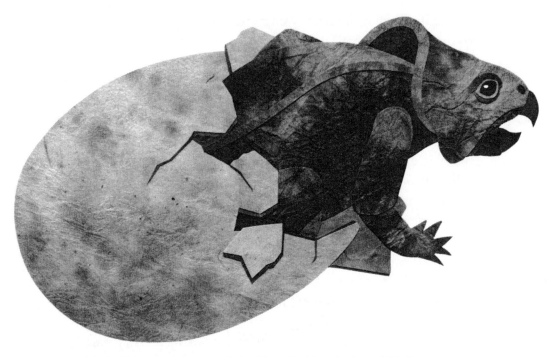

A baby *Protoceratops,* actual size (from *Prehistoric, Actual Size*)

sun, and the slow death of species no longer supplied with what they need to survive? Revel in this death and destruction as in *The Day the Dinosaurs Died* by Charlotte Lewis Brown, and you've got a good read with accurate science. Even better are books that put the peril narrative into perspective, helping us understand how these patterns of long periods of slow change followed by big events have altered life on Earth repeatedly over a few billion years. Franklyn M. Branley's *What Happened to the Dinosaurs?* manages to capture the complexity without sacrificing clarity.

A good dinosaur book can also be one that — gasp! — does not focus solely on dinosaurs. The Cretaceous period was teeming with amazing flora and fauna, some of which were also wiped out at the time of asteroid impact. Giant ferns! Super bugs! Why should dinosaurs get the starring role all the time? How about a book about bacteria? Those critters survived multiple mass extinctions over the history of Earth. I guess no one's figured out how to make bacteria cute — or ferocious.

Too often, science books focus on individual organisms rather than species interrelationships in an ecosystem. A good dinosaur book allows dinosaurs to share the spotlight with others. Plants and smaller animals didn't exist just so that dinosaurs could eat them — they were part of a complex balance of organisms dependent on one another. Aliki's classic *Fossils Tell of Long Ago* includes dinosaur fossils among those of many other organisms whose fossilized remains help us understand the past. Patricia Lauber's *Living with Dinosaurs* turns the typical dinosaur book on its head, as Douglas Henderson's illustrations show us the world from the dinosaur's perspective, allowing the complex ecosystem to take center stage.

While branching out from just dinosaurs is a good thing, it's also important that a good dinosaur book stick to its proper time period. Dinosaurs and woolly mammoths (not to mention *Homo sapiens*) did not coexist, so please don't put them in the same book. Doing so makes it very difficult to convey the vast periods of time that separate these species and the incremental evolutionary development that explains when and if they're related. (A good book about that second most popular extinct creature, though, is Sandra Markle's *Outside and Inside Woolly Mammoths*.)

Most importantly, a good dinosaur book fully embraces the complex and fundamental scientific theories that underlie this seemingly straightforward topic. Nearly every major branch of science intersects with dinosaurs in some way. The rise and fall of the dinosaurs is a case study in evolution, particularly in understanding the origins of modern birds. Books such as *A Nest of Dinosaurs: The Story of Oviraptor* by Mark A. Norell and Lowell Dingus showcase the evidence that supports these findings and the ways that scientists piece it all together. The structure of the universe and the early history of the solar system help explain the asteroid impact that devastated the dinosaur population. The chemical reactions and meteorological patterns in the atmosphere and on land explain why some living things suffered and others didn't. Geological processes explain why dinosaur fossils are found in some places on Earth and not others, and why they even still exist millions of years after the organisms that made them died. *Asteroid Impact* by Douglas Henderson is one of the few books that dig into these areas of science, and Henderson's dramatic, detailed art illustrates the major events without overdoing it. The field of paleontology is based on a relatively limited set of evidence, which provides plenty of opportunities to discuss the community of scientists and how they convince one another of their ideas. Indeed, this is an area of strength in dinosaur books, with plenty of good ones to mention. *Dinosaurs at the Ends of the Earth: The Story of the Central Asiatic Expeditions* by Brian Floca gives historical perspective on turn-of-the-last-century science. Nic Bishop's *Digging for Bird-Dinosaurs* updates readers with a modern field expedition to Madagascar to see how fossils are uncovered, while Sandra Markle's *Outside and Inside Dinosaurs* gives us the technology used when those fossils return to the laboratory. Kathleen V. Kudlinski in *Boy, Were We Wrong about Dinosaurs!* dares to admit that scientific ideas change as new theories and evidence are introduced.

But if all this wealth fails to satisfy; if only a comprehensive compendium of information will do, try Thomas R. Holtz, Jr.'s *Dinosaurs: The Most Complete, Up-to-Date Encyclopedia for Dinosaur Lovers of All Ages*. If there is anything paleontology enthusiasts wish to know, they will find it here: geology and geological history, fossil hunting and dating, evolution, prehistoric ecology, and, of course, the dinosaurs themselves — forty-two chapters of exceptionally detailed information about the major classifications, including sidebars written by practicing paleontologists that emphasize cutting-edge research areas.

Each of the books above illustrates components of what makes a good dinosaur book: taking on challenging topics as accurately yet as creatively as possible, illuminating aspects of scientific theory and practice that help readers understand their nature, and never losing the wonder and excitement felt by scientists and children alike when imagining what Earth must have been like when dinosaurs were around.

MORE GREAT SCIENCE BOOKS

Nic Bishop, *Frogs*
  48 pp. Grades K–3. This informative book covers anatomical, behavioral, and reproductive facts about frogs. The photographs in vivid colors are stunningly crisp and beautifully printed.

Sarah C. Campbell, photographs by Sarah C. Campbell and Richard P. Campbell, *Wolfsnail: A Backyard Predator*
  32 pp. Grades PS–2. A predatory wolfsnail tracks an unlucky garden snail. The spare text highlights the wolfsnail's single-minded focus, and each step of the attack is illustrated with an exceptional close-up photograph.

Jason Chin, *Redwoods*
  40 pp. Grades 1–4. A young boy waiting for the subway starts reading a book about redwood trees and embarks on an imaginative journey through the redwood forest. What sets this book apart is the pairing of the fantastical visual narrative with a straightforward nonfiction text. A contagious celebration of the relationship between information and imagination.

Nicola Davies, illustrations by Neal Layton, *Just the Right Size: Why Big Animals Are Big and Little Animals Are Little*
  64 pp. Grades 4–6. Davies and Layton explore the rules that control what bodies can and can't do, taking a close look at the difference between "little things" and "big things" to explain why there are no giant spiders and why humans can't fly. The book integrates humor (especially in the cartoon illustrations) and riveting scientific information.

James M. Deem, *Bodies from the Ice: Melting Glaciers and the Recovery of the Past*
  64 pp. Grades 4–6. After introducing the oldest ice mummy (5,300-year-old Otzi), Deem gives readers a tour of mummified bodies found in ice the world over. The design, with its variety of photographs, captions, and sidebars, seals the appeal.

Steve Jenkins, ***Dogs and Cats***

40 pp. Grades 3–5. Jenkins clearly presents scientific information in this uniquely styled flip-book comparison of dogs and cats featuring his trademark cut-paper illustrations. An inviting, multidimensional introduction to the pets we love.

David Macaulay with Richard Walker, ***The Way We Work: Getting to Know the Amazing Human Body***

336 pp. Grade 9 and up. Macaulay (*The Way Things Work*) turns his prodigious curiosity and formidable talents to human anatomy and physiology. Humor occasionally leavens the information, which, though often complex, is clearly and succinctly presented in double-page spreads, accompanied by an illuminating array of illustrations.

Sy Montgomery, photographs by Nic Bishop, ***Kakapo Rescue: Saving the World's Strangest Parrot*** (Scientists in the Field)

74 pp. Grades 4–6. Montgomery and Bishop trek to Codfish Island off New Zealand's coast to cover, with in-depth description and glorious photography, naturalists' efforts to save the kakapo. Layered into the engrossing account is information on New Zealand's unique biodiversity and the devastating consequences of human settlement on its ecosystem.

Catherine Thimmesh, ***Lucy Long Ago: Uncovering the Mystery of Where We Came From***

64 pp. Grades 4–6. Thimmesh examines the discovery of and research surrounding Lucy, one of the most important early hominid skeletons found to date. The text details what scientists are able to extrapolate from Lucy's bones. Explanatory sidebars, diagrams, and plentiful photographs of fossils and reconstructed hominids provide excellent support.

Up the Bookcase to Poetry
Alice Schertle

There was, in the house I lived in as a child, a large bookcase extending from floor to ceiling in the living room. In it books were arranged, logically, with the easier books at the bottom, within a child's reach, and the more difficult adult titles higher up. I aspired to the top shelf. I remember from time to time during my childhood dragging a chair over, standing on it, and pulling from the top shelf a book called *Pride and Prejudice*. I knew this to be a wonderful book from the reverence with which older members of my family spoke of it. So it was always with a sense of failure and frustration that I flipped through the pages, trying to read the occasional paragraph or sentence. I was missing something. Each time, I had to slide *Pride and Prejudice* back into place on the top shelf and set my sights a bit lower.

The very first book I can remember loving was the large, well-worn Mother Goose on the bottom shelf. Because I had been read to from that book since before I could stand, and knew the rhymes by heart, I put it in my lap, looked at the pictures, recited the verses, and thought I was reading. And soon, of course, I was reading — and rereading—the poems in Robert Louis Stevenson's *A Child's Garden of Verses.*

On the second shelf I found a collection of books bequeathed me by an older cousin: the Nancy Drew books. I read all thirty-two. Or did I read one of them thirty-two times? They all seem to blend. I don't remember what Nancy did in any of those books, but whatever it was, she always did it awfully well. Eventually, and probably none too soon, I wound my way out of the high-crime community of River Heights and up to the next shelf, where I found those noble, faithful, often abused, long-suffering animals: *Black Beauty; Smoky, the Cowhorse; My Friend Flicka; Lassie Come-Home; The Yearling.* I cried my way through those books with the growing suspicion that writers of animal fiction suffered from an unhealthy compulsion to kill off their title characters.

About this time, my mother imposed a curfew on my reading. She thought I needed my sleep. You would think that a parent who wanted to restrict a child's reading after a particular hour would hide the flashlight. On one memorable occasion I emerged from under the covers with a book just as the sky was beginning to go gray in the east. I had found the book that kept me reading until dawn not in the tall living-room bookcase but in a kitchen cupboard. Many of us—teachers, librarians, writers, editors, parents—grapple with the problem of how to get a child to read. I recommend wrapping a book in a dish towel and hiding it behind the cookbooks. When I found *Forever Amber* so wrapped, wedged behind *101 Ways with Jell-O,* nothing would have stopped me from reading it. And I have to say that it expanded my horizons considerably. Fortunately, back at the bookcase, I found reading that kept me from thinking of romance solely in terms of *Forever Amber.*

Thank goodness for poetry. For "Evangeline," "The Lady of Shalott," for "Lochinvar," who rode out of the west, and "The Highwayman," who rode through the night to meet Bess beneath her casement, and

rose upright in the stirrups; he scarce could reach her hand,
But she loosened her hair in the casement! His face burnt like
    a brand
As the black cascade of perfume came tumbling over his breast;
And he kissed its waves in the moonlight,
(O sweet black waves in the moonlight!)
Then he tugged at his rein in the moonlight, and galloped away
    to the West.

Who could resist?

And so, I read my way up the bookcase, until the day came when, once again, I took from the top shelf *Pride and Prejudice.* I opened to the first page and read, "It is a truth universally acknowledged that a single man in possession of a good fortune must be in want of a wife." I read every word. It was worth waiting for.

But, of all my childhood reading, it is the poetry that has stayed with me. I can't remember a line from *Raggedy Ann,* or from the animal stories I cried over, or from *Treasure Island, The Secret Garden, The Jungle Book,* or *Little Women* — all of which I loved. Though it is still probably my all-time favorite novel, I can quote only the first sentence of *Pride and Prejudice.* But I know every rhyme from that old Mother Goose book. I still know many of the poems from *A Child's Garden of Verses.* And I can still recite from memory all seventeen stanzas, one hundred and two lines, of "The Highwayman."

It took me twenty-seven books to get around to writing poetry. My first twenty-six were picture books. In a way, writing picture books is a lot like writing poetry. I'd say that, considered in terms of the amount of time spent per sentence, or per line, or per word, it takes more time to write the shortest work — a poem — than anything else. Next is probably the picture book. Benjamin Franklin, who, as far as I know, didn't write picture books, said, "I don't have time to be brief."

Poetry is language compressed, an intensification of language. It's saying more in fewer words. Developing a picture-book story, too, is a question of peeling away the layers, of eliminating the extraneous, of trying to discover, to understand what this story is "about." Which means you have to find the core, the center, the heart — and in order to sustain a whole story, that heart has to be beating. Which is just a way of saying that a picture-book story has to be parked on something substantial. Humor will provide it. Humor is its own excuse for being. But even in a story that isn't funny, this thing at the center has to be there. It doesn't have to be profound or complex; just a kernel of significance will do. It has to be there in a poem, too.

Writers collect words almost compulsively. In Tom Stoppard's play *The Real Thing*, the main character has this to say about words: "I don't think writers are sacred, but words are. They deserve respect. If you get the right ones in the right order, you can nudge the world a little, or make a poem children will speak for you when you're dead."

He's right about words; they deserve respect. There's nothing like laboring over one or two lines for a few hours to foster that respect. It's made of me a listener. It's one reason I am a compulsive rereader of sentences and paragraphs, lines and stanzas. I listen to what I'm reading, in my head, and when I hear something really wonderful, I have to go back and find out how the author did that. Or, if it's less than wonderful, I want to try to discover what went wrong.

Writing formal poetry, lines using traditional metrical form, makes you analytical of words in a way that can become almost obsessive. You tend to hear words — people's names, for example — in terms of the metrical feet they represent. Humphrey Bogart: two trochees. Esa-Pekka Salonen: trochee, trochee, dactyl. Pierre Cardin: iambic. Eleanor Roosevelt, Engelbert Humperdinck: double dactyls.

These are the kinds of thoughts that come unbidden into the mind of a person who spends a few hours every day writing poetry using form — traditional, metrical, scannable, often rhymed. I don't mean to imply that I write, or read, only formal poetry. But I love the music of lines written in form. I think children respond particularly to such poetry, and I think form is the inescapable and essential foundation of all that came after it, including poetry that rejects it. So here are some thoughts about the process of writing such poetry.

If I am working on a poem in form, do I say to myself, "Now I think I'll use mostly trochees here" or "Here's where I'll throw in some anapests"? No. But at least I'll be aware of the effect of certain poetic feet, certain rhythms, on the speed of a line, for example.

It is sometimes suggested that certain kinds of feet, rhythmical units of sound, create specific "moods"—that anapests, for instance, are light, happy, appropriate only in light or humorous verse. (Anapests, you'll recall, are feet of three syllables, the first two unstressed, the last syllable stressed. The word *persevere* is an anapest. "She's a calico cat" would be two anapests.) I don't like to invest poetic feet with too much personality. I've seen too many poems in which lines with anapests in them are serious, or lyrical, or even somber to think of them as giddy or irresponsible feet. But when I use them, I'll try to remember that anapests, and dactyls, will speed up a line, as certain other kinds of feet, or rhythms, will slow a line down.

There is a Robert Frost couplet that I like to use with classes of children to show them how the rhythm of a line can echo what's happening in the poem. The first line is slow, halting, almost awkward—because he's talking about something that is old, and slow, and stiff. But the second line is as fast and bouncy as its subject. The couplet is:

The old dog barks backward without getting up.
I can remember when he was a pup.

Which brings us to the question of just how much analysis of poetry you can do with children. I'd never start out a poetry session with fourth-, fifth-, or sixth-graders with a lesson on metrics. But after we'd done a few poems, and they were into it, and I could see that the poetry had them, then I might slip in a little metrics, in a painless and nonthreatening way.

We might collect names or words that are dactyls: *Jennifer, Abraham, Melanie, Deborah, suddenly, relative, mayonnaise, sycamore.* Many classes can construct whole dactylic sentences if you start them out:

Jennifer / wouldn't play / basketball.
Jennifer / probably / wouldn't play / basketball / after
she'd / eaten a / hamburger.
Jennifer / probably / wouldn't play / basketball / after
she'd / eaten a / hamburger / smothered in / onion rings / if she
were / counting her / calories.

In my experience, children love form. They respond to the regularity of it; they find its predictability satisfying. (Adults do, too.) In some instances, it's as pleasurable as solving a puzzle when they discover the pattern. And it is the pattern of sound in rhymed poetry that helps them to memorize, to make a poem their own.

Most classes of fifth- or sixth-graders have heard the Robert Frost poem "Stopping by Woods on a Snowy Evening," and it's easy for them to hear the rhyme pattern: in the four-line stanzas, lines one, two, and four rhyme. Line three does not. But what they don't hear—not consciously—and what they love to discover is that the stanzas are linked; they are tied together by the unrhymed sound at the end of the third line. It's that sound that provides the rhyme for the next stanza.

If poetry is about sound, and writing poetry a matter of learning to listen, poetry is also about image, and writing poetry a matter of noticing things. Images are all around, and there are poems in those images, if I can just learn to see them.

Writing poetry is about sound, and about image, and about a third thing that comes from inside. I think it is a tantalizingly shy thing. I do not know how to summon it at will. And I cannot name it. But Emily Dickinson could. She said:

To make a prairie it takes a clover and one bee, —
One clover, and a bee,
And revery.
The revery alone will do
If bees are few.

Gazing at Things
Naomi Shihab Nye

No one will ever approach you and say, "This looks like a good day to curl up and read poetry." You have to do that for yourself. One great thing is — you can sneak it in, between all the other things you are doing. The poet William Stafford carried his own poems on small cards in his pockets — we may carry our own or someone else's. Poetry books are often elegantly slim, which allows them to fit easily into purses or briefcases. The brevity is beneficial. You may read and reread in the same amount of time it might take to eat a few crackers with cheese. Your day will feel deeper, calmer, better. Once, a natty businessman seated next to me on an airplane began weeping when he saw me reading a book of poems. He said, "When I was young, poetry gave me so much hope. Why have I denied it to myself all these years?"

Recently, while preparing dinner in our renovated hundred-year-old kitchen, now jazzed up with a new black sink, handmade green Mission tile from Mexico, and our first dishwasher (we're very slow), a sense of negligence washed over me. What about the sunset? I thought. Have I sat with the sunset lately? Why not? What time is it?

Leaving the garbanzos resting in the blender with their little moon of garlic, I hoofed it to the front porch and sat on the steps. Sure enough, the wide sky toward the west was softening into lovely pink stripes — all in unobtrusive silence. Cars were whizzing home, buses rounding the corner. But the beautiful big sky — that ripe pink and purple sky above the pecan trees, the Mexican cafés, and the abandoned Judson candy factory — radiated outward in stripes. Taking a long breath, I closed my eyes, then opened them again to see the plum-colored swirls intensify and merge.

Right then my neighbor Amparo walked by, noticed me sitting there, and called out across our fence, "What's wrong?" Usually she speaks Spanish to me, but these conversations often end abruptly, so now she tries English. "What's wrong?"

I laughed, pointing. "Nothing is wrong! It's *right*! Look up at the sky!"

She turned and looked, shrugged, and said, "I thought you locked out." She walked on.

This is what we have come to in our culture — you sit down to rest, to breathe and to stare, without doing anything, and it appears peculiar.

I'd like to go back in time.

"What do you hope to do with your life?"

"Gaze at things. Thank you."

Beginning at about the age of three, I was regularly attracted outside onto the square concrete porch of our Saint Louis home to watch the softening light. A gray midwestern glow or a lonesome yellow beam said, "Take heed. Notice me. I am going now, and you will soon be shipping off to bed." It made me feel poignant — already I was nostalgic for a different kind of slow-paced life.

The only good thing about going to bed was hearing our father's wonderful Palestinian folktales, which made us laugh happily, and, afterward, our mother's voice, winding us down with resonant poems, spoken in a calm, deliberate tone. Frequently her daily voice was harried and nervous, so this nocturnal care for each syllable felt delicious. She read Robert Louis Stevenson, Emily Dickinson, Carl Sandburg. . . . I loved poetry's leaping interweave, the selectiveness of each magical word. Poetry wasn't worrying about anything. It was contemplating. I loved the rich descriptions of lines and scenes. Poetry wasn't trying to get us to do anything, it was simply inviting us to think, and feel, and see. It was language we could tuck under our chins. A cool sheet, a cotton quilt.

Poetry's understated quality of hinting somehow felt better than the words that got passed around the rest of the day. With intimate immediacy, poetry took me to a deeper place, a time-pillow of heightened consciousness. I am sitting on the step of the book, soaking something in. . . .

I also liked the way poetry looked on the page — all that white space around the words suggested that each word had honor.

Henry David Thoreau said that "to see the sun rise or go down every day . . . would preserve us sane forever."

It's the pause we humans are desperate for. If you don't think everyone is desperate, ask a gymnasium of kindergartners how many of them feel they have too much to do and are always rushing, and nearly every hand will go up. They don't have to ask what you mean, either. They know.

Poems can really help.

MORE GREAT POETRY

Gwendolyn Brooks, illustrations by Faith Ringgold, *Bronzeville Boys and Girls*
48 pp. Grades 4–6. With acute observation and feeling, Brooks captures moments of childhood. The strong colors of the illustrations place the poems both in the real world and the imaginary world of childhood, where a tea party seems to float in the air on a raft of blue.

Douglas Florian, *Comets, Stars, the Moon, and Mars: Space Poems and Paintings*
48 pp. Grades 4–6. Moving from planet to universe, Florian sums up the heavens in twenty snappy rhymes. With its gorgeous palette, sweeping vistas, and ingenious effects, this is an expansive and illuminating view of the subject.

Paul B. Janeczko, illustrations by Chris Raschka, *A Kick in the Head: An Everyday Guide to Poetic Forms*
64 pp. Grades 4–6. The twenty-nine poems in this attractive collection — from light verse to a Shakespearean sonnet — are arranged by form (tercet, haiku, roundel, etc.) and are accompanied by bright, playful illustrations. Companion volumes include *A Poke in the I: A Collection of Concrete Poems* and *A Foot in the Mouth: Poems to Speak, Sing, and Shout.*

Ron Koertge, *Shakespeare Makes the Playoffs*
170 pp. Grades 6–8. Writer/first baseman/eighth-grader Kevin writes poems about his life, from baseball playoffs to romantic complications. The pleasing variety of verse — a villanelle here, a sestina there — is a seamless fit for Koertge's story and characters. Sequel to *Shakespeare Bats Cleanup.*

Naomi Shihab Nye, illustrations by Terre Maher, *A Maze Me: Poems for Girls*
118 pp. Grades 7–12. In this quiet, personal collection of more than seventy free-verse poems aimed especially at girls between twelve and seventeen, Nye captures the struggle of a young teen to connect with and understand her world.

Linda Sue Park, illustrations by Istvan Banyai, *Tap Dancing on the Roof: Sijo (Poems)*

40 pp. Grades 4–6. Twenty-seven engaging poems in a traditional three-line Korean poetic form on themes such as seasons, home, and school. The illustrations add an extra element of wit and imaginative freedom.

Jack Prelutsky, illustrations by Brandon Dorman, *Be Glad Your Nose Is on Your Face and Other Poems: Some of the Best of Jack Prelutsky*

194 pp. Grades K–3. Containing a wide selection of Prelutsky's euphonious, often challenging, usually humorous verse, this collection is everything a fan could ask for. An accompanying CD sets many poems to music. For more Prelutsky, see *Something Big Has Been Here* and *My Dog May Be a Genius*.

Alice Schertle, illustrations by Petra Mathers, *Button Up!: Wrinkled Rhymes*

40 pp. Grades K–3. Fifteen adroitly phrased rhymes, voiced by various pieces of clothing, reflect children's amiable relationships with these intimate possessions. Schertle's contagiously rhythmic, playful verse is perfectly reflected in the art, which ranges from delicately comical to downright funny.

Joyce Sidman, illustrations by Rick Allen, *Dark Emperor & Other Poems of the Night*

32 pp. Grades K–5. Beautifully crafted poems celebrate the world that comes alive after dark; each poem is accompanied by a corresponding paragraph of information. The subtle colors of Allen's linocut prints encourage readers to seek out the featured plant or animal gradually, just as eyes become accustomed to the dark.

Marilyn Singer, illustrations by Josée Masse, *Mirror Mirror: A Book of Reversible Verse*

32 pp. Grades K–3. Through a poetic invention she dubs the reverso, Singer meditates on twelve familiar folktales and, via shifting line breaks and punctuation, their shadows. Each free-verse poem has two stanzas set on facing columns, where the second is the first reversed. Similarly bifurcated illustrations, Day-Glo bright, face the cleverly constructed and insightful poems.

Chapter Seven

GIRL BOOKS AND BOY BOOKS

Introduction
Roger Sutton

Questions about gender and reading are perennial. Otherwise free-to-be types talk about "boy books" and "girl books" with aplomb, until they notice that a boy is *not* reading the novel that the gender experts suggested, and that the sea of pink covers keeps some girl readers firmly on the shore. In the adult world, gender divisions in reading don't cause much concern, even though, consistently, women read far more books than do men. But if fans of Oprah's picks are mainly female, and more men are content with the sports section, so be it. When those same adults consider books for younger readers, however, the issue becomes more fraught — are girls being limited by reading only books about girls "just like me"? Are boys losing some basic socialization by reading about things, not people? Or are those categorizations even true?

I've asked *Horn Book* reviewer and unrepentant Girl Reader Christine Heppermann to join me in wondering why boys don't read more and if it's bad for girls to read romance. Here's some advice, though: the best thing you can give to a would-be, could-be reader, boy or girl, is access to a wide variety of reading possibilities among which he or she can find what seems just right, labels be damned.

Telling the Truth
Christine Heppermann

Contemporary realistic fiction written for girls reassures readers that what's going on in their everyday lives *matters*. School stories, friendship stories, stories about falling off the stage during a ballet recital: to anyone too old to have to worry anymore about being picked last in gym, such fare can seem trivial. But the authors of these books understand that sometimes the most mundane dilemmas can be the weightiest. Sometimes it *is* vitally important whether you wear jeans and a tank top or a lacy thrift-store dress for the first day of school because, as Lizzie (in Claudia Mills's *Lizzie at Last*) observes when grappling with this issue, "Decisions made on the first day of seventh grade would affect her for the rest of the year, maybe for the rest of her life." Mom and great-aunt Martha will tell you that you look lovely whatever you wear; Mills and writers like her will tell you the truth.

Honesty is a pivotal element in one of the novels that ushered in modern realistic fiction for children, Louise Fitzhugh's 1964 classic *Harriet the Spy*. Paradoxically, Fitzhugh comes about this honesty by promoting the message that, as sounded by Harriet's formidable nanny, Ole Golly, "Sometimes you have to lie." When Harriet's classmates get hold of her spy notebook, in which she has written, among other things, scathingly critical comments about them, they express their hurt and outrage by ostracizing her, sending her into emotional turmoil. Although Harriet eventually issues a formal apology to everyone in the sixth-grade newspaper, she doesn't waver in her conviction that writers need to tell the truth as they see it, and, inside, she remains the same judgmental Harriet, albeit with a heightened respect for the power of words. Adults didn't always consider Fitzhugh's warts-and-all characters, including Harriet's rather self-absorbed, ineffectual parents, to be appropriate for children, but young readers immediately embraced *Harriet the Spy,* and it continues to inspire new generations of tomato-sandwich eaters and keyhole listeners.

A lot of what *Harriet the Spy* brought to children's fiction — imperfect parents, the virtues of disobedience, a gimlet-eyed view of sixth-grade society — is now old hat, but in 1964 the book was a pioneer, opening up territory hitherto unexplored or at least carefully circumscribed. With *The Long Secret,* the sequel to *Harriet the Spy* published in 1965, Fitzhugh became the first writer for children to take on the topic of menstruation, with a frankness that would be matched (and popularity surpassed) five years later with the publication of Judy Blume's *Are You There God? It's Me, Margaret.*

Novels by this grand dame of the genre exemplify how the right book at the right time can leave a lasting impression on a reader. In Jennifer O'Connell's collection *Everything I Needed to Know About Being a Girl I Learned from Judy Blume* (2007), essays by twenty-four women writers reveal some of the qualities that give Blume's books staying power. A number of the contributors remember using her texts as survival guides to help them through the dense woods of adolescence. "I can't even count the number of times I read and reread *It's Not the End of the World,*" reflects essayist Kristin Harmel. "That's because when you're eleven and your parents are splitting up, no one realizes that you might have some real adult questions that you don't exactly know how to ask. . . . I didn't know how to ask those things. But Judy Blume did. And through [her character] Karen Newman, she told me the things I ached to know."

The term *problem novel* is usually a pejorative, indicating that the formula behind it is short and sweet. (Here's a book about Divorce! Here's a book about Bullying! And everything is going to Turn Out Fine!) Though Blume's stories often center on a single issue, they usually manage to transcend one-word synopses, thanks to her extraordinary empathy and insight. She doesn't preach or lecture. She's like the ideal older sister who's been there, done that, and won't laugh at you or roll her eyes when you go to her for advice.

Of course, not everyone reads realistic fiction for profound guidance. Realistic fiction can be a fantasy social club: it's a way to meet people you might not have the courage to approach in real life. Want to get in with the popular crowd or at least know how they think? Claudia Mills forges that connection in her West Creek Middle School series when she writes, in two separate volumes, from the points of view of Alex and Marcia, the "it" boy and girl of their class. Good-looking, wisecracking Alex Ryan often intimidates the other students with his sharp-edged sense of humor, but in *Alex Ryan, Stop That!*, we see *him* intimidated by his overbearing father. Similarly, *Makeovers by Marcia* shows that, though the ultra-confident-seeming narrator may sport meticulously painted purple nails, her self-esteem has a few chips. The message here is more complex than "beautiful people have problems, too." Because Mills is such a skilled writer, she also manages to highlight the qualities that make Alex and Marcia natural leaders. Still, it's comforting for all of us lower-ranking pack members to be able to look beneath their skin and realize that no one is invulnerable.

As the essays in *Everything I Needed to Know About Being a Girl I Learned from Judy Blume* confirm, it's a powerful experience to open a book and realize you are not alone. The best contemporary realistic fiction for children brings out the individuality of the characters while communicating their universal qualities. One thing we all have in common, whether we're poised and polished Marcia or tomboy Harriet, is that, on some essential level, we all feel like misfits.

That's certainly the case for Millie in Lisa Yee's *Millicent Min, Girl Genius,* a novel that cracks open a stereotype and looks at it from the inside. Millicent isn't just a brainy Chinese American girl; she's a bona fide prodigy, an eleven-year-old high-school senior, much more jazzed about her college-level summer-school class on poetry than the volleyball league her mother forces her to join so she can have, in the words of her school psychologist, "a more normal and well-rounded childhood." As she sees nothing wrong with the current state of her childhood, Millicent is skeptical: "If my parents are implying that I'm not 'normal,' does that mean I am subnormal? And their brilliant solution is . . . volleyball? What is normal about forcing someone to move in rotation?"

Not only is Millicent the opposite of the boy-or-clothes-crazy airhead parents often expect to find in realistic fiction for girls, but Yee's novel, accessible and humorous as it is, introduces a fairly sophisticated literary device, that of the unreliable narrator. For all her assertions that she has no need for play, friends her own age, or other childish distractions, Millie spends a fair amount of time deciding how she would sign yearbooks — most of her planned inscription is in Latin — if she *had* friends, or brooding about past cruelties and injustices inflicted upon her by schoolmates. When Emily, a new girl in town and fellow prisoner of volleyball league, asks Millie to sleep over, she keeps her sky-high IQ a secret and hopes that Emily "will not be put off by [her] credentials."

Yee gives Millicent a nemesis with an entirely different problem. Stanford Wong, the son of family friends, is popular and athletic; but, unlike Millie, he wasn't reading Truman Capote at age six. In short, his English grades stink, and his parents hire Millicent to tutor him for the summer, an arrangement both she and he find about as pleasant as extended oral surgery. The contrast between Stanford and Millicent adds comedy and reminds readers that, although some people think otherwise — when Millie orders huevos rancheros at the college cafeteria, the cashier remarks, "I didn't think you people liked that kind of food"— all Asians aren't walking cerebral cortexes, and they aren't all the same. Millicent may be an example of a type, albeit an extreme example, but she is also distinctly individual, like her peace-activist grandmother, former-homecoming-queen mother, and intermittently employed father, who enjoys playing with toys more than his daughter does.

Do writers like Yee remember the trials of their youth better than the rest of us, or are they just more eloquent in expressing them? In some realistic novels for girls, the descriptions of feelings and events are so perceptive, so resonant, they practically turn into poetry. "Summer ripened like a piece of fruit. But it was a piece of fruit with an unseen bruise, and it was ripening and spoiling at the same time. The bruise's name was Glenna." Here author Lynne Rae Perkins, in the voice of narrator Debbie, foreshadows the irreparable rift between best friends that occurs in her novel *All Alone in the Universe*. Her story speaks to how the most devastating events in a child's life aren't always dramatic or obvious. Debbie and her best friend, Maureen, never get into a knockdown, drag-out fight. Their gradual unraveling happens much more quietly. Another girl, Glenna, starts spending time with Maureen, and at first Debbie considers her too trivial to cause concern. "To me, she was like one of those crumbs of wax that flake off the milk carton into your glass and you drink it anyway. It's too much trouble to fish it out, and it's not going to kill you." But when Debbie's friendship-twosome with Maureen more and more frequently becomes a threesome, Debbie slowly and painfully awakens to the reality that something is changing, and it is beyond her control.

Novels like *All Alone in the Universe* are important. They let kids know that someone *is* paying attention to the awkward, joyous, triumphant, and sad moments in their everyday lives; that even if there is no national memorial devoted to broken middle-school friendships, such books are here, like lit candles, to commemorate their passing.

BECOMING JUDY BLUME

COE BOOTH

The library in Mrs. Koff's third-grade classroom was sad, just a few milk crates stacked to form a small makeshift bookcase. I remember dreading "free read" time because inevitably I would stand in front of that classroom library, scanning those familiar books, hoping something new would magically appear, a book that would suddenly make me *like* to read. But, truthfully, I was starting to give up on that dream.

Back then I read only when I was forced to for school. I would have liked to read books about kids like myself, but most of the African American books available at the time were historical fiction and, while I read and liked them OK, I just didn't feel that spark of connection, that invisible *something*, that made the books impossible to put down. The characters in those novels didn't speak the way my friends and I spoke. They didn't live where I lived. And their problems weren't the kinds of problems my friends and I ever had to deal with. Bottom line: I couldn't relate.

Enter Judy Blume.

I was in fourth grade when my teacher encouraged me to read *Are You There God? It's Me, Margaret*. I admit I was reluctant. I mean, was I, a little girl from the Bronx, supposed to care about Margaret, a girl who in the beginning of the book actually *complains* about having to move into a big, beautiful house in a nice suburban neighborhood? Really?

But in spite of myself, I was hooked by page four. No, Margaret didn't look like me, and certainly her life wasn't anything like mine. But *she* was real to me. More real than the characters in any of the other books I had read up to that point. Inside — the way she thought and felt, her secret desires and fears — she was just like me.

Pretty soon I was reading more of Judy Blume's books. I found it easy to put myself in her characters' shoes and understand their conflicts, no matter how different they were from mine. I enjoyed losing myself in their worlds. For the first time, I enjoyed *reading*!

Those books inspired me. As a matter of fact, if you had asked me back then, I would have told you I was going to grow up to be the black Judy Blume! I wanted to write girl books. But more specifically, I wanted to write books about black girls, primarily *for* black girls. More than anything, I wanted to write books that would reach those girls at just the right time in their lives and, hopefully, become as meaningful to them as Judy Blume's books were (and still are) to me.

Everygirl
Kitty Flynn

Life, as far as I could see, was going to be a sort of obstacle
course, with detours, yield signs, stop signs, and cautions.
—*Alice in Lace*

To legions of tween and teen girl readers, Alice McKinley has been
a trusted friend and guide for more than twenty years. Phyllis
Reynolds Naylor's Alice has been navigating life's obstacle course
from her first appearance in *The Agony of Alice* (1985), when she was
in sixth grade; at this writing, she's a senior in high school. Each
book in the series takes place over a few months, typically a school
semester or summer vacation, mirroring the rhythm of readers'
lives. Alice leads a middle-class existence in suburban Maryland
with her widowed father and older brother. (Alice's mother died
when she was in kindergarten; her absence prompts Alice to consciously study the women around her as a measure of her own identity and for a better understanding of what her future might look
like.) While Alice's interests and problems change realistically along
the way, she can be counted on to offer honest and authentic obser-
vations about family and friends, school and boys, body image and
self-perception, sexuality and values.

That's not to say Alice has all the answers. She'd be the first
to say she doesn't, and that's a big part of what makes her such a

likable and easy-to-relate-to character. Whereas her best friends, Pamela and Elizabeth, are firmly entrenched in their positions (thrill-seeking risk taker and naive, good Catholic girl, respectively), Alice doesn't approach life with ready solutions, sending girls a reassuring message that it's OK *not* to know everything. Realistically imperfect, Alice makes mistakes and faces the consequences. She models how to survive life's inevitable embarrassments and errors of judgment — reassuring readers that they, too, will survive.

One of the series' hallmarks is straightforward, nonthreatening information about sex and sexuality, which speaks to girls' normal curiosity and evolves naturally as Alice grows more aware of herself as a sexual being. At twelve, for example, Alice ponders the logistics of French kissing: "You probably had to start planning it early in the morning and be careful what you ate all day so your mouth wouldn't taste like onions or anything." By eighth grade, her questions are more advanced, as when she bravely asks her cousin, "Carol, what does intercourse really, really feel like for a woman?" (The trickiest aspect of the Alice books is to know where to jump into the series — tweens may want to stick with the earlier titles, when Alice is in middle school; the titles set in Alice's late-high-school years are more appropriate for older teens.)

Alice's father and (more reluctantly) her brother field the bulk of her forthright questions with respect and humor — often at the dinner table. This family openness is idealized, but it's an ideal to strive for: Alice's frank talk about sexuality over roast chicken might inspire her readers to talk with a trusted adult about a sensitive topic. And for some readers — probably many — Alice gives voice to what they can't.

Sharing shelf space with the many girl-focused tween/teen series about queen-bee cliques, princesses, and Hollywood starlets, the Alice books stand out as a whole lot more substantial. Escaping into the world of prom queens and promiscuous nannies is easy; what's hard is finding one's way in the ordinary, everyday world. Reading about Alice's experiences with bullying, prejudice, peer pressure, and boyfriends — to name just a few topics — is a rehearsal of sorts for modern-day real life. At their heart, these books are encouraging lessons in developing and maintaining all kinds of healthy relationships: with family, with friends, with boyfriends or girlfriends, and, most importantly, with oneself.

GROW UP WITH US, YOU'LL BE FINE

MITALI PERKINS

Growing up in a Bengali household in the Bay area, I wasn't eager to leave girlhood. My two older sisters had done it, and it didn't look like fun. American guys started pursuing them, which meant an increase in monitoring and interrogation at home. Relatives discussed their potential to marry good Bengali boys, evaluating positives and negatives as though my sisters were mangoes for sale at the market. I watched with trepidation as my sisters' free, strong selves disappeared behind a *burka* of femininity. And it wasn't just in the culture of our origin. Most of the American masculine world seemed more interested in my sisters' curves than in their opinions.

If growing up meant that gender commandeered your person-hood, who wanted that? Not me. That's why my fourteen-year-old crush, redheaded Brian McElroy, stayed locked in my daydreams where he belonged, and I shunned him at school. I knew exactly why Peter Pan flew back to Neverland.

It took a trio of fictional characters to convince me that I could survive the move to womanhood, and their names were Jo, Anne, and Laura. I kept the library's copies of *Little Women*, *Anne of Green Gables*, and the Little House books in constant circulation.

Despite the constraints experienced by women in those times and places, all three protagonists retained a strong sense of self as they matured. Oh, they changed; no doubt about that. They married, had children, left childish ways behind. But I could tell that Plumfield's Mrs. Jo was still as impulsive and determined as she had been in *Little Women*. When an older Laura in *Little Town on the Prairie* rocked a desk furiously to protest a teacher's unjust treatment of her younger sister, I recognized the feisty little girl who had dragged in the Ingallses' entire woodpile to prepare for a storm. And when the talkative orphan in *Anne of Green Gables* grew up to become the chatelaine of Ingleside, she kept the same sense of humor, the same delight in nature, the same independence of thought.

If my fictional friends could move into the adult world without losing themselves, I, too, might be able to keep myself. Like Jo, Anne, and Laura, I could stride bravely into womanhood. And so I did.

MORE GREAT GIRL BOOKS

Jeanne Birdsall, *The Penderwicks: A Summer Tale of Four Sisters, Two Rabbits, and a Very Interesting Boy*

262 pp. Grades 4–6. Along with their loving but preoccupied botanist father and clumsy dog, the motherless Penderwick sisters spend a summer in the Berkshires. Suffused with affectionate humor, this charming, old-fashioned story feels familiar in the way the best books seem like old friends. In the sequel, *The Penderwicks on Gardam Street,* Birdsall again delivers genuinely funny scenes and tender moments.

Meg Cabot, *Allie Finkle's Rules for Girls: Glitter Girls and the Great Fake Out*

199 pp. Grades 3–5. Allie is thrilled to attend a twirling competition with her best friends—until she finds out that "frenemy" Brittany is having a glamorous birthday party on the same day. Cabot provides a gentle way to learn that you should "always be true to your friends, just as you are to yourself," in this typically funny and age-appropriate series entry.

Barry Deutsch, *Hereville: How Mirka Got Her Sword*

142 pp. Grades 4–6. Eleven-year-old Mirka Herschberg, a Hasidic Jew, is not your average dragon-slaying heroine. The Shabbat-observing protagonist finds herself first battling a furious talking pig, then competing in a knitting contest against a troll. This graphic novel is laugh-out-loud funny and thoroughly engrossing.

Shannon Hale and Dean Hale, illustrations by Nathan Hale, *Rapunzel's Revenge*

144 pp. Grades 5–8. In this gutsy graphic novel, Rapunzel is a spunky, (hair-) whip-toting cowgirl. She joins with rapscallion Jack to rescue her mother and end her wicked stepmother's reign. Full of high action, sensory thrills, and amusing wisecracking.

Kate Klise, *Grounded*

196 pp. Grades 4–6. After Daralynn's father and siblings die in a plane crash, her angry mother, a stylist for a funeral home, lets her daughter out of the house only to assist at work. When Clem's Crematorium threatens Mom's livelihood, Daralynn decides to investigate the owner. Told from Daralynn's entertainingly candid perspective, this is an improbably light-hearted mystery.

Cynthia Lord, **Touch Blue**

186 pp. Grades 4–6. Tess,who lives on a small Maine island, is excited when her family decides to foster a child, but thirteen-year-old Aaron is not exactly thrilled to be there. Tess's narration gives readers a real feeling for island life, while her sense of humor keeps things light.

Lauren Tarshis, **Emma-Jean Lazarus Fell Out of a Tree**

199 pp. Grades 4–7. Hyper-rational seventh-grader Emma-Jean doesn't understand her classmates' illogical behavior. This gently probing book tackles tween-relevant issues with sensitivity and skill.

Jacqueline Wilson, illustrations by Nick Sharratt, **Candyfloss**

339 pp. Grades 3–6. Preteen Floss adores her down-on-his-luck dad and decides to stay with him when Mum, stepfather, and baby brother move to Australia for six months. Comic-strip panels introduce each chapter, setting tone, illustrating Floss's feelings, and extending the action.

Jacqueline Woodson, **After Tupac & D Foster**

151 pp. Grades 5–7. A tone of fierce warmth and closeness permeates this novel about two black girls—best friends—whose mothers don't allow them to leave their block in 1994 Queens. Woodson eloquently limns the duo and their community in this ruminative, bittersweet novel.

Go Big or Go Home

Roger Sutton

Will Hobbs begins his 2008 *Go Big or Go Home* with a bang — literally, as a meteorite crashes through the roof into fourteen-year-old Brady's bedroom: "It was heavy, and almost too hot to handle, as well it might be after blazing a fiery hole through the atmosphere. We'd been hit by an intruder from outer space! I couldn't think of anything cooler that had happened in my entire life." Christened "Fred" by Brady and his best-bud cousin, Quinn, the meteorite leads the boys through all manner of adventure involving neighboring bullies and their Turkish war dog, Attila, "extreme" bicycle riding through the Black Hills, fishing, spelunking, an astrobiologist named Rip Ripley, and a space virus that gives Brady near-super-powers before putting him into a paralysis that the doctor mistakes for death. Awesome!

Go Big or Go Home is unmistakably a "boy book," and Hobbs is one of the most reliable practitioners of the genre. This is not to say that girls won't read it or that boys read nothing else. Instead, "boy book" means a story that might appeal to boys who otherwise won't voluntarily pick up a novel.

Concern over boys reading is perennial: what they read, why they don't, whether it matters. Part of the problem, though, is the way the debate gets framed: by adult, largely female teachers and librarians who define reading by what and how they themselves read. Boys read plenty (magazines, online news, for example), but as a group they read fewer books and less fiction than girls do. It's a distinction maintained right through adulthood.

But thank goodness for do-gooders, because the zeal with which librarians and teachers have tried to turn boys into fiction readers has resulted in some of children's literature's most boy- *and* girl-friendly first-class novels.

What makes a book a "boy book" rather than a book about a boy? I think Hobbs has it right in his title: Go Big or Go Home. What reluctant readers want are big plots, big themes, and lots of action focused on a hero the reader could imagine himself being, with maybe just a little work. Gary Paulsen's Brian, forsaken in the Canadian wilderness with nothing but a *Hatchet,* is an ordinary boy of whom great things are demanded. So is Harry Potter.

In Louis Sachar's *Holes,* Stanley Yelnats, sent to a boys' prison camp for a crime he didn't commit, is tubby, ordinary — and afflicted with more than a palindromic name. He attributes his misfortune to a family curse, first placed upon his great-great-grandfather for failing to keep his promise to carry the one-legged fortune-teller Madame Zeroni up the mountain to the life-giving spring. That was way-back-when in Latvia, but even in Stanley's contemporary Texas, the curse comes back in all its power — until Stanley closes the circle. At once a tense tale of survival and a poker-faced shaggy-dog story, and written in a laconic style that leaves plenty of, er, holes for the reader to fill in, *Holes* is the rare book that found critical acclaim, popular appeal, and instant entry into the canon. It was a boy book for everybody.

While habitual readers enjoy and are at ease with books along a spectrum that includes the ruminative and low-key, occasional readers want a bang for their buck. And for their time: when reading isn't easy, and when it's freighted with others' expectations of you, you want to feel that it's worth what you probably think of as a sacrifice.

At the risk of overindulging Dr. Freud, "bigness" is important to boy books. If you don't read very much, you want to feel that what you *do* read is Important. The bigness can be expressed in length, like the Harry Potter books, or in an elaborate structure, as in *Holes,* or in the ideas — think of the generations of brainy boys who have sustained the science-fiction industry. Big ideas can also operate on a smaller scale, as in Andrew Clements's string of best sellers about elementary school life. In his *Frindle,* a boy sets out to add a new word to the dictionary and succeeds; in *Lunch Money,* a boy builds a publishing empire from his and his classmates' spare change.

Clements's books star girls as often as boys, and it's important to note that the presence of a female main character is not in itself a deterrent to reluctant boy readers. Harry Potter's Hermione proved that. What these reluctant readers don't want are books filled with interpersonal emotional drama that propels the plots of such girl favorites as Phyllis Reynolds Naylor's Alice books (see "Everygirl," page 247) or Ann Brashares's Traveling Pants series. It's not that boy readers are afraid of emotions, exactly, it's that they want to feel them in service to high stakes — like a gun, in Walter Dean Myers's *Scorpions,* or a mutiny, as in Avi's *True Confessions of Charlotte Doyle,* a boy book about a girl. Or in controlling the world, as in Anthony Horowitz's James Bond–like Alex Rider series. Boys like to think Big.

Brian Selznick, an illustrator who frequently collaborates with Andrew Clements, won the 2008 Caldecott Medal with a boy book par excellence. While the Caldecott Medal, for "most distinguished picture book of the year," generally goes to a book of thirty-two pages, *The Invention of Hugo Cabret* is 534 pages long, with 158 pictures and 26,159 words. (The provision of this information by the narrator is evidence of the book's understanding of one thing boys like to get from a book: facts and statistics, preferably ones involving large numbers.) The book begins in a way that even the most reluctant of readers can appreciate: with twenty-one consecutive word-less double-page spreads. Beginning with a close-up of the moon, the pictures move down to the skyline of 1931 Paris, where dawn is beginning to break and a boy is walking, then running, through a train station. Is that a secret entrance? Yes. The boy goes behind the wall to spy, through a peephole cut into a clock, on an old man with a small stall of toys. The text finally begins: "From his perch behind the clock, Hugo could see everything."

The story that proceeds from there is complicated but speedy: Hugo has a broken handwriting automaton left by his late father, and he's been pilfering parts from the toy vendor in order to make it work. The message the restored automaton delivers only deepens the mystery, which involves the real-life early special-effects wizard / filmmaker Georges Méliès. Relying on text to convey conversation and motivation, and pictures to convey the considerable action, *Hugo Cabret* mimics the style of the early silent films, which alternated moving images with title cards to tell a story. The separation of pages where you look and pages where you read stimulates both ways of following the story (literally: there are some great chase scenes), and both its novelty value and textual breaks contribute to the book's attractiveness.

As any fifth-grade teacher will tell you, boys are jumpy, their brains as well as their limbs. Novelty both stimulates and soothes them, thus the perennial boy appeal of joke books (see "Banana Peels at Every Step," page 154) and *Guinness World Records,* a presage of the Internet that allows you to go from fact to fact to fact in a direction determined by the reader rather than by the book. Fiction fans (which, remember, include most of the people involved in teaching and encouraging a boy to read) don't always understand this pleasure in random facts, but what they need to know is that the boy so inclined is making up the story for himself, just as he does when scrutinizing a map or the statistics on a ball game or player.

Not every reader likes fiction. Many boys (and men) comfortable with paragraphed text still prefer nonfiction: biographies, history, how-to books, or books about science. Marc Aronson speaks to that in his essay on nonfiction ("Cinderella Without the Fairy Godmother"), but also bear in mind that these readers are likely to go beyond the offerings of bound books in search of disparate sources of information that can be put together like Legos by the reader. There's a difference, some boys will insist, between being interested in dinosaurs and being interested in *reading about* dinosaurs, which only looks like a distinction without a difference to a reader.

Your best chance of getting a non-book reader to value books is to show him what books can do that other media cannot. While the Internet contains more information, useless and otherwise, than *Guinness,* that book remains one of the most popular in the world and derives its considerable status and lucrative spinoff franchises because it *is* a book. It has boundaries and a defined scope. It is *printed:* no take-backs until the next year's edition. Specious or not, it has authority and gets respect. It has the last word. Expert, true, definitive, big: books are really good at being all these things.

THE MASCULINITY CHART

ROBERT LIPSYTE

Two bogus books I found in a public library a week apart when I was young are the reason I write novels for teenage boys. I am forever grateful.

Back in the forties and fifties, my dad took me and my sister to the library every week. We could take out as many books as we could carry, and he never censored our choices.

I found the first bogus book in the science section, where I often trolled for sex ed books. After a quick peek inside for revealing pictures, *The New You and Heredity* looked promising. I tucked it in the middle of my usual stack to check out: Steinbeck, John R. Tunis, Spanish explorer epics.

I read *The New You and Heredity* under the covers with a flashlight in case I found what I was looking for. But before that naked lady could show up, I came across the "masculinity chart."

Standing atop the chart were test pilots, engineers, and athletes. At the bottom were teachers, librarians, and writers. Even then, I knew which end of the chart I was headed toward. And I believed the chart was true. It was in a *book,* something I dreamed of writing someday. And it was about *science,* something of which I knew nothing but its infallible power. (It would be a long time before I found out that *junk books* and *junk science* are not necessarily oxymorons.)

I was in despair. Just as I was coming into the age when boys start wondering what it takes to be a real man, I had proof I'd never make it. I wanted to talk it over with Dad, but he was a teacher. I didn't want to make him feel bad.

Even now, I can't laugh at that long, miserable week. The battle of boyhood is tough enough without a bad book sneering at your future.

But I hadn't given up hope. The following week, when I returned *The New You and Heredity* to the library, I began searching the shelves in sections I rarely visited. It was in the travel section that I found *The Royal Road to Romance* by Richard Halliburton.

His energy and enthusiasm lifted my spirits. I was particularly taken by the way he would swim across crocodile-infested waters with a typewriter strapped to his back and a knife in his teeth. He'd carve up anything that tried to stop him. And then he'd write about it. Even then, I didn't totally buy his stories, and now they seem as spurious as the masculinity chart. But they throbbed with possibility.

When I finally returned that book several months later — I kept renewing it — I swaggered past the science shelves. Just try to put Richard at the bottom of your dumb chart, old *New You*. He'll carve his way to the top. And I'll be right behind him.

STATS

MARC ARONSON

As far as I can recall, I did not have a clear sense of "boy" or "girl" reading as a child. I enjoyed the books we were assigned in school, especially the nonfiction, like Loren Eiseley's *The Immense Journey* (the book that taught me the meaning of ecology) and Gavin Maxwell's *Ring of Bright Water* (a beautiful book on otters). But my sense of reading changed the summer I was eleven, going on twelve.

I was at Camp Thoreau, as Red Diaper a camp as could be. Two of the counselors were Robbie and Mike Meeropol (the astute reader will recognize them as the sons of Julius and Ethel Rosenberg). I believe Paul Robeson's grandson was there. We sang "Last Night I Had the Strangest Dream" and believed in disarmament. I distinctly recall being in a common room with older kids who were reading the publications of Youth Against War and Fascism, one of which included the Port Huron Statement—the founding document of SDS (Students for a Democratic Society), the very personification of the New Left.

That summer, though, neither science nor politics held my attention. A boy a few years older than me introduced me to APBA. We never knew what the initials stood for, but these were cards filled with numbers, derived from the actual stats of a baseball player (we played teams from the previous year, but you could also buy famous teams, such as the 1927 Yankees). You rolled a pair of dice and looked at what that roll meant for your batter; then, depending on the defensive points of the nine players your opponent had selected, you knew what had happened. I still remember that seven was a single, and if there was a runner on first, he reached third and the batter advanced to second on the throw. Six was a double, twelve a home run.

That summer, I found reading numbers to be an emotional experience. That summer, I learned that numbers can carry a whole narrative, that numbers can be devastating. That summer cured me of any impulse to gamble — it hurt too much to lose. That summer I began to love not just playing sports but poring over stats and picturing what they meant.

I did not stop reading the books we were assigned in school. And I joined a socialist party (I think it was the Socialist Workers). But what really happened to me that summer was that for the first time I felt the terrifying power of sports stats — the scorecard of life. I truly hated losing; I yearned to win. Only as an adult would I look back on that summer and think of what I was doing as "boy" reading. To me, then, it was the whole world, everything, on the roll of a die and a number on a card.

P.S. This morning my older son was waiting in line with the other six- and seven-year-olds for the bus to take him to school. He had a pack of shiny new baseball cards. Soon the line turned into a huddle — every boy pressing to get in closer, to catch a glimpse of those amazing numbers: I could hear them chattering away about lifetime stats. I was seeing in the twenty-first century precisely what I recalled from 1962: avid, passionate boy reading.

AN INTERVIEW WITH

JON SCIESZKA

ROGER SUTTON: You've built a second career on getting boys to read. Why don't they? What are you trying to fix?

JON SCIESZKA: I'm trying to fix that boys never give reading a chance. They're so impulsive and so into instant gratification, or else they turn off reading because of an experience like having to read a particular book for school. Which is what happened to my son in third grade: *Little House on the Prairie* was the one required summer-reading book. To his credit, he read the whole thing, but he just kept saying, "Nothing's happening!" Finally he decided, "All right, that's reading, then. That's not for me. I'll play hockey instead." It killed me to see him give up on reading before he had the chance to find something he really liked.

Of course, not everybody has to read really well, because I think we also tyrannize kids that way and say everybody has to love reading; reading is magic. And it's *not* magic for those guys — and many girls as well — it's really hard work. I think we come across to kids as too heavy-handed, saying that reading is wonderful, and if you don't find it so, you're a bad person.

RS: Or even if we do say reading is fun, we sometimes give them books that *we* think are fun but kids don't.

JS: Yeah. I think a lot of boys get the impression that reading equals school. And they see school as a bunch of adults telling them what to do. Reading gets tangled up in that, like a bad taste for them. It's interesting: in a lot of studies, boys will say they're not readers, but when the studies (like those reported in *"Reading Don't Fix No Chevys"* by Smith and Wilhelm) actually tracked what boys did read, they read a ton of stuff! Nonfiction, magazines, newspapers, computer manuals. Those are the storytelling styles that boys prefer — humor or nonfiction or comic books or graphic novels. Those are all different literacies, but they're never counted as reading. And audiobooks should count, too. Our definition of "real reading" is way too narrow.

MORE GREAT BOY BOOKS

P. B. Kerr, *One Small Step*

309 pp. Grades 5–7. NASA asks thirteen-year-old Scott, son of an air force flight instructor, to man a pre-*Apollo 11*, top-secret spaceflight to the moon with a crew of chimponauts. Kerr makes the wouldn't-it-be-cool-to-be-an-astronaut dream a reality here, with a story that's entirely plausible yet thoroughly imaginative.

Jeff Kinney, *Diary of a Wimpy Kid: Rodrick Rules*

217 pp. Grades 4–6. Greg might not be the most reliable narrator, but in his characteristic hand-printed diary format with line drawings on every page, he reports life as a middle brother with humor and just the right accent of whiny pessimism.

Ann M. Martin, *Everything for a Dog*

211 pp. Grades 4–7. The stories of two boys (Charlie, who finds solace in his dog after his older brother dies in an accident, and Henry, who longs for a dog but can't have one) and a stray dog named Bone begin separately but intersect in a moving conclusion. Far from an ordinary dog story, this is a fine book about life, death, forgiveness, and love.

Rosanne Parry, *Heart of a Shepherd*

163 pp. Grades 4–6. Set in the cattle-and-sheep country of eastern Oregon, this first novel chronicles sixth-grader Brother's year of hard work (lambing, calving), danger (a rattlesnake, a fire), and worry about his father's safety as a soldier on duty in Iraq. Brother's honest voice conveys an emotional terrain as thoughtfully developed as the western landscape Parry evokes.

Gary Paulsen, *Lawn Boy*

88 pp. Grades 5–7. When the twelve-year-old narrator's grandmother gives him a lawn mower, he decides he might as well earn a few bucks. Before he knows it, he's an entrepreneur. With all the energy of a bull market, this is a brief, accessible farce, with summer escapism written all over it.

Pam Muñoz Ryan, illustrations by Peter Sís, *The Dreamer*
374 pp. Grades 3–6. Although terrified by his autocratic father, Neftalí
Reyes grows up with a voracious love of words, books, nature, and ideas.
Sís's imaginative illustrations and the Chilean-rainforest-green type are
striking complements to Ryan's perceptive fictional account of poet Pablo
Neruda's early life.

Roland Smith, *Peak*
246 pp. Grades 5–8. Fourteen-year-old Peak is a natural-born climber.
Smith takes classic plot elements—kid in trouble, physical challenge,
overly ambitious parent—and plays them perfectly. The gripping story
pulls no punches about the toll Everest exacts on body and psyche.

Gary Soto, *Mercy on These Teenage Chimps*
147 pp. Grades 5–8. Ronnie and his best friend, Joey, (both thirteen)
are changing, with long gangly arms and awkward chimplike behavior. A
rollicking novel about the painful beginnings of adolescence.

Elissa Brent Weissman, *The Trouble with Mark Hopper*
229 pp. Grades 4–7. Sixth-grader Mark Geoffrey Hopper deserves his reputation for being a mean-spirited, superior smarty-pants; shy, nice fellow
sixth-grader Mark Geoffrey Hopper has just moved to town. When the two
Marks are thrown together for a project, they begin to learn skills from
each other and become tentative friends. Realistic school interactions and
believable characters give this novel both kid appeal and substance.

Tim Wynne-Jones, *Rex Zero and the End of the World*
186 pp. Grades 5–7. At the height of the Cold War, Rex's family moves to
Ottawa, where he joins a neighborhood gang tracking down an escaped pan-
ther. Wynne-Jones sets the enormity of the possibility of world destruction against the equally cataclysmic concerns of childhood, all magnified
by Rex's vivid imagination. Sequels: *Rex Zero, King of Nothing; Rex Zero, the
Great Pretender.*

Chapter Eight
MESSAGES

Introduction
Roger Sutton

I was in junior high school when "the American tribal-love rock musical" *Hair* was huge with kids, that generation's *Rent*. Few of us were actually allowed to see it (the show famously featured nudity, and it was briefly banned in Boston for that and for the onstage desecration of an American flag), but we had the record and knew all the songs. We also knew enough not to play it within earshot of our parents, but one afternoon when I *thought* I was safe, my mother overheard a lyric containing the word *motherfucker* and hollered. I also had a paperback that had been made from the show's script, which, upon discovery, my mother literally—and ceremoniously—put in the trash.

My parents were not generally censorious people, but something about *Hair* set my mother off. And something about the way I deeply resented her actions still exhibits itself in me forty years later: when there's a question of parental prerogative versus a child's reading interests, I'm with the kid.

Hair seems tame now, as usually happens with objects of censorship viewed in hindsight, and parents today have by and large been diverted by hotter (in several senses) mediums to leave their children's reading in peace. But the impulse to control such material remains, maybe not in *you,* but in parents of a less enlightened sort. Unless there is something that shocks / horrifies / angers you in your kids' book choices, (a) they are hiding something from you, or (b) they aren't reading enough.

Part of what reading is all about is the way it allows us to independently define ourselves. Children should be reading books that contradict their parents' declared interest: it's a way to test those interests, to see if they work or how they might work better. And even when a parent honestly embraces a child's right to read freely, there still will be times when your child needs to read secretly a book you don't know about. Don't make them talk.

Censorship is just one controversial topic that has attended children's reading throughout time. Others include perennial questions about didacticism (Does a book "send the right message"?); bibliotherapeutic usefulness (Does reading a book about death help a grieving child? What do we mean by "help"?); the changing notions of what constitutes a family; and, most persistently, sex. The following essays try to provide some answers.

What Makes a Good Sex Ed Book?

Christine Heppermann

Growing up Catholic, I was always afraid of something: unconfessed sins; demonic possession; Sister Alice, my grade-school principal, who once clamped her talons on my shoulder and marched me to her office for having a boy's name Magic-Markered across my palm while receiving Holy Communion. But the one thing that gave me recurring nightmares was the idea that just praying to have a baby could get me knocked up.

One Sunday, maybe riffing on the Old Testament plight of Abraham and Sarah, our pastor's sermon involved the story of two parishioners, a husband and wife, who had been trying for years to have a child. This was in the 1970s, pre–Louise Brown, and apparently the only infertility treatment readily available to the couple was prayer. They prayed together; our pastor prayed with them; and, lo and behold, these prayers were answered: a week earlier, our pastor had baptized the couple's one-month-old daughter.

The adults in the congregation applauded this happy ending, while my seven-year-old mind began spinning faster than Linda Blair's head in *The Exorcist*. Of course I wasn't *planning* on praying for a baby, but what if I did so *accidentally*? What if I asked God for a hamster or black Converse high-tops but somehow worded my request unclearly and wound up pregnant instead?

According to psychologist Anne C. Bernstein's book *Flight of the Stork,* in which the author analyzes a series of interviews she conducted with children in the 1970s to see what they knew about human reproduction, there were lots of other confused kids out there besides me. There was the young boy Bernstein interviewed who, presumably having been told the sperm-and-egg story by his parents, figured that, since he came from an egg, he must be a chicken. There was the preschool-age girl who stopped eating because she believed she had "a baby in her tummy," just like her pregnant mother did, and she feared that "were she to eat, all that yucky food would bury her wonderful baby." Not every child with creative ideas about their origins develops such fears, but Bernstein's research led her to the logical conclusion that providing children with straightforward, accurate information about sex and reproduction lessened their anxiety.

It's a mission that sex education books for children ideally should be able to help parents fulfill, because, let's face it, parents need the help. I certainly don't want my two daughters to be on constant red alert for virgin birth. Yet when my seven-year-old plunked down next to me while I was folding laundry and asked me how I *knew* I wasn't ever going to have another baby, I started stammering, momentarily terrified by the realization that I couldn't very well explain birth control without also explaining what needed to be controlled.

Even with the best of intentions, writes Bernstein, "Many parents still find it difficult to talk about reproduction with their children. Their own emotional discomfort in talking about sex is one stumbling block, and their lack of information about what the child is really asking and is likely to understand is another." Reading a good sex education book with my daughter gives me a script to consult when I get flustered. It's not as if I need someone to feed me all my lines, but I also don't want to just stumble onto the stage to improvise and, in my stage fright, risk conveying a message I didn't mean to convey.

It's too bad Robie H. Harris and Michael Emberley's *It's NOT the Stork!: A Book about Girls, Boys, Babies, Bodies, Families, and Friends* wasn't around for the parents of the little girl with the baby-in-the-tummy belief — a still-common explanation for pregnancy, one I've unthinkingly used myself. Bernstein's interviewee would have been quickly set straight by their "Pregnant Woman at the Movies" page. Here Emberley's welcoming cartoon art depicts a mother-to-be in her theater seat, chomping on snacks, while an interior view of her torso clearly shows the distinction between "popcorn in the stomach" and "fetus in the uterus."

Since the 1994 publication of *It's Perfectly Normal: Changing Bodies, Growing Up, Sex, and Sexual Health* for adolescents, Harris and Emberley have established themselves as the go-to duo for thorough, accessible books on human sexuality for children, and their audiences just keep getting younger. Next in the series is *It's So Amazing!: A Book about Eggs, Sperm, Birth, Babies, and Families*, which speaks to readers ages seven and up, while *Stork!* is designed for kids as young as four.

A 2005 *New York Times* article by Jodi Kantor titled "Sex Ed for the Stroller Set" articulates the sensible rationale behind the growing trend toward early sex education: "According to this approach, toddlers should learn words like 'vulva' at the same time they learn 'ears' and 'toes,' benign-sounding myths about storks and seeds constitute harmful misinformation, and any child who can ask about how he or she was created is old enough for a truthful answer." Thus, Harris and Emberley label the anus as well as the elbow on their side-by-side drawings of a boy and girl at bath time, and relate anatomical details that even adults might find enlightening, such

as the distinction between the vagina (interior) and the opening to
the vagina (exterior), and the illustration depicting a circumcised
versus an uncircumcised penis.

But naming body parts is one thing; talking about what they can
be used for is another. Even parents comfortable doing the former

This cartoon sequence from Robie Harris and Michael Emberley's accessible *It's
So Amazing!: A Book about Eggs, Sperm, Birth, Babies, and Families* (intended
for readers ages seven and up) uses humor and a matter-of-fact approach to
present sex as an integral part of what it means to be a person.

activity with their preschooler might still have to steady themselves when they reach chapter ten of *It's NOT the Stork!* and see Emberley's illustration of a blissful couple lying together in bed — woman on top — hearts floating in the air above them, a blanket covering their naked midsections. Although Harris includes a disclaimer for readers about how "children are much too young to do the special kind of loving — called 'sex' — that grownups do," she does directly address the mechanics of baby making, i.e., "this kind of loving happens when the woman and the man get so close to each other that the man's penis goes inside the woman's vagina."

Her definition almost makes intercourse sound accidental — "Whoops, got too close to each other again!" — but at least children aren't left to concoct their own possibly unsettling renditions of exactly how the egg and the sperm meet. They'll know sperm doesn't travel via hand-to-hand contact, like cold germs, or squiggle across the swings at the park.

Harris's emphasis on sex as an adult activity could also be construed as reassurance. Children tend to view sexual intercourse as "silly" or "gross," so most will probably be relieved to hear they don't have to engage in such shenanigans any time soon. When I was a teenager, I babysat for a ten-year-old girl who told me she planned to adopt babies instead of giving birth to them herself, not because she wanted to avoid the pain of labor, but because she was never, ever going to do "that," at which point she frowned and shuddered, as if she were talking about enduring multiple root canals.

Or is Harris's adults-only directive really there to reassure parents, who might assume that the humorously entwined couple in Emberley's cartoon will prompt five-year-olds to leap into bed together? Sex educator Deborah M. Roffman, in her book *Sex and Sensibility: The Thinking Parent's Guide to Talking Sense About Sex*, bemoans the "two uniquely American myths" that hamper our society's ability to openly discuss sex with children. "The first is that although knowledge is a good thing, sexual knowledge might not be (the old 'tell them about it and they'll go right out and do it' bugaboo). The second is that giving information . . . is the same thing as giving permission." Having worked with children for many years and having observed the more forthright approach to sex education prevalent in most other developed countries, Roffman has concluded that "talking openly about sex tacitly gives a child permission, all right, but only to do just that: to talk and to think, to reason, to understand, to clarify, to ask questions, and to come back later and talk some more. And to see us as credible and trusted sources of information."

And here's my question: even if books like *Stork!* do heighten children's curiosity about their bodies, is this really such a bad thing? I suspect that Harris and Emberley would say no, but have their voices been tempered by today's socially conservative culture? In journalist Judith Levine's book *Harmful to Minors: The Perils of Protecting Children from Sex*, a sex educator is quoted as saying that twenty-first-century America has mainstream sex education and right-wing sex education but no left-wing sex education. Sure, sex education books no longer admonish children that they will develop epilepsy or start wetting the bed if they "self-abuse," the way Victorian-era treatises did. Still, what's published today, even Harris and Emberley's body-positive, celebratory fare, stops short of letting kids in on the whole truth: one of the best things about human sexuality, in addition to generating the miracle of birth, is that it gives people pleasure.

Ironically, for a truly progressive approach to sex education for children, I had to look to the past. I was combing through the juvenile birds-and-bees section at my local library one day when I happened upon several copies of a small, battered paperback called *A Kid's First Book About Sex*. Written more than two decades ago by Joani Blank (founder of the revolutionary San Francisco female-friendly sex-toy store Good Vibrations), it made *Stork!* seem almost puritanical by comparison.

A Kid's First Book About Sex sounds like it belongs on the board-book shelf—colors, shapes, numbers, and . . . sex!—and in fact it proclaims right off the bat that it is aimed at "girls and boys whose bodies haven't started to change into grown-ups' bodies." Then it goes on to freely admit that, unlike most sex ed books for the younger set, it won't "say much about how babies are made and born" because "making babies is an important part of sex, but there are lots of other things kids want to know about sex!"

Like what things? How about how an orgasm feels? Blank, with accompanying black-and-white cartoons by Marsha Quackenbush, compares it to, among other satisfying sensations, "climbing up the ladder of a big slide and whooshing down" and "sneezing after your nose has been tickling." And she encourages dialogue, asking readers questions ("Isn't [masturbation] a big word for something almost everyone does? Did you ever hear any other words for masturbation?") and humorously indicating the different reactions such questions might provoke in parents. ("If you ask your mom or dad a question about sex, how will they look? This one is pleased or happy. This one is scared. This one is embarrassed. . . . This one is running away.")

As a parent of girls who have been known to dance around with their friends in Disney Princess gowns, lip-synching to Avril Lavigne, shaking their booties, and calling each other "sexy," I particularly appreciate the section in Blank's book where she tries to help kids come up with their own definition for that ubiquitous word. Instead of dismissing *sexy* as a grown-up term not applicable to children, the way I clumsily did once with my oldest daughter, she names different feelings—giggly, excited, happy, weird, warm, or "just different"—and asks "How does a sexy feeling feel to you?" Blank leads kids to the refreshing conclusion that "sexy" isn't just about Hannah Montana (I suppose back then it would have been Christie Brinkley) in tight pants. Ideally, it's about exuding confidence and having a healthy body image. In Blank's words, "A sexy person is someone who . . . really likes herself or himself, and shows it."

Do young children really need the kind of explicit information Blank proffers? Well, as Harris points out in *It's NOT the Stork!*'s section on male anatomy, "Baby boys even have erections before they are born, while they are growing inside their mothers' bodies." It's hard to deny that we are all sexual beings from birth. Telling kids the nuts and bolts of where babies come from seems easy in comparison to helping them sort through the sexual feelings and moral and emotional issues that only grow more complex as they get older. Blank and Harris and Emberley don't present sex as an isolated act but as an integral part of what it means to be a person. The more comfortable we make children early on with this mindset, the better equipped they will be to grapple with their sexuality in all its glory.

Reading about Families in My Family

Megan Lambert

In my family there are two moms and five kids. I've yet to find a children's book that depicts a cast of characters that looks *anything* like our particular multiracial, foster-adoptive family constellation. I know there are lots of artistic, social, political, and market-driven reasons for this; for one thing, such a book would risk getting so bogged down in introducing everyone that it would be hard to come around to the story.

I used to worry about this. When my oldest child (a biracial, biological son) was also my only child, I scoured libraries, bookstores, and book lists to try to make sure that his books would be not only windows into others' experiences but mirrors of his own. Fat chance of finding such a mirror that went beyond a reflection of surface appearance and into a fully realized story. In the end, despite my best efforts to find books to celebrate his nontraditional familial reality, Rory didn't much care that Heather had two mommies or that black is brown is tan; he was far more interested in the adventures of Captain Underpants and Sylvester and his magic pebble, thank you very much, and I couldn't really blame him.

I began to think that much of my fretting over building a multicultural, LGBT-inclusive children's book collection was the product of visiting adult preoccupations on my child. I had the good intentions of wanting to provide a literary world that reflected the life experiences that we shared as a multiracial, two-mom family. But I realized that this was the world I'd built as an adult. My son was included in that world, but he also had a world of his own devising: informed by me and by his other mom, of course, but more and more uniquely *his* as he grew up and made his own friends, followed his own passions, tastes, and interests, and formulated his own visions for the world.

Of course, following such a line of thinking is itself an argument for the creation of books that tell stories from different vantage points. A child raised by straight parents who will grow up to be gay would be well served by children's books that depict families with two mommies or two daddies, right? After all, my son's world, occupied as it was by the stuff of preschool, was also one in which he imagined the adult he would become. Once, while reading *Homemade Love* by bell hooks and Shane W. Evans, Rory said something to me along the lines of, "I like reading this book about a family with all brown people because maybe someday I will grow up and have a family like that, too." Eureka! I exhaled alongside overburdened Heather and her mommies and the black and brown and tan family and realized that Rory had a point. Reading children's books isn't all about looking at the here-and-now; it's also about thinking about up-ahead-and-later.

But there are limits to this vision of aspirational children's literature, based on a child's perceptions of adult life. One day Rory announced that he was going to marry his friends Andy, Tim, and Rose. Never once did it cross my mind that I was raising a future bisexual polygamist. What I understood from this declaration was that four-year-old Rory really liked his friends Andy, Tim, and Rose. A preschooler doesn't really get what marriage is, because it's an adult institution. That's why, when the prince-in-search-of-a-*prince* picture book *King & King* came out (as it were), I felt that this was a book aimed more at well-intentioned, anti-homophobic adults than at children.

Nevertheless, I think there *is* space for children's books that address what it is to grow up and what it is to be an adult, books that move beyond glorifying and romanticizing childhood with a nostalgic tone that smacks of a tragic loss of innocence; after all, one of the main tasks of childhood is to leave it. Don't get me wrong; I'm not saying that I believe the children are our future. It's more complicated than that: I believe the children are *their* future, and yes, I guess I believe the children are our future, too. But I am leery of songs, children's books, and platitudes that focus only on this last belief. It's all just a little too "and a little child shall lead them" for me. I don't much like burdening children, real or imaginary, with the expectation that through their perceived innocence and charming naiveté they will save the world as they inherit it. This is different from acknowledging, celebrating, and supporting the fact — in literature and in life — that growing up is not a tragedy but a birthright.

And, just as importantly, I believe the children are our present, too, and *their* present. And that's why I am still on the lookout for books that depict different kinds of families and different kinds of being in the world. Even if it's a stretch to imagine that my particular family (Puerto-Rican-Caucasian-Jamaican-African-American-biracial-two-moms-with-five-kids-foster-adoptive-with-some-bio-ties) will ever see itself in print, I like to think that if there's room for Heather and her mommies, there's room for more of their friends, too.

What Ails Bibliotherapy?
Maeve Visser Knoth

Mention the word *bibliotherapy* and children's librarians and book-sellers have similar tales to tell. The stories go something like this: a well-intentioned parent comes in and asks for a book about death. When questioned further, she explains that her child's grandmother is dying and the child needs some books to help her understand what is happening. The librarian or bookseller suggests several picture books that deal, in one way or another, with death. Each time the woman is handed a book, the librarian or bookseller tells her a little about it. Each time, the woman rejects the choice. "No, *The Tenth Good Thing About Barney* won't do. That's about a *dog* dying. I told you it was a *grandmother*. No, *Grandpa Abe* won't do either, because it's about a grand*father*. Oh, no, I know you said this next lovely book is about a grandmother, but the grandma in this book has cancer. My daughter's grandmother is dying from congestive heart failure." And so it goes. The parent is looking for something that exactly mirrors her own life.

Teachers also, with the very best of intentions, search for books that will address the emotional lives of the children in their care. One student's family is going through a divorce, so let's gather some divorce stories to help him. Another child is experiencing the jealousy that often comes along with a new baby in the house, so let's read her some of those new-baby picture books. There are excellent books on each of these subjects; why am I so reluctant to hand them over?

The more I think about my aversion to this kind of bibliotherapy, the more I define my own approach to children and books as a kind of "advance" bibliotherapy. Rather than address what is happening in the present, I'm inclined to prepare children for the many kinds of emotional experiences they will have *before* they occur. I would rather inoculate children than treat the symptoms of the emotional trauma. We give children vaccinations against measles. We can't vaccinate against divorce, but we *can* give children some emotional knowledge to use when they, or their friends, do go through a divorce. I advocate that we read picture books about death and divorce and new babies when no one is dying, when a marriage is strong, before anyone is pregnant.

When I was in sixth grade, the mother of one of my classmates died from cancer. Ours was a small school, so we all knew Jill's mother. We knew what kind of cupcakes she was likely to pack in Jill's lunch and what kind of car she drove on field trips. The death of a parent had been, up to that time, unthinkable to me. I remember that I worried about my own mother, but more than that, I remember knowing that Jill's behavior might be affected by her mother's death. I remember thinking that if Jill refused to take turns on the monkey bars or if she pushed her way to the head of the lunch line, she might be doing these things because she was sad. No adult ever told me this, but I had read scores of books about children without parents. I knew that the orphaned Mary Lennox in *The Secret Garden* was a terrible brat because she was miserable, not because she chose to be; I understood, on an emotional level, what it might be like to be motherless.

Fast-forward many years. I now have two children and can observe and contribute to their own reading choices. I try to avoid direct bibliotherapy, although of course we read books for factual information when facts help to prepare for new experiences: Fred Rogers's *Going to the Dentist* and Janet and Allan Ahlberg's *Starting School,* for example. But I also make a point of reading books about the "hard" stuff long before my children might need their emotional information. We have read books about racism, books about adjusting to a new school and town, and books in which children are dealing with alcoholic parents.

Sharing emotionally complex books before a difficult experience occurs may give children the ability to practice their own personal bibliotherapy. Several days after her pet rat died, my daughter, Anya, found Robie H. Harris's *Goodbye Mousie* on a bookshelf and read it to herself again and again. When, at age four, she broke her arm, she searched the shelves for Lynne Rae Perkins's *The Broken Cat* and kept it on her bedside table as a daily selection until her arm finished healing. In both these cases she already knew these stories and sought them out herself: Anya decided when she was ready to read about the death of a beloved pet; Anya decided that she needed to revisit a story of injury and healing. My only contribution was a full, varied home bookshelf and a willingness to read to her.

As a parent and librarian, I continue to recommend that parents read all kinds of emotionally complex books to their children. Read *Bridge to Terabithia* aloud to your kids, even if it does make you cry. Consider it a kind of vaccination.

AN INTERVIEW WITH

KATHERINE PATERSON

KATHERINE PATERSON: I get in trouble because my stories aren't propaganda. With propaganda, you think you have an answer and you try to impart it. In story, you're searching: you've got a question and your story is your way of looking for an answer, not giving one. You can't lay down answers for people in stories. Stories are always open for the reader to learn what he or she is able to learn or needs to learn or wants to learn. I think that's one reason people like Jesus better than they like Saint Paul, because Jesus tells stories, and they're open-ended. Wonderful stories, the parables. You get to the end of one and you think, "Well, then what happened?" And it's left open for you.

ROGER SUTTON: I got an e-mail recently from an outraged person who saw our review of an evangelical book that we had panned for its pedestrian prose and amateurish illustrations. This person thought that what children need are answers, and this book had answers, in spades. So she would probably not accept a book of yours — you're saying that you, as the writer, are exploring right alongside the reader.

KP: Of course I am.

RS: When you write, are you seeking to answer a question, or are you still asking the question?

KP: I'm still asking the question. *Bridge to Terabithia* is the classic example, I guess. I wrote *Bridge* because my son's best friend was struck and killed by lightning, and I had cancer. I wrote it because everything was awful. How can you explain to your child why his best friend was struck by lightning? Well, you can't. But if you write a story, you've got to shape it. You've got to have a beginning and a middle and an end, and, at the end, the beginning and the middle have to make sense. So maybe in the story you can make sense of something that doesn't make sense in life. By the time I had finished with the book, it wasn't that I knew why a little girl had been struck by lightning or why I had cancer, it was that it made sense below the level of rational explanation.

RS: It's interesting, too, because you clearly wanted to explain a tragedy to your son, but you were also facing questions about yourself — why did I get cancer? It's not just about explaining something to your son, or to children in general.

KP: I realized at a very early point that the book was for me and not for David. Your first thought is that you're being altruistic and helpful and all that kind of stuff, but pretty soon you realize who you're writing for! You're not doing it for the kid. I mean, if you were doing it for somebody else, then it would be propaganda, right? Because you would think you had something to impart that this poor, ignorant person didn't know. And that's not the way you write a real story.

RS: I think of your books as being much more family fiction than children's fiction.

KP: I would love for families to read a book like *Bridge to Terabithia* or *The Great Gilly Hopkins* or *Flip-Flop Girl* together. I found, with my own children, that the books we read together became a sort of vocabulary for us, a way of talking about things that were hard to talk about. Sometimes all you have to do is invoke the name of a character, and the other person knows how you feel. I'd love to feel that my books were read that way.

PART FOUR
LEAVING THEM ALONE

Overview

Roger Sutton

O h, you're not out of the picture. You're *never* out of the picture. But adolescence is the stage in which readers begin to most acutely require privacy in their book selection and reading. This is only partly because of sex.

By the time they become teens, readers will be accustomed to making independent choices. It is the job of adults — parents, teachers, librarians — to make sure that a rich array of books is available for these readers to choose from.

Choice is the operative word — we would no more recommend giving *Forever . . .* , Judy's Blume's pre-condom, pre-AIDS classic of first love and sex, to a teen reader than we would endorse keeping it from her. A huge part of the pleasure of reading is picking out books for yourself, especially books that speak to a place inside you that you're currently keeping under wraps. The late Mike Printz (after whom the Michael L. Printz Award for Young Adult Literature was named) was a high-school librarian in Topeka, Kansas, and in his library he always kept a box of books that kids were free to take and return privately, with no need for checkout or a library card. They were books about sex and physical development, of course, but also on topics such as child abuse or alcoholism. Mike reasoned that the kids who most needed these books were also those who would be most afraid to be seen reading them. But even the healthiest, happiest teen needs to be able to be alone with a book, one that he has pursued, chosen, and read on his own.

Chapter Nine

BOOKS FOR TEENS

The Discovery of Like-Minded Souls
Roger Sutton

For a long time, young adult literature was narrowly conceived, first as "junior novels" about romance, careers, or sports, and then, in the late 1960s, concerned with social issues as exemplified in the lessons learned by a teen protagonist. Gangs (*The Outsiders*), drugs (*Tuned Out*), runaways (*Go Ask Alice*), mental illness (*Lisa, Bright and Dark*), child abuse (*Don't Hurt Laurie!*), alcoholism (*The Late Great Me*), and incest (*Abby, My Love*) were all favorite topics. While these books were intended as a kind of bibliotherapy, allowing young teen readers an easy, nonthreatening entry into sensitive topics, they were more often read as adventure stories, providing bookish junior-high kids with vicarious thrills about life on the wild side. I'm a little old to have been an audience for these books, but I remember the similar charge I got out of David Wilkerson's *The Cross and the Switchblade*, a 1963 memoir of Wilkerson's ministry to hardened teens on the streets of New York. I completely ignored the book's heavy Christian evangelical message to focus on the sordid but enthralling tales of gang fights and heroin addiction. But if I did not become "born again" as a result of reading this book, neither did I start mainlining "horse." I stayed the dweeby little egghead I was. Critics of these books (and *Go Ask Alice* is still frequently banned in school libraries today) made the same mistake that proponents did: each assumed that such books would "do something" to (or for) young readers. Both positions assume that reading does something it does not. While a novel about, say, drug abuse, will give a reader information and points to consider, it won't get him high. It also won't scare him straight, either — books don't work this way.

You know this. When you read some morbid Swedish murder mystery or sex-soaked Jackie Collins romp, you know it's a story, not a set of instructions. But our laudable and instinctive desire to protect our young (or, less charitably, our shortsighted and futile desire to *control* our young) leads us to believe that they read differently from us, that they are "impressionable." We all are. If reading didn't have an effect on us, we wouldn't do it; the mistake is in thinking that the effect is as simple as how-to, for kids or for ourselves.

In its beginnings, young adult literature was a subset of children's literature, YA books being published by the same publishing divisions as children's books were. But while you could find a children's book on just about any subject, YA limited itself to realistic (more or less) treatments of contemporary teen life. Through the 1980s, the genre was overwhelmingly populated by short novels set in the present, often with a first-person teen narrator (who was most often white), about some aspect of teen life. The canvases and casts of characters were small, and the plots generally followed a formula: a teen has a problem of a personal nature, has some melodrama, learns (along with readers) about the problem's parameters, and overcomes it. Happy endings were the rule, one most famously broken by Robert Cormier, who, in novels such as *The Chocolate War* and *I Am the Cheese* let the bad guys win. There were some expert practitioners, such as M. E. Kerr (*Dinky Hocker Shoots Smack!; Gentlehands*) and Richard Peck (*Are You in the House Alone?; Remembering the Good Times*), who brought distinctive voices and humor to the genre, but it was a fairly narrow field. But YA books were only ever meant to be one aspect of teenage reading. Along with problem novels and teen romance paperbacks, teens were reading such popular adult authors as Stephen King, V. C. Andrews, and Mary Higgins Clark. Teenagers provided the backbone of science fiction and fantasy publishing, and almost all of their non-fiction interests were served by books for adults. "YA literature" has never been synonymous with "what teenagers read."

Problem novels have remained popular while they gained in sophistication. In Laurie Halse Anderson's 1999 *Speak*, high-school freshman Melinda isn't talking, barely managing monosyllabic responses in class and at home, silently enduring the taunts of classmates for her having called the cops to a party the previous summer. Her inner narration, though, is powerfully acidic as she epigrammatically catalogs the meannesses, both petty and deep, of high-school life: "Nothing good ever happens at lunch. The cafeteria is a giant sound stage where they film daily segments of Teenage Humiliation Rituals. And it smells gross." Eventually, we learn that Melinda was raped by an older boy, Andy, at that party, and the book ends with Melinda holding a shard of glass to his neck while she reminds him of what she had said at the party: "I said no." While the success of *Speak* inspired a flurry of teen novels about elective muteness, those rather missed what made Anderson's book so magnetic. *Speak* is about a girl on her own with a terrifying secret. She is silent but watchful and smarter than just about everyone else in the story. You can see how this might be appealing. Silent and watchful and feeling smarter is part of what being a reader is all about. And *Speak* spoke to undedicated readers as well: the voice is smart and ironic but the style is crisp and immediate, and the fact that we don't know for quite a while exactly why Melinda isn't talking gives the book suspense.

It's worth repeating that *Speak* and other "problem novels" aren't meant to be read as problem solvers: in real life, a girl in Melinda's situation doesn't need a book; she needs help. Books help, yes;

reading helps, but it's not a case of connecting the dots. If you were a girl in Melinda's situation, the last thing you might want is a book that comes that close. But if you're a girl who feels different, misunderstood, maybe isolated (that is, if you feel like a reader), then this book could speak to you.

A counterpoint to *Speak* for boys could be Walter Dean Myers's *Monster,* published the same year. In the beginning of the book, Steve is jailed and awaiting trial for his alleged participation in a Harlem drugstore holdup that left the proprietor dead. No one is accusing Steve of the shooting or even of being in the store at the time; he's instead charged with casing the joint to make sure no customers would be there to witness the robbery. In court, Steve insists he wasn't even in the store that day, much less a co-conspirator, but . . . let's just say that Myers applies the standard of reasonable doubt to a whole lot of things in this novel, trusting his readers to find the truth. The first recipient of the Printz Award, *Monster* manages to be that rare thing, both reader-friendly and risk-taking. Structured as a screenplay for a movie written, directed, and "starring sixteen-year-old Steve Harmon as the Boy on Trial for Murder!" the book looks easy and fun to read, comprised mostly of dialogue and directions for settings and camera shots, with occasional grainy screen caps and handwritten excerpts from Steve's journal. At the same time, though, Myers is insistently reminding us that everything we're learning is from Steve's POV. It's a remarkably strategic use of first-person perspective in a genre where narrators can almost always be taken at their word. As is usual in YA literature, we're encouraged to identify with the protagonist, but the close questioning of his public defender and the prosecutor and the testimony of the robbers nibbles at our empathy, putting us in the interesting situation of identifying with the perhaps-guilty, not a frequent position for young adult readers, as readers, to be in. They can handle it.

From the 1990s, though, and perhaps precipitated by an increase in the numbers of teens, YA publishing broadened. The books got longer, and fantasy and science fiction, horror fiction, historical fiction, verse novels, and nonfiction joined traditional contemporary realism. There is more humor, too, mostly chick-lit romance

comedy of the *Bridget Jones's Diary* ilk. Perhaps most significantly, the YA books of today more often assume a high-school readership rather than the younger teens who once provided the largest audience for problem novels and Sweet Dreams romances: the "Gr. 7 and up, Age 12 and up" designation became "Gr. 9 and up, Age 14 and up." This is not necessarily because they are racier but because they are becoming more complex and in some cases indistinguishable from serious adult fiction.

The wild success of *Bridget Jones's Diary* not only inspired a whole genre of adult chick lit; it spawned junior versions as well, like Louise Rennison's popular, likable books about Georgia Nicolson. Ye Shall Know Them By Their Pink Covers! In turn, these lightly romantic comedies were inevitably joined by some faster big sisters. Series like Gossip Girl feature fairly hard-core "mean girls," boozing, and sex. While paperback junk has always been part of the teenage reading menu, Gossip Girl and the like don't make even the feeblest of gestures toward being "good for you." They provide a kind of *Go Ask Alice* vicarious thrill, but that of hot boys and glamorous clothes rather than drugs and running away.

When does a young adult book become an adult book? Whether there is a genuine distinction between books for children and books for adults, and what that distinction might be, are questions at the heart of children's literature scholarship. Writing in 1974, British critic John Rowe Townsend, acknowledging its difficulty, essentially threw up his hands at the question, saying "a children's book is one that appears on a publisher's children's list." But young adult books won't let us off that easily. Some books, for example, are adult books in one country and YA books here, or the other way round — *The Curious Incident of the Dog in the Night-Time* is an adult book here, but in the UK it was published as both young adult *and* adult — likewise for *The Spell Book of Listen Taylor* by Jaclyn Moriarty, published as an adult book in Australia but then re-edited for YA here. These

publishing vagaries are generally dictated by marketing departments and differing national conceptions of "teen reading," but
readers need not pay attention. High-school readers should and will
choose their books from all over the place. They read best sellers:
teens in no small part were responsible for the blockbuster success
of *Flowers in the Attic* and *A Child Called "It."* The teen audience is
crucial to sales of science fiction, fantasy, and graphic novels.

Adolescence is also a time for first efforts in ambitious reading,
like the Russian classics, or big-theory (and big-ass) books like Ayn
Rand's *Atlas Shrugged* or Neal Stephenson's *Cryptonomicon*. Despite
their appeal for generations of teen readers, such books contradict
received wisdom on What Teens Like. They do not star teen characters, they are not about the problems of everyday life, and they
often employ an array of narrative strategies beyond the first person. But the same teen who is tackling big-theme, large-cast books
may at the same time be reading Gossip Girl or even, at the end of a
very tough day, *Harry the Dirty Dog*. The point of being a skilled
reader is not to read increasingly difficult books, it's to allow you
scope: the pianist who has mastered the Piano Sonata in D by
Mozart doesn't forswear his earlier Sonata in C simply because it's
easier to play.

Books don't know who reads them, but books for adults assume
the reader is their equal. And it follows that, as readers, you and
your teenage children are equals, too. (If not competition — my
mother and I spent a week stealing Sidney Sheldon's *The Other Side
of Midnight* back and forth from each other.) Feel free to share, but
leave your kid plenty of room and privacy. The current vogue for
book clubs might lead one to think that the primary goal of reading is to have something to talk about with your friends. While
books do provide a durable kind of social glue, you might find that
your child is not especially interested in sticking to you. He or she
will probably be more interested in the pursuit or discovery of

like-minded souls, both within the pages of books and in like-minded fellows who see the brilliance of, for example, Neil Gaiman or Terry Pratchett or Francesca Lia Block. Should your child invite you in, by all means accept, but don't make the first move. Let your kid lead. Books require — and provide — privacy and independence.

Where Snoop and Shakespeare Meet

Janet McDonald

William Shakespeare asked, "To be, or not to be?" The Clash sang, "Should I stay or should I go?" Same conflict, different cadence. Charles Darwin posited the survival of the fittest. Snoop Dogg touts the dominance of the illest. Same attitude, different argot.

Brows come in high- and low-. Unfortunately for artist Frida Kahlo, actor Josh Hartnett, and Bert the Muppet, they also come in uni-. But unlike unibrows on faces, unibrow *literature* — the union of academy and street into a work that enlightens and entertains — is a thing of beauty. It has the power to bring into the literary fold young adults who are not merely *reluctant* readers but those who are downright averse to the written word.

As a young adult novelist, I aim for the tale and the telling that together will convey, in the cultural vernacular of the reader, my *intellectual* values. The transmission of *moral* values I leave to the literati preachers. My books house teen mothers, high-school drop-outs, shoplifting homeboys, preppy drug dealers, and girl arsonists. A few characters are gay; others are straight. Most strive to achieve a positive goal; some seek little more than their idle, pointless status quo. But it is not only the down-and-(nearly-)out who are represented. The cast also includes paralegals, college kids, teenage entrepreneurs, computer-savvy project girls, and budding artists.

I have been asked why the books I write don't paint a clear, bright line of judgment with regard to situations I depict, such as teenage pregnancy, vandalism, or fistfights. One person asked me simply why I didn't "get on a soapbox." Well, soapboxes are for soap, and soap is for washing clean. Books give off light, and light reveals the dirty, the clean, and the in-between. It is more important to me that young people read than that they behave well. Put more provocatively, closed legs are good, but an open mind is better.

I am not drawn to the pulpit — it is the podium that inspires me. And from my podium I write up, not down, to readers. I write about, although obviously not exclusively for, black teenagers. And contrary to what appears to be conventional wisdom, I see no problem evoking both T. S. Eliot and Missy Elliott, lacrosse and basketball, buggin' out and *Sturm und Drang*, pumpkin soup and BBQ spareribs, and generally whipping up a rich unibrow mix of do-rags, private schools, collard greens, blazers, hoodies, Bill Clinton, rap music, Basquiat, *ya mama* jokes, Harlem redstones, violin adagios, housing projects, three-story Colonials, baggy jeans, Dostoyevsky, graffiti, and flaming calla lilies.

My novel *Brother Hood* opens with Nathaniel, a black teenage boy, on a train reading *Crime and Punishment* — prompting a major publishing figure to suggest that I stop "showing off." Now, I admit to having something close to a fetish for Fyodor. I have read *Crime and Punishment* at least three times and his short story "The Double" half a dozen times. So naturally I want others to discover Dostoyevsky's powerful and engrossing tales. What *should* Nathaniel have been reading on that train ride home to Harlem? The latest sex, drugs, and gangbanger literature aimed at black teenagers? *VIBE* magazine? Why not expose kids to the classics along with more contemporary writing? After all, these works have endured through the centuries for a reason — they capture the human experience at its essence and thus withstand time and transcend race.

I receive numerous e-mails from young people. Many are self-described nonreaders who discovered a taste for literature through my books. They identify with and can understand certain language and vocabulary, which reflects how they or their friends talk. They like the humor, which leaves them, as one girl put it, "on tha flo" laughing. They identify with my taste in music and movies ("*Don't Be a Menace to South Central While Drinking Your Juice in the Hood* is my favorite movie, too!").

My fantasy is that some of those readers will be so delighted that they will follow with brimming curiosity the trails of crumbs I've dropped all along their path, right alongside the Ebonics wise-cracks and rap lyrics. They will read *Crime and Punishment* because Nathaniel in *Brother Hood* made it sound thrilling. They will get a dictionary and look up *doppelgänger, enigma, succubus,* and *xenophobia,* words that filled my character Raven Jefferson's head in *Spellbound.* Like *Chill Wind*'s Aisha Ingram, they will marvel at the fact that anyone would sell Manhattan for twenty-four dollars' worth of trinkets. I hope that everyone will learn the French words that pop up throughout my books and will be so intrigued by my shameless and constant promotion of Paris as the place to be that reader after reader will come and knock at my door. Inside, we'll dance to Snoop's latest and, over dinner, discuss *Hamlet.*

How long will I live? asks Snoop in "Murder Was the Case (Death After Visualizing Eternity)." Shakespeare gives the rapper an "hour upon the stage" to strut and fret. Their respective musings on mortality resonate and flow together like a Sunday sermon's call and response. It is by offering *both* that young adult literature will enrich readers.

What Makes a Good Thriller?

Nancy Werlin

For years, when my publisher tried to call my books mysteries, I insisted that they're thrillers. It's a lowbrow term, connoting blood, guns, and nefarious activities. Basically, thrillers tend to be about nasty people doing bad, illegal, and / or unethical things, although usually there's also a blameless individual around as protagonist who is endangered body and soul by these bad people and their immoral plans.

Louisa May Alcott wrote thrillers back before she turned into a respectable children's author. It's fascinating to get a glimpse of the joy Alcott took in penning tales of seductresses, drug addicts, and murderers. Similarly, readers of thrillers are looking for the vicarious, well, *thrill* of consorting with people who are no better than they should be, people who are doing things that shock us, make us afraid, and, if we are honest, excite us. Thrillers are a guilty-pleasure type of reading. Mysteries are almost respectable, but thrillers? No.

So it's certainly tempting to get defensive and declare that a good thriller is constructed from the same ingredients that make any good book: close intellectual attention to the braid of character, plot, and theme; strong writing that uses a considered mix of dialogue, exposition, and action and a minimum of adverbs; etc., etc. But this would be an evasion. Suspense thrillers are indeed different beasts, and writing a good one is not the same as writing any good mainstream literary novel, even when the two share many qualities.

Traditionally, a thriller requires a heroic (or at least semi-heroic) main character and a villain. The two alternately chase and circle each other around some crime. In my novel *The Killer's Cousin,* the crimes are concealed in the past. The hero, David Yaffe, is tormented and guilt-ridden. (The tormented hero is a popular American heroic variant: think Raymond Chandler.) So far, so standard. But in this, my first thriller, I got lucky in the characterization of the young villain, Lily. Because Lily is a child, David can't confront her physically, no matter how threatening she is. He's trapped. And therefore, so are the readers of the novel, as they imagine themselves in his place. You cannot, after all, bludgeon an eleven-year-old girl to death. Not even in your imagination. No matter how much you might want to.

The creation of suspense is not simple, I realized. And it is not really about "what happens at the end." You can't rely on making the reader afraid by keeping the eventual safety of the main character in doubt, for example. Frankly, the modern reader knows it's unlikely the hero will die or even sustain a major injury.

This realization caused me to make the reckless choice to give away the ending in my latest thriller. *The Rules of Survival* is about three children who are at the mercy of a woman who should never have been a mother in the first place. Right on page one, the oldest sibling, Matthew, explains that he is telling the story in retrospect. That all three kids are alive and doing fine. That everybody made it.

Having given away the ending, I was thrown on my resources as a writer to make the journey of the novel terrifying. This meant trying to make "what happens next" exciting and suspenseful, of course. But it also meant trying to find innovative ways to induce shared fear in the reader.

Contemplating the third draft, I had an idea. I rewrote the novel, abandoning the straightforward narrative I had used previously, and turned it into a long letter written by Matthew to his youngest sister. This means that there's not only an "I" telling the story, but also a "you" listening to the story. And although the "you" is nominally five-year-old Emmy, it's also you-the-reader — a fact that some readers will notice but that others will accept without considering how it operates on them.

This technical choice — writing in first person but using direct address — replaces the usual "How does it end?" uncertainty by seizing you-the-reader by the throat and taking you along on the Walsh children's journey through hell, not as observer but as participant.

Thus, you are Emmy Walsh. You are five years old. As the story begins, you do not even speak. But you're smart and observant, and, most of all, you're willful. Therefore, you don't always listen to your much-older brother and sister when they explain to you how to maneuver around Mommy and her scary, unpredictable ways.

Now, as you read that bit of description, you-the-reader should feel a little uneasy, perhaps even a little fearful. Because as you become Emmy, you realize: who cares about the safe ending? First, you have to get there. First, you have to go through hell.

The manipulative use of tension is what makes a thriller different from any other good book. But as you will also perceive, it is not quite as simple as saying that the tension must build higher and higher and higher. The skilled writer must also know when to lessen the tension, when to give the reader a break before, very soon, tightening the screws yet again. Harder. And the skilled writer will do that tightening in as innovative a way as possible, using whichever of the many tools in her writer's toolbox is best suited to the story at hand.

I have one more secret about writing thrillers to share. This one is not about technique, but about heart.

Fear has ruled me ever since I can remember. Not because my childhood was extraordinarily fear-filled. I think it is simply my temperament. I remember distinctly, for example, being ten years old and looking at illustrations of North America during the Ice Age. I plotted how my family would escape to Florida if the ice suddenly returned. I imagined us taking the last airplane out, fighting our way past other frantic refugees. We might have to kick, even to kill. I planned for that. Survival at all costs, I thought. For me. For those I love.

This same sentiment powers Matthew in *The Rules of Survival*. He says to his little sister — and to you-the-reader:

> This is what I think happens when you live with fear. . . . I think the fear gets into your blood. It makes your subatomic particles twist and distort. You change, chemically. The fear changes, too. It becomes . . . your master. You are a slave to it.

In writing suspense, I draw heavily on my own fear. In *The Rules of Survival*, I used that fear to write about a not-uncommon night-mare situation that I myself have never experienced. In my other novels, likewise: I have never killed anyone (*The Killer's Cousin*), never been kidnapped (*Locked Inside*), never stumbled onto a ille-gal drug distribution network (*Black Mirror*), and never found shady scientific experiments going on in the basement (*Double Helix*). But this is not to say that I have not experienced fear. Like Matthew and my other characters, I have lived it. And like Matthew, I work out my fears using writing. Thus I know exactly how to map my fear onto my characters, so that you-the-reader can feel its reality. You will feel it because my writing will force you, in turn, to map the characters' fears onto your own fears. To become one with them, and with me.

We all — adult, child, and teen alike — know what it is to fear. And we all want to learn how to handle our fear. Safely. Safely, within the pages of a book.

This, to me, is the pull of the thriller.

AN INTERVIEW WITH

SARAH DESSEN

ROGER SUTTON: You have very fervent fans.

SARAH DESSEN: They're fantastic — they buy the book the day it's released and read it incredibly quickly and then immediately e-mail me and ask when the next one is coming out! It's really the highest compliment. Young adults are an amazing audience to be writing for, because you're catching people at their most enthusiastic about reading. Adults are a little more reserved. I still get excited about good books, but I don't get jumping-up-and-down-screaming excited. It's such a passionate time, adolescence. I remember the feeling in high school, and even in middle school, of reading a book and really connecting with it on that elemental level of "somebody understands me." It's so powerful. It's a great market to be writing for because you connect so strongly with your audience.

RS: I think part of that connection is that you create these characters that girls — and I'm assuming that most of your readers are girls — can see themselves in and relate to. Yet they are all individuals. I see a lot of common themes in your books, but each one of those girls is a different person. How do you balance making a character particular with making her universal?

SD: There are certain things about the teenage experience in our culture that are always going to be there: the issues you have with your parents; the boy you have a crush on who doesn't know your name; the friend who isn't nice to you, but for some reason you're friends with her anyway. But then there's room within those experiences to make each character unique.

The thing that all my narrators have in common is that they are girls on the verge of a big change. And how they deal with that change is where the story comes from. When I was in high school, I was never happy with myself and I always wanted to believe that there was the potential for something big to happen in my life. You know — that I was going to meet some amazing guy and come to some stunning realization about myself that was going to make my life better. I think that's very appealing at that age, because it can happen. At that age, a girl can go away for the summer and when she comes back in the fall, she's completely different. She's taller, she's blossomed. There's so much potential. That's why I like writing about this age, because there's still so much room to come into one's self, so much change happening fast and furious. There's a wealth of material there.

RS: I notice that you often start with a precipitating offstage event. For instance, in *The Truth About Forever,* the death of the father happens before the book actually begins, but it sets in motion all the things that happen to the heroine.

SD: I think that's often how you feel as a teenager, that the world is happening around you, and you're sort of whirling and getting bounced around within it. I remember feeling that way, that I didn't have much control over my own destiny. Everything was *happening* to me, and I was just trying to keep my head above water.

RS: *Do* you think of yourself as a writer for girls?

SD: I do. I don't kid myself; I don't think a lot of boys are reading my books. My books are so firmly fixed in the girl mindset and the girl point of view. Women tend to want to share our experiences more, to talk about what's going on with us. Especially when things are going badly or you're stressed out, to find some commonality or sense of recognition in a story is very comforting. Boys are different that way. They don't want to talk about everything that's going on with them. One comment I get again and again from girls is, "I read your book and it is my life — it's like it's my school and my teachers."

RS: And that's also the theme of your books. It's not just that you have readers, who, because they are girls, explore their emotions through reading. Your books are *about* young women trying to understand themselves and their place in the world.

SD: My setup, typically, involves a character feeling disjointed and out of place — maybe because she once felt more in place and then something happened to make her lose her footing, or maybe she's never felt that she fit anywhere and has been looking for a way to find her place. It's a pretty universal experience: much of adolescence is just trying to figure out where you fit in, where your spot is, who your people are.

RS: Do you think that that's something particular to girls?

SD: No, but I think the willingness to explore it is. Girls are much more willing to face the fact that they're looking for it, and more willing to reach out for it, than boys. People have said to me many times that I should write a book from a boy's point of view. All I can say is that I spent four years of high school sitting around with my friends analyzing what boys were thinking. That's all we did. We would sit at lunch and be like, "He said hi to me in the hall—what did that mean?"

RS: Nothing!

SD: Right, completely cryptic! So I can't even imagine saying what some boy means. Or what he's thinking. I don't know how boys think. I wish I did.

RS: In the 1980s, there was an earlier wave of "let's have more books for boys" going on. A number of women writers tried their hand at a male perspective. But the characters weren't real boys. They were male, but they would talk to each other and to other people as if they were women. It was as if the goal of these books was to take these tough characters and turn them into women. Put 'em in touch with their feelings. Make 'em cry. Make 'em talk about things. And I wasn't convinced.

SD: Teen readers can tell if someone's writing about them and it's not right. One of the most important things in writing for teens is to be genuine, and not to write down to them, not to proselytize or try to force-feed them a message. My books are not about social issues. I'm just telling the kind of story that I want to hear, writing the kind of book I wanted to read when I was in high school.

RS: Do you have an opinion about the term *chick lit*?

SD: I'm not as offended by it as others are. But I also think it's become too wide a term. We sort of throw anything with a pink cover into the category now. It used to be targeted very specifically,

and now anything that isn't Literature and has women in it is *chick lit*. It seems like you're one or the other, you're "literary" or you're "chick lit." And that's unfortunate, because there are lots of shades in between. But I'm not offended by it, because I *am* writing books for girls. I *like* that my covers are kind of pink and cute. I'm not gonna lie. In high school that's the kind of cover I wanted to pick up — and that's *still* the kind of cover that I'm drawn to.

Holden at Sixteen
Bruce Brooks

It was 1964 and I was fourteen when I first read *The Catcher in the Rye* by J. D. Salinger. After considering the last bit of what Holden Caulfield had to say to me — "Don't ever tell anybody anything. If you do, you start missing everybody" — I decided this was the second-best book I'd ever found, after Robert Ruark's *Something of Value*. And found is the right word: I had picked Holden's tale from the rather cheesy paperback rack at Packett's Pharmacy during my endless browses there, choosing it over Leonard Wibberley's *The Mouse That Roared* (not about mice) and George Orwell's *Animal Farm* (not about animals or farming), because *Catcher* seemed much stranger. Strange was good.

I felt pretty serious about bestowing my number-two all-time honor on Salinger — the man ought to feel honored. Nobody I knew took books as seriously as I did, except my dad, but he read only Harold Robbins and Erle Stanley Gardner and James Michener. Alas for Pops: I felt *The Catcher in the Rye* was simply too much book for him. He was better off tucking up with Perry Mason in that attorney's predictable murder courtroom, or with Mr. Michener in Hawaii, than he would be trying to hang with old Holden in his goddamned prep school, or his dive New York City hotel, or his little sister's room — good old Phoebe — after midnight.

So I did not recommend *Catcher* to my dad, though I owed him one for his urging me to read *The Carpetbaggers*. It would not have been fair. One could not expect adults to handle the kind of rough stuff Holden was laying down.

Ah, well. Little did I know what I would soon find out — that I was measurably something called a Young Reader, and that *The Catcher in the Rye* was a special-reserve official Adult Novel, technically more appropriate for my father than for little me. I had no right to possess this book, never mind how naturally me and old Holden hit it off; I had no authority to parse its distribution among grown-ups like my dad, no matter how baffled I knew they would be by its life. Not my call: *The Catcher in the Rye* was fully a Brilliantly Offbeat Work of Serious Literature, and one that already belonged to Them. The adults would prove their provenance with elite awards, doctoral dissertations, and critical-intellectual studies embodied in entire books! Holden Caulfield was the precious property of the grandest high-literary thinkers.

And I thought he was just a kid like me, running through a cool and shuddering story. But I was wrong, or at least only partially perceptive. Holden stood adamantine as some kind of icon, voice, symbol, avatar, age-displaced induction of pan-generational mimesis, etc. Holden, and Salinger, were highly Major. Whereas I and my teen buddies, along with our descendants for the next fifty years, were measurably Minor.

In 1998, my son Alex, then age fourteen, wrote me a letter that began:

> Dear Bruce,
> Hey, Happy Birthday, 48, hard to believe. Hope you had a great day. Listen, I have to tell you about a book I just read. You need to check it out, I know you will get it all.

It's called "Catcher in the Rye," the author is JD Salinger.
You know how much I hate the idea that there is something general that adults try to call "teen experience"
(like there's "adult experience" right?). Well, as much as
I hate the idea and those words, I have to say Salinger
got teen experience just right, at least for ONE teen,
a kid named Holden. Read this book, and we can talk
about it!

Alex's letter was still fresh in my mind when I opened a *New
Yorker* in 2001 and found a long article titled "Holden at Fifty" by
one of our leading intellects of high culture, Louis Menand.

Menand said essentially this: *The Catcher in the Rye* is a great
book, but really it has nothing to do with young people. Holden
Caulfield is nothing like a young person. He is too astute, too precise with language, and too sensitive to be so young; Salinger was
playing around, trying to pass this wonderful character off as a kid.
Furthermore, *Catcher* itself is not really a book that should be read
by young people — they are insufficiently astute, precise with language, and sensitive to appreciate the book. In fact, young readers don't even truly like the novel: they read it only because adults
say they should, and they pretend to enjoy it for the same reason.
According to Menand, no young reader ever discovered *The Catcher
in the Rye* on his or her own; a sophisticated but misguided adult
must have been involved.

But what did I expect from a piece called "Holden at Fifty"?
Holden was not fifty in 2001. Holden will never be fifty. Holden
was sixteen in 1951, and he is sixteen today. That will not change,
whether the novel is fifty, seventy-five, or a hundred. It may take
the sixteen-year-olds of those times to tell, though.

It is a truism among people in the young adult field that *The
Adventures of Huckleberry Finn, To Kill a Mockingbird,* and *The Catcher
in the Rye* would likely be published today as YAs. Or, at least, they

could be, successfully — and not just because they are narrated by young people. The reason they make the grade as YA novels is simple: Huck, Scout, and Holden act their ages. These three characters look like kids, walk like kids, and quack like kids. Not because they are exactly like existing kids, or because they may be deemed "accurate" by the critics who use that chilly word as a virtue and count accuracy as "truth." Rather, these three narrators tell us unique stories, in unique voices, which allow us to believe that their lives fit.

Ultimately, the fact that *The Catcher in the Rye* is not designated an official Young Adult Book hasn't limited its availability to young readers, much less its appeal to them. (The novel is frequently challenged or banned for kids, but so are many YA books.) Holden Caulfield's tale is probably the book most widely read by teenagers, generation after generation, and perhaps most widely enjoyed. *The Catcher in the Rye* is windy and stony and hot and cool, brilliantly subtle and disarmingly overt, straightforward, manipulative, sentimental, pragmatic, crazy, controlled, always precise. But perhaps most important, to adult readers in ignorance, and to young readers in wisdom, *The Catcher in the Rye* is ineffably young.

THE GUYS' CLUBHOUSE

VIRGINIA EUWER WOLFF

I didn't even ask why I was turning into Holden Caulfield. I was fifteen, a brochure girl for postwar innocence. And I was a farm kid, three thousand miles away from Holden's Manhattan; I took violin lessons, rode my bike through orchards, memorized social-studies facts, picked strawberries to make money, earned Camp Fire Girl honor beads. I also sought the right bras, the right pimple medicine, the boys most likely to alarm my family.

The Catcher in the Rye came into my life at a rummage sale, and I read it in one evening. Within the next few days, I heard myself reciting whole paragraphs from memory, and in doing so I began to notice that I was driving nearly everyone away. My usually affectionate family loathed Holden and me enough to shoot scornful looks over to our side of the dinner table and forget to pass us the potatoes. It went on for months.

The gender difference didn't occur to me.

Why not? I now ask myself. Didn't it seem really, really, *really* odd that I was this boy who was hanging Sunny's sad green dress on a hanger in a New York hotel room? I don't think I gave it a thought.

I look back on whom I was choosing to be: an academic failure who had done nearly everything wrong that he'd been asked to do right; a boy who was making his own journey into the underworld and taking meticulous note of its sinister mien; a narrator whose flair for vulgarity was almost choral and who was intimately attuned to the sanctity of life; a solitary wanderer who, like many teenagers, was just learning how to take the full measure of his undisciplined temperament; a protagonist who wanted to save falling children and who was saved by his little sister; a borrower and a lender who was teaching me about responses to defilement, a lesson I would continue to need as the beleaguered twentieth century stumbled forward.

Somehow I've gotten through the intervening years without ever examining whether or not I was unconsciously seeking a gender change (no, I was not), whether or not I had penis envy, whether or not I wanted to try on boyhood. But as I ask these questions even now, it seems that it was a literary identification of convenience. Getting to be Holden let me use his brain, which was so much more interesting than mine. When I was Holden, I had form, shape, demeanor. He gave me someone to *be*.

I had loved living with Betsy and Tacy, had enjoyed bustling around solving mysteries with Nancy Drew, but I hadn't *become* them. They were book friends, and they didn't give my mother the migraines that my immersion in Holden's life gave her.

What I do know at this distance: Holden was teaching me about structure and narration, about the subjectivity, the turn-on-a-dime bias inherent in fiction. I had heard certain kinds of storytelling all my life. His kind was new, alluring in its impertinence, the perfect vehicle for me to use as an armored car in an adolescence that really didn't need one. And there was a poignant gravity to Holden that has never left me. Could I have guessed that the mere mention of his name could still upset people, all these decades later? Not a bit.

As a grown-up reader I love the sweet agony of becoming Jane Eyre, Clarissa Dalloway, Natalie Babbitt's Winnie Foster, and some of Alice Munro's exquisitely sculpted characters. But I think my early subversive partnership with Holden has also made it possible for me to come closer to becoming David Copperfield, Jerry Renault, Jesse Aarons, Will Parry, King Lear, and my favorite, Gogol's Akaky Akakievich Bashmachkin. Holden let me sneak briefly into the guys' clubhouse, and I'll always be grateful.

MORE GREAT BOOKS FOR TEENS

Sherman Alexie, illustrations by Ellen Forney, *The Absolutely True Diary of a Part-Time Indian*

232 pp. Grades 8–10. Junior makes the difficult commute from his Spokane Indian reservation to an off-rez high school where he's the only Indian. His inimitable and hilarious narration is intensely alive with short paragraphs, poetry in prose, one-liners, and take-no-prisoners cartoons.

Coe Booth, *Kendra*

293 pp. Grade 9 and up. Kendra, fourteen, lives with her strict but loving grandmother. Hot guy Nashawn has Kendra doing things that shame as well as excite her. Does Nashawn love her? Does her recently returned mother? Kendra's present-tense narration is intelligent and honest, grounded by her basic common sense.

Sarah Dessen, *Lock and Key*

422 pp. Grade 10 and up. After her mother leaves, seventeen-year-old Ruby is placed in the care of her sister. The intricacy of relationships shines in this in-depth exploration of family, trust, and responsibility. The complex, deeply sympathetic characters are pure pleasure to spend time with.

Sharon Dogar, *Annexed*

341 pp. This audacious novel is Peter van Pels's first-person, present-tense chronicle of life in the Annex with the Frank family. The novel provides a new look at Anne Frank—speculative, of course, but in no way contradicting her own famous diary.

Saci Lloyd, *The Carbon Diaries 2015*

330 pp. Grades 7–10. In a brilliantly conceived speculative drama set in the future, Lloyd extrapolates a logical, world-changing application of global warming that is both optimistic and terrifying. This gripping, perceptive, and impassioned book contains equal parts political immediacy and tart humor.

E. Lockhart, *The Disreputable History of Frankie Landau-Banks*
342 pp. Grades 8–10. Frankie's boyfriend, Matthew, is the co-leader of an all-male secret society at her elite prep school. A clinical-sounding narrator addresses readers directly, giving the book a case-study vibe and presenting Frankie's exploits in a dispassionate way so that readers are left to make up their own minds about this unique, multifaceted young woman.

Catherine Gilbert Murdock, *Dairy Queen*
278 pp. Grade 9 and up. Coaching the rival high school's quarterback in a summer fitness program, farm girl (and football player) D.J. realizes she's attracted to Brian, even as they face off on the field. D.J.'s practical, understatedly humorous voice drives this engrossing tale of love, family, and football. Sequels: *The Off Season* and *Front and Center*

Jandy Nelson, *The Sky Is Everywhere*
281 pp. Content to shadow her high-wattage older sister, seventeen-year-old clarinetist and secret poet Lennie is devastated when Bailey dies unexpectedly. Lennie's profound loss awakens unanticipated new feelings, including an unwelcome attraction to Bailey's bereft boyfriend and healthy first love with an exuberant new boy. Tender, romantic, and loaded with passion.

Marcus Sedgwick, *Revolver*
204 pp. His family's Arctic Circle cabin is Sig's entire world—a secure one until the day his father dies and the menacing Gunther Wolff arrives, demanding the gold Sig's father owes him from the Alaska Gold Rush. Tight plotting and a wealth of moral concerns will appeal to fans of Gary Paulsen, Jack London, and even Cormac McCarthy.

Francisco X. Stork, *Marcelo in the Real World*
316 pp. Grade 9 and up. Seventeen-year-old Marcelo is at the high-functioning end of the autism spectrum. A summer job in the mailroom at his father's cutthroat law firm tests Marcelo's coping and social skills, moral compass, and loyalty. Stork ratchets up the tension as the plot winds to its memorable denouement.

Conclusion
Roger Sutton

Rereading *The Catcher in the Rye,* or any of the books discussed here that I had read as a young person, I'm reminded of C. S. Lewis's famous adage that "no book is really worth reading at the age of ten which is not equally — and often far more — worth reading at the age of fifty and beyond." I don't agree with him: *Catcher in the Rye* was far more compelling to me as an adolescent than as an adult (although its poignancy became apparent to me only in my thirties), and we can all think of examples of books that were lifelines in childhood that simply do not resonate the same way now. But Lewis was arguing for a continuity of literature that I believe has been amply demonstrated by the landmarks and exemplars Martha Parravano and I and our colleagues have provided here. While *Where the Wild Things Are* speaks intensely to young children about conflict and the refuge of fantasy, it also stands with any work of art that champions the imagination. Similarly, while we may now be of an age with the (almost always) patient Quimby parents rather than the put-upon Ramona, we continue to wrestle with the problem of being misunderstood. Not only can *Where the Wild Things Are* and *Ramona the Pest* continue to speak to — to grow up with — an individual reader throughout a lifetime, they also remain alive, for both children and literary culture, a half century after their publication. Ageless, then, in two ways.

We hope you do go on to read and enjoy many of the titles discussed here, and remember that they are only a taste from the feast. Whether you talk to your local librarian or bookseller, follow up on the suggestions given in this book, or peruse the lists we have on the *Horn Book* website (www.hbook.com), you'll find no lack of recommendations. And if you have acquired a taste for reading *about* children's literature, there is a sturdy tradition of that as well; see "Further Reading" on page 339.

The best way to understand how children read is to read for yourself. There is no need to put yourself in the shoes of a ten-year-old even if you are fifty and encountering *Holes* for the first time. Your own shoes will be sufficient to walk you through the story. Only by experiencing it as a *reader* — not a grown-up, not a parent — will you be in a position to recommend it to another: not a child, but a fellow reader.

RESOURCES

BIBLIOGRAPHY OF RECOMMENDED TITLES

Introduction

Betty Baker, illustrations by Arnold Lobel, *Little Runner of the Longhouse* (Harper-Collins).

Elizabeth Guilfoile, illustrations by Mary Stevens, *Nobody Listens to Andrew* (Follett).

Robert Lawson, *They Were Strong and Good* (Viking).

Dorothy Sterling, *Mary Jane* (Doubleday).

Part One: Reading to Them

Janet and Allan Ahlberg, *Each Peach, Pear, Plum* (Viking); *Peek-a-Boo!* (Viking).

Aliki, *How a Book Is Made* (HarperCollins).

Zoë B. Alley, illustrations by R. W. Alley, *There's a Wolf at the Door* (Roaring Brook).

Jim Aylesworth, illustrations by Barbara McClintock, *The Mitten* (Scholastic).

Molly Bang, *Ten, Nine, Eight* (Greenwillow).

Byron Barton, *Boats* (HarperCollins); *Dinosaurs, Dinosaurs* (HarperCollins); *Machines at Work* (HarperCollins); *Planes* (HarperCollins); *Trains* (HarperCollins); *Trucks* (HarperCollins).

Chris Barton, illustrations by Tom Lichtenheld, *Shark vs. Train* (Little, Brown).

Jonathan Bean, *At Night* (Farrar, Straus and Giroux).

Bonny Becker, illustrations by Kady MacDonald Denton, *A Visitor for Bear* (Candlewick).

Sandra Boynton, *Blue Hat, Green Hat* (Simon & Schuster); *Moo, Baa, La La La!* (Simon & Schuster).

Raymond Briggs, *The Mother Goose Treasury* (Coward-McCann). *The Snowman* (Random House).

L. Leslie Brooke, *Ring o' Roses* (Warne).

Craig Brown, *Tractor* (Greenwillow).

Margaret Wise Brown, illustrations by Clement Hurd, *Goodnight Moon* (Harper-Collins); *The Runaway Bunny* (HarperCollins).

Margaret Wise Brown, illustrations by Ashley Wolff, *Little Donkey Close Your Eyes* (HarperCollins).

Anthony Brown, *Me and You* (Farrar, Straus and Giroux).

Ashley Bryan, *Beautiful Blackbird* (Atheneum).

John Burningham, *Mr. Gumpy's Outing* (Holt).

Virginia Lee Burton, *Mike Mulligan and His Steam Shovel* (Houghton Mifflin).

Eric Carle, *The Very Hungry Caterpillar* (Philomel).

Peter Catalanotto, *Matthew A. B. C.* (Atheneum).

Margaret Chodos-Irvine, *Ella Sarah Gets Dressed* (Harcourt).

Eileen Christelow, *Five Little Monkeys Jumping on the Bed* (Clarion).

Vicki Cobb, *I Face the Wind* (HarperCollins); *I Fall Down* (HarperCollins); *I See Myself* (HarperCollins).

Nancy Coffelt, illustrations by Tricia Tusa, *Fred Stays with Me!* (Little, Brown).

William Cowper, illustrations by Randolph Caldecott, *The Diverting History of John Gilpin* (Pook).

Donald Crews, *Freight Train* (Greenwillow); *School Bus* (Greenwillow); *Truck* (Greenwillow).

Doreen Cronin, illustrations by Harry Bliss, *Diary of a Fly* (HarperCollins).

Shutta Crum, illustrations by Carol Thompson, *Thunder-Boomer!* (Clarion).

Chris L. Demarest, *Alpha Bravo Charlie* (McElderry); *Firefighters A to Z* (McElderry).

Tomie dePaola, *Tomie dePaola's Mother Goose* (Putnam).

Leo and Diane Dillon, *Mother Goose: Numbers on the Loose* (Harcourt).

Rebecca Kai Dotlich, illustrations by Sachiko Yoshikawa, *What Is Science?* (Holt).

Olivier Dunrea, *Gossie* (Houghton Mifflin); *Gossie & Gertie* (Houghton Mifflin).

Lois Ehlert, *Eating the Alphabet* (Harcourt).

Ed Emberley, *Go Away, Big Green Monster!* (Little, Brown).

Mary Engelbreit, *Mary Engelbreit's Mother Goose* (HarperCollins).

Lisa Campbell Ernst, *The Turn-Around, Upside-Down Alphabet Book* (Simon & Schuster).

Muriel Feelings, illustrations by Tom Feelings, *Jambo Means Hello* (Dial).

Denise Fleming, *Alphabet Under Construction* (Holt); *Barnyard Banter* (Holt).

Brian Floca, *The Racecar Alphabet* (Atheneum).

Mem Fox, illustrations by Judy Horacek, *Where Is the Green Sheep?* (Harcourt).

Mem Fox, illustrations by Helen Oxenbury, *Ten Little Fingers and Ten Little Toes* (Harcourt).

Wanda Gág, *Millions of Cats* (Macmillan).

Paul Galdone, *The Three Little Pigs* (Clarion).

Taro Gomi, *Spring Is Here* (Chronicle).

Bob Graham, *April and Esme, Tooth Fairies* (Candlewick).

Emily Gravett, *Orange Pear Apple Bear* (Simon & Schuster).

Janice N. Harrington, illustrations by Shelley Jackson, *The Chicken-Chasing Queen of Lamar County* (Farrar, Straus and Giroux).

Kevin Henkes, *Julius, the Baby of the World* (Greenwillow); *Little White Rabbit* (Greenwillow).

Eric Hill, *Where's Spot?* (Putnam).

Tana Hoban, *Black on White* (Greenwillow); *Of Colors and Things* (Greenwillow); *White on Black* (Greenwillow).

Shirley Hughes, *Alfie Gives a Hand* (Red Fox).

Rachel Isadora, *The Fisherman and His Wife* (Putnam).

Joseph Jacobs, illustrations by John D. Batton, *English Fairy Tales* (CreateSpace).

Stephen T. Johnson, *Alphabet City* (Viking).

Barbara M. Joosse, illustrations by Barbara Lavallee, *Mama, Do You Love Me?* (Chronicle).

G. Brian Karas, *The Village Garage* (Holt).

Helen Lester, illustrations by Lynn Munsinger, *Tacky Goes to Camp* (Houghton Mifflin); *Tacky the Penguin* (Houghton Mifflin).

Mike Lester, *A Is for Salad* (Putnam).

Arnold Lobel, *The Arnold Lobel Book of Mother Goose* (Random House).

William Low, *Machines Go to Work* (Holt).

Janette Sebring Lowrey, illustrations by Gustaf Tenggren, *The Poky Little Puppy* (Golden Books).

Amy MacDonald, illustrations by Maureen Roffey, *Let's Make a Noise* (Candlewick).

Leonard S. Marcus, illustrations by Amy Schwartz, *Mother Goose's Little Misfortunes* (Simon & Schuster).

James Marshall, *The Three Little Pigs* (Dial).

Bill Martin Jr, illustrations by Eric Carle, *Brown Bear, Brown Bear, What Do You See?* (Holt).

Bill Martin Jr and John Archambault, illustrations by Lois Ehlert, *Chicka Chicka Boom Boom* (Simon & Schuster).

Salley Mavor, *A Pocket Full of Posies: A Treasury of Nursery Rhymes* (Houghton Mifflin).

Sam McBratney, illustrations by Russell Ayto, *One Voice, Please: Favorite Read-Aloud Stories* (Candlewick).

Robert McCloskey, *Blueberries for Sal* (Viking); *Make Way for Ducklings* (Viking).

Bob McLeod, *SuperHero ABC* (HarperCollins).

Kate and Jim McMullan, *I Stink!* (HarperCollins).

Susan Meddaugh, *Martha Speaks* (Houghton Mifflin).

Eve Merriam, illustrations by Dan Yaccarino, *Bam Bam Bam* (Holt).

Zoran Milich, *The City ABC Book* (Kids Can).

Margaret Miller, *I Love Colors* (Little Simon); *Now I'm Big* (Greenwillow); *What's on My Head?* (Little Simon).

Barry Moser, *The Three Little Pigs* (Little, Brown).

Chihiro Nakagawa, illustrations by Junji Koyose, *Who Made This Cake?* (Front Street/Boyds Mills).

Satoru Onishi, *Who's Hiding?* (Kane/Miller).

Iona Opie, illustrations by Rosemary Wells, *Here Comes Mother Goose* (Candlewick); *My Very First Mother Goose* (Candlewick).

Helen Oxenbury, *All Fall Down* (Aladdin); *Clap Hands* (Aladdin); *Say Goodnight* (Aladdin); *Tickle, Tickle* (Aladdin).

Leslie Patricelli, *Baby Happy, Baby Sad* (Candlewick); *Higher! Higher!* (Candlewick).

David Pelletier, *The Graphic Alphabet* (Orchard).

Jerry Pinkney, *The Lion & the Mouse* (Little, Brown).

Beatrix Potter, *The Tale of Peter Rabbit* (Warne).

Laura Rankin, *The Handmade Alphabet* (Dial).

Peggy Rathmann, *Good Night, Gorilla* (Putnam).

Lynn Reiser, photographs by Penny Gentieu, *My Baby & Me* (Knopf); *You and Me, Baby* (Knopf).

H. A. Rey, *Curious George* (Houghton Mifflin).

Anne Rockwell, *Big Wheels* (Dutton).

Anne and Harlow Rockwell, *The Toolbox* (Macmillan).

Phyllis Root, illustrations by David Walker, *Flip, Flap, Fly!* (Candlewick).

Glen Rounds, *Three Little Pigs and the Big Bad Wolf* (Holiday House).

Robert Sabuda, *The Movable Mother Goose* (Simon & Schuster).

Coleen Salley, illustrations by Janet Stevens, *Epossumondas Saves the Day* (Harcourt).

Liz Garton Scanlon, illustrations by Marla Frazee, *All the World* (Beach Lane/Simon).

Richard Scarry, *Richard Scarry's Cars and Trucks and Things That Go* (Golden Books).

Laura Amy Schlitz, illustrations by Max Grafe, *The Bearskinner: A Tale of the Brothers Grimm* (Candlewick).

Jon Scieszka, illustrations by Lane Smith, *Math Curse* (Viking); *The Stinky Cheese Man and Other Fairly Stupid Tales* (Viking); *The True Story of the 3 Little Pigs!* (Viking).

Ann Herbert Scott, illustrations by Glo Coalson, *On Mother's Lap* (Clarion).

Laura Vaccaro Seeger, *Dog and Bear* (Roaring Brook); *First the Egg* (Roaring Brook).

Maurice Sendak, *In the Night Kitchen* (HarperCollins); *Outside Over There* (HarperCollins); *We Are All in the Dumps with Jack and Guy* (HarperCollins); *Where the Wild Things Are* (HarperCollins).

David Shannon, *No, David!* (Blue Sky/Scholastic).

Bob Shea, *Dinosaur vs. Bedtime* (Hyperion).

Judy Sierra, illustrations by Melissa Sweet, *The Sleepy Little Alphabet* (Knopf).

Marc Simont, *The Stray Dog* (HarperCollins).

Joseph Slate, illustrations by Ashley Wolff, *Miss Bindergarten Gets Ready for Kindergarten* (Dutton).

Esphyr Slobodkina, *Caps for Sale* (HarperCollins).

Peter Spier, *To Market! To Market!* (Doubleday).

William Steig, *Brave Irene* (Farrar, Straus and Giroux); *Doctor De Soto* (Farrar, Straus and Giroux); *Sylvester and the Magic Pebble* (Farrar, Straus and Giroux).

David Ezra Stein, *Pouch!* (Putnam).

John Steptoe, *Baby Says* (HarperCollins); *Mufaro's Beautiful Daughters* (HarperCollins); *My Special Best Words* (Viking); *Stevie* (HarperCollins); *The Story of Jumping Mouse* (HarperCollins).

Nancy Tafuri, *Have You Seen My Duckling?* (Greenwillow).

Eugene Trivizas, illustrations by Helen Oxenbury, *The Three Little Wolves and the Big Bad Pig* (McElderry).

Chris Van Allsburg, *Jumanji* (Houghton Mifflin).

Shigeo Watanabe, illustrations by Yasuo Ohtomo, *How Do I Put It On?* (Philomel).

Rosemary Wells, *Max's ABC* (Viking); *Max's First Word* (Dial).

David Wiesner, *The Three Pigs* (Clarion).

Mo Willems, *Don't Let the Pigeon Drive the Bus!* (Hyperion).

Vera B. Williams, *"More More More," Said the Baby* (Greenwillow).

Margot Zemach, *The Three Little Pigs* (Farrar, Straus and Giroux); *The Three Wishes* (Farrar, Straus and Giroux).

Gene Zion, illustrations by Margaret Bloy Graham, *Harry the Dirty Dog* (Harper-Collins).

Part Two: Reading with Them

Tedd Arnold, *Hooray for Fly Guy!* (Scholastic).

Monika Bang-Campbell, illustrations by Molly Bang, *Little Rat Makes Music* (Harcourt).

Annie Barrows, illustrations by Sophie Blackall, *Ivy and Bean: Bound to Be Bad* (Chronicle).

Charlotte Lewis Brown, illustrations by Phil Wilson, *The Day the Dinosaurs Died* (HarperCollins).

Beverly Cleary, *Ramona the Pest* (HarperCollins).

Patricia Reilly Giff, illustrations by Blanche Sims, *The Beast in Ms. Rooney's Room* (Delacorte).

Judyann Ackerman Grant, illustrations by Sue Truesdell, *Chicken Said, "Cluck!"* (HarperCollins).

Stephanie Greene, illustrations by Martha Weston, *Owen Foote, Frontiersman* (Clarion); *Happy Birthday, Sohpie Hartley* (Clarion).

Nikki Grimes, illustrations by R. Gregory Christie, *Almost Zero: A Dymonde Daniel Book* (Putnam).

Betty Hicks, illustrations by Adam McCauley, *Basketball Bats* (Roaring Brook); *Goof-Off Goalie* (Roaring Brook); *Swimming with Sharks* (Roaring Brook).

Jennifer and Matthew Holm, *Babymouse: Queen of the World!* (Random House).

Kimberly Willis Holt, illustrations by Christine Davenier, *Piper Reed, Navy Brat* (Holt).

Lee Bennett Hopkins, illustrations by Susan Gaber, *Small Talk: A Book of Short Poems* (Harcourt).

Johanna Hurwitz, illustrations by Lillian Hoban, *Rip-Roaring Russell* (HarperCollins).

Jessica Scott Kerrin, illustrations by Joseph Kelly, *Martin Bridge: Ready for Takeoff!* (Kids Can).

Grace Lin, *Ling & Ting: Not Exactly the Same!* (Little, Brown).

Arnold Lobel, *Frog and Toad Are Friends* (HarperCollins).

Lenore Look, illustrations by LeUyen Pham, *Alvin Ho: Allergic to Girls, School, and Other Scary Things* (Random House).

Edward Marshall, illustrations by James Marshall, *Fox and His Friends* (Dial).

Megan McDonald, illustrations by Peter Reynolds, Judy Moody (series) (Candlewick).

Kate McMullan, illustrations by R. W. Alley, *Pearl and Wagner: Two Good Friends* (Dial).

Claudia Mills, illustrations by Heather Maione, *How Oliver Olson Changed the World* (Farrar, Straus and Giroux).

Else Holmelund Minarik, illustrations by Maurice Sendak, *Little Bear* (HarperCollins).

Peggy Parish, illustrations by Fritz Siebel, *Amelia Bedelia* (HarperCollins).

Sara Pennypacker, illustrations by Marla Frazee, *Clementine* (Hyperion).

Dav Pilkey, *The Adventures of Captain Underpants* (Scholastic).

James Proimos, *Johnny Mutton, He's So Him!* (Harcourt).

Cynthia Rylant, illustrations by Suçie Stevenson, *Henry and Mudge* (Simon & Schuster).

Barbara Seuling, illustrations by Paul Brewer, *Robert and the Great Pepperoni* (Cricket).

Dr. Seuss, *The Cat in the Hat* (Random House).

Erica Silverman, illustrations by Betsy Lewin, *Cowgirl Kate and Cocoa* (Harcourt).

Shelley Moore Thomas, illustrations by Jennifer Plecas, *Good Night, Good Knight* (Dutton).

Sarah Weeks, illustrations by Jane Manning, *Pip Squeak* (HarperCollins).

Mo Willems, *Are You Ready to Play Outside?* (Hyperion); *I Am Invited to a Party!* (Hyperion); *Pigs Make Me Sneeze!* (Hyperion).

Lisa Yee, illustrations by Dan Santat, *Bobby vs. Girls (Accidentally)* (Levine/Scholastic).

Part Three: Reading on Their Own

Jon Agee, *Orangutan Tongs: Poems to Tangle Your Tongue* (Hyperion); *Sit on a Potato Pan, Otis!: More Palindromes* (Farrar, Straus, and Giroux).

Janet and Allan Ahlberg, *Starting School* (Viking).

Joan Aiken, *The Wolves of Willoughby Chase* (Doubleday).

Louisa May Alcott, *Little Women* (Little, Brown).

Lloyd Alexander, *The Book of Three* (Holt).

Aliki, *Fossils Tell of Long Ago* (HarperCollins).

Laurie Halse Anderson, *Chains* (Simon & Schuster); *Forge* (Simon & Shuster).

M. T. Anderson, *The Astonishing Life of Octavian Nothing, Traitor to the Nation, Volume I: The Pox Party* (Candlewick); *The Astonishing Life of Octavian Nothing, Traitor to the Nation, Volume II: The Kingdom on the Waves* (Candlewick).

M. T. Anderson, illustrations by Kurt Cyrus, *Jasper Dash and the Flame-Pits of Delaware: A Pals in Peril Tale* (Beach Lane).

Jennifer Armstrong, *Shipwreck at the Bottom of the World: The Extraordinary True Story of Shackleton and the* Endurance (Crown).

Marc Aronson and Marina Budhos, *Sugar Changed the World: A Story of Magic, Spice, Slavery, Freedom, and Science* (Clarion).

Ruth Ashby, *Young Charles Darwin and the Voyage of the Beagle* (Peachtree).

Avi, *The Traitors' Gate* (Atheneum); *The True Confessions of Charlotte Doyle* (HarperCollins).

Natalie Babbitt, *Tuck Everlasting* (Farrar, Straus and Giroux).

Paolo Bacigalupi, *Ship Breaker* (Little, Brown).

Deidre Baker, *Becca at Sea* (Groundwood).

Catherine Bateson, *Being Bee* (Holiday House).

L. Frank Baum, illustrations by W. W. Denslow, *The Wizard of Oz* (Rand McNally).

Nathaniel Benchley, illustrations by Arnold Lobel, *Sam the Minuteman* (HarperCollins).

Franny Billingsley, *Chime* (Dial).

Jeanne Birdsall, *The Penderwicks* (Knopf).

Nic Bishop, *Digging for Bird-Dinosaurs* (Houghton Mifflin); *Frogs* (Scholastic).

Judy Blume, *Are You There God? It's Me, Margaret.* (Atheneum); *It's Not the End of the World* (Atheneum).

Louise Borden, illustrations by Niki Daly, *The Greatest Skating Race: A World War II Story from the Netherlands* (McElderry).

Frank Cottrell Boyce, *Cosmic* (Walden Pond).

Franklyn M. Branley, illustrations by Marc Simont, *What Happened to the Dinosaurs?* (HarperCollins).

Ann Brashares, *The Sisterhood of the Traveling Pants* (Delacorte).

Gwendolyn Brooks, illustrations by Faith Ringgold, *Bronzeville Boys and Girls* (HarperCollins).

Charlotte Lewis Brown, illustrations by Phil Wilson, *The Day the Dinosaurs Died* (HarperCollins).

Don Brown, *All Stations! Distress!: April 15, 1912, The Day the Titantic Sank* (Flash Point/Roaring Brook).

Joseph Bruchac, *Code Talker* (Dial).

Frances Hodgson Burnett, *The Secret Garden* (Candlewick).

Sheila Burnford, *The Incredible Journey* (Little, Brown).

Meg Cabot, *Allie Finkle's Rules for Girls: Glitter Girls and the Great Fake Out* (Scholastic).

Sarah C. Campbell, photographs by Sarah C. Campbell and Richard P. Campbell, *Wolfsnail: A Backyard Predator* (Boyds Mills).

Kristin Cashore, *Graceling* (Harcourt).

Andrew Chaikin with Victoria Kohl, illustrations by Alan Bean, *Mission Control, This Is Apollo: The Story of the First Voyages to the Moon* (Viking).

Jason Chin, *Redwoods* (Flash Point/Roaring Brook).

Beverly Cleary, *Dear Mr. Henshaw* (HarperCollins).

Andrew Clements, *Frindle* (Simon & Schuster); *Lunch Money* (Simon & Schuster).

Lesa Cline-Ransome, illustrations by James Ransome, *Young Pelé: Soccer's First Star* (Schwartz & Wade).

James Lincoln Collier and Christopher Collier, *My Brother Sam Is Dead* (Four Winds).

Suzanne Collins, *The Hunger Games* (Scholastic); *Catching Fire* (Scholastic); *Mockingjay* (Scholastic).

Susan Cooper, *The Dark Is Rising* (McElderry); *King of Shadows* (McElderry).

Audrey Couloumbis and Akila Couloumbis, *War Games: A Novel Based on a True Story* (Random House).

Christopher Paul Curtis, *Bud, Not Buddy* (Delacorte); *Elijah of Buxton* (Scholastic); *The Watsons Go to Birmingham — 1963* (Delacorte).

Karen Cushman, *Catherine, Called Birdy* (Clarion).

Nicola Davies, illustrations by Neal Layton, *Just the Right Size: Why Big Animals Are Big and Little Animals Are Little* (Candlewick).

Jean de Brunhoff, *The Story of Babar* (Egmont).

James M. Deem, *Bodies from the Ice: Melting Glaciers and the Recovery of the Past* (Houghton Mifflin).

Barry Deutsch, *Hereville: How Mirka Got Her Sword* (Amulet).

Siobhan Dowd, *The London Eye Mystery* (Random House).

Jeanne DuPrau, *The City of Ember* (Random House); *The Diamond of Darkhold* (Random House).

Hans Magnus Enzensberger, *The Number Devil* (Holt).

Louise Erdrich, *The Porcupine Year* (HarperCollins).

Tom Feelings, *The Middle Passage: White Ships / Black Cargo* (Dial).

Louise Fitzhugh, *Harriet the Spy* (HarperCollins); *The Long Secret* (HarperCollins).

Candace Fleming, *The Lincolns: A Scrapbook Look at Abraham and Mary* (Random House).

Brian Floca, *Dinosaurs at the Ends of the Earth* (DK Ink).

Douglas Florian, *Comets, Stars, the Moon, and Mars: Space Poems and Paintings* (Harcourt).

Esther Forbes, *Johnny Tremain* (Houghton Mifflin).

Russell Freedman, *Lincoln: A Photobiography* (Clarion); *The Voice That Challenged a Nation: Marian Anderson and the Struggle for Equal Rights* (Clarion).

Neil Gaiman, illustrations by Dave McKean, *Coraline* (HarperCollins); *The Graveyard Book* (HarperCollins).

Jack Gantos, *Hole in My Life* (Farrar, Straus and Giroux); *Joey Pigza Loses Control* (Farrar, Straus and Giroux); *Dead End in Norvelt* (Farrar, Straus and Giroux).

Alan Garner, *The Owl Service* (Harcourt Odyssey [orig. Collins]).

Jean Craighead George, *Julie of the Wolves* (HarperCollins).

James Cross Giblin, *Good Brother, Bad Brother: The Story of Edwin Booth and John Wilkes Booth* (Clarion).

Fred Gipson, *Old Yeller* (Perennial Classics).

Kenneth Grahame, *The Wind in the Willows* (Atheneum).

K. M. Grant, *How the Hangman Lost His Heart* (Walker).

Jan Greenberg and Sandra Jordan, *Ballet for Martha: Making Appalachian Spring* (Flash Point/Roaring Brook); *Christo and Jeanne-Claude: Through the Gates and Beyond* (Flash Point/Roaring Brook).

Shannon Hale and Dean Hale, illustrations by Nathan Hale, *Rapunzel's Revenge* (Bloomsbury).

Robie H. Harris, illustrations by Jan Ormerod, *Goodbye Mousie* (McElderry).

Robie H. Harris and Michael Emberley, *It's NOT the Stork!: A Book about Girls, Boys, Babies, Bodies, Families, and Friends* (Candlewick); *It's Perfectly Normal: Changing Bodies, Growing Up, Sex, and Sexual Health* (Candlewick); *It's So Amazing!: A Book about Eggs, Sperm, Birth, Babies, and Families* (Candlewick).

Deborah Heiligman, *Charles and Emma: The Darwins' Leap of Faith* (Holt).

Douglas Henderson, *Asteroid Impact* (Dial).

Charles Higson, *SilverFin: A James Bond Adventure* (Hyperion).

Will Hobbs, *Go Big or Go Home* (HarperCollins); *Wild Man Island* (HarperCollins).

Terry Hokenson, *The Winter Road* (Front Street/Boyds Mills).

Thomas R. Holtz, Jr., *Dinosaurs: The Most Complete, Up-to-Date Encyclopedia for Dinosaur Lovers of All Ages* (Random House).

bell hooks, illustrations by Shane W. Evans, *Homemade Love* (Hyperion).

Phillip Hoose, *Claudette Colvin: Twice Toward Justice* (Farrar, Straus and Giroux).

Anthony Horowitz, *Stormbreaker* (Philomel).

Polly Horvath, *Everything on a Waffle* (Farrar, Straus and Giroux).

Will James, *Smoky, the Cowhorse* (Scribner).

Paul B. Janeczko, illustrations by Chris Raschka, *A Kick in the Head: An Everyday Guide to Poetic Forms* (Candlewick).

Tove Jansson, *Finn Family Moomintroll* (Farrar, Straus and Giroux).

Steve Jenkins, *Dogs and Cats* (Houghton Mifflin); *Prehistoric, Actual Size* (Houghton Mifflin).

Ji-Li Jiang, *Red Scarf Girl: A Memoir of the Cultural Revolution* (HarperColllins).

Catherine Jinks, *Evil Genius* (Harcourt); *Genius Squad* (Harcourt).

Marthe Jocelyn, *How It Happened in Peach Hill* (Random House).

Diana Wynne Jones, *Howl's Moving Castle* (Greenwillow).

Jacqueline Kelly, *The Evolution of Calpurnia Tate* (Holt).

Barbara Kerley, illustrations by Edwin Fotheringham, *What to Do about Alice?: How Alice Roosevelt Broke the Rules, Charmed the World, and Drove Her Father Teddy Crazy!* (Scholastic).

P. B. Kerr, *One Small Step* (McElderry).

Jeff Kinney, *Diary of a Wimpy Kid: Rodrick Rules* (Amulet/Abrams).

Rudyard Kipling, *The Jungle Book* (Books of Wonder).

Jim Kjelgaard, *Big Red* (Holiday House).

Ellen Klages, *The Green Glass Sea* (Viking); *White Sands, Red Menace* (Viking).

Kate Klise, *Grounded* (Feiwel and Friends).

Eric Knight, *Lassie Come-Home* (Holt).

Ron Koertge, *Shakespeare Makes the Playoffs* (Candlewick).

Kathleen Krull, illustrations by Boris Kulikov, *Isaac Newton* (Viking); *Leonardo da Vinci* (Viking); *Albert Einstein* (Viking).

Kathleen V. Kudlinski, illustrations by S. D. Schindler, *Boy, Were We Wrong about Dinosaurs!* (Dutton).

Mark Kurlansky, illustrations by S. D. Schindler, *The Cod's Tale* (Putnam); *The Story of Salt* (Putnam).

Tom Lalicki, *Grierson's Raid: A Daring Cavalry Strike Through the Heart of the Confederacy* (Farrar, Straus and Giroux).

Patricia Lauber, illustrations by Douglas Henderson, *Living with Dinosaurs* (Simon & Schuster).

Ursula K. Le Guin, *A Wizard of Earthsea* (Atheneum).

Gail Carson Levine, *Ella Enchanted* (HarperCollins).

C. S. Lewis, *The Lion, the Witch and the Wardrobe* (HarperCollins).

Grace Lin, *Where the Mountain Meets the Moon* (Little, Brown).

Cynthia Lord, *Touch Blue* (Scholastic).

David Macaulay, *Built to Last* (Houghton Mifflin Harcourt).

David Macaulay with Richard Walker, *The Way We Work: Getting to Know the Amazing Human Body* (Lorraine/Houghton Mifflin).

Patricia MacLachlan, *Sarah, Plain and Tall* (HarperCollins).

Margaret Mahy, *The Changeover: A Supernatural Romance* (Atheneum).

Sandra Markle, *Outside and Inside Dinosaurs* (Atheneum); *Outside and Inside Woolly Mammoths* (Walker).

Ann M. Martin, *Everything for a Dog* (Feiwel).

William Mayne, *Earthfasts* (Dutton).

Emily Arnold McCully, *Marvelous Mattie: How Margaret E. Knight Became an Inventor* (Farrar, Straus and Giroux).

Hilary McKay, *Forever Rose* (McElderry).

Kierin Meehan, *Hannah's Winter* (Kane/Miller).

Claudia Mills, *Alex Ryan, Stop That!* (Farrar, Straus and Giroux); *Lizzie at Last* (Farrar, Straus and Giroux); *Makeovers by Marcia* (Farrar, Straus and Giroux).

A. A. Milne, illustrations by Ernest H. Shepard, *Winnie-the-Pooh* (Dutton).

Lucy Maud Montgomery, *Anne of Green Gables* (Modern Library).

Sy Montgomery, photographs by Nic Bishop, *Kakapo Rescue: Saving the World's Strangest Parrot* (Scientists in the Field) (Houghton Mifflin).

Jim Murphy, *An American Plague: The True and Terrifying Story of the Yellow Fever Epidemic of 1793* (Clarion).

Meja Mwangi, *The Mzungu Boy* (Groundwood).

Walter Dean Myers, *Scorpions* (HarperCollins).

Phyllis Reynolds Naylor, *The Agony of Alice* (Atheneum); *Alice in Lace* (Atheneum).

Kadir Nelson, *We Are the Ship: The Story of Negro League Baseball* (Hyperion).

Vaunda Micheaux Nelson, illustrations by R. Gregory Christie, *Bad News for Outlaws: The Remarkable Life of Bass Reeves, Deputy U.S. Marshal* (Carolrhoda).

Mark A. Norell and Lowell Dingus, *A Nest of Dinosaurs: The Story of Oviraptor* (Doubleday).

Naomi Shihab Nye, illustrations by Terre Maher, *A Maze Me: Poems for Girls* (Greenwillow).

Scott O'Dell, *Island of the Blue Dolphins* (Houghton Mifflin).

Scott O'Grady with Michael French, *Basher Five-Two: The True Story of F-16 Fighter Pilot Captain Scott O'Grady* (Doubleday).

Mary O'Hara, *My Friend Flicka* (HarperCollins).

Irene Gut Opdyke with Jennifer Armstrong, *In My Hands: Memories of a Holocaust Rescuer* (Knopf).

Kenneth Oppel, *Airborn* (Eos/HarperCollins).

Linda Sue Park, illustrations by Istvan Banyai, *Tap Dancing on the Roof: Sijo (Poems)* (Clarion); *Keeping Score* (Clarion).

Ruth Park, *Playing Beatie Bow* (Atheneum).

Rosanne Parry, *Heart of a Shepherd* (Random House).

Elizabeth Partridge, *John Lennon: All I Want Is the Truth* (Viking); *Marching for Freedom: Walk Together, Children, and Don't You Grow Weary* (Viking).

Katherine Paterson, *Bridge to Terabithia* (HarperCollins); *Flip-Flop Girl* (Dutton); *The Great Gilly Hopkins* (HarperCollins).

James Patterson, *The Angel Experiment: A Maximum Ride Novel* (Little, Brown).

Gary Paulsen, *Hatchet* (Simon & Schuster); *Lawn Boy* (Random House); *Guts: The True Stories behind* Hatchet *and the Brian Books* (Delacorte).

Philippa Pearce, *Tom's Midnight Garden* (HarperCollins).

Kit Pearson, *A Handful of Time* (Viking).

Richard Peck, *A Season of Gifts* (Dial); *A Year Down Yonder* (Dial).

Robert Newton Peck, *Hang for Treason* (Doubleday).

Lynne Rae Perkins, *All Alone in the Universe* (Greenwillow); *The Broken Cat* (Greenwillow).

Matt Phelan, *The Storm in the Barn* (Candlewick).

Licoln Peirce, *Big Nate: In a Class By Himself* (HarperCollins).

Dav Pilkey, *The Adventures of Captain Underpants* (Scholastic).

Daniel Pinkwater, *Looking for Bobowicz* (HarperCollins).

Terry Pratchett, *Nation* (HarperCollins); *The Wee Free Men* (HarperCollins).

Jack Prelutsky, illustrations by Brandon Dorman, *Be Glad Your Nose Is on Your Face and Other Poems: Some of the Best of Jack Prelutsky* (Greenwillow).

Jack Prelutsky, illustrations by James Stevenson, *Something Big Has Been Here* (Greenwillow); *My Dog May Be a Genius* (Greenwillow).

Philip Pullman, *The Golden Compass* (Knopf).

Marjorie Kinnan Rawlings, *The Yearling* (Collier).

Philip Reeve, *A Darkling Plain* (HarperCollins); *Mortal Engines* (HarperCollins).

Rick Riordan, *The Lightning Thief* (Disney/Hyperion).

Ken Roberts, illustrations by Leanne Franson, *The Thumb in the Box* (Groundwood).

Fred Rogers, *Going to the Dentist* (Putnam).

J. K. Rowling, illustrations by Mary GrandPré, *Harry Potter and the Sorcerer's Stone* (Scholastic).

Marisabina Russo, *Grandpa Abe* (Greenwillow).

Pam Muños Ryan, Peter Sís, *The Dreamer* (Scholastic).

Robert Sabuda and Matthew Reinhart, *Encyclopedia Prehistorica: Dinosaurs* (Candlewick).

Louis Sachar, *Holes* (Farrar, Straus and Giroux).

Antoine de Saint-Exupéry, *The Little Prince* (Harcourt).

Alice Schertle, illustrations by Petra Mathers, *Button Up!: Wrinkled Rhymes* (Harcourt).

Laura Amy Schlitz, *A Drowned Maiden's Hair* (Candlewick).

Laura Amy Schlitz, illustrations by Robert Byrd, *Good Masters! Sweet Ladies!: Voices from a Medieval Village* (Candlewick).

Brian Selznick, *The Invention of Hugo Cabret* (Scholastic).

Dr. Seuss, *Bartholomew and the Oobleck* (Random House).

Anna Sewell, *Black Beauty* (Puffin).

Margery Sharp, *The Rescuers* (Little, Brown).

Steve Sheinkin, *The Notorious Benedict Arnold: A True Story of Adventure, Heroism, & Treachery* (Flash Point/Roaring Brook).

Neal Shusterman, *The Schwa Was Here* (Dutton).

Joyce Sidman, illustrations by Rick Allen, *Dark Emperor & Other Poems of the Night* (Houghton Mifflin).

Seymour Simon, *Gorillas* (HarperCollins).

Seymour Simon and Nicole Fauteux, *Let's Try It Out* (Simon & Schuster).

Isaac Bashevis Singer, illustrations by Maurice Sendak, *Zlateh the Goat and Other Stories* (HarperCollins).

Marilyn Singer, illustrations by Anna Vojtech, *Tough Beginnings: How Baby Animals Survive* (Holt); illustrations by Josée Masse, *Mirror Mirror: A Book of Reversible Verse* (Dutton).

Peter Sís, *Starry Messenger* (Farrar, Straus and Giroux); *The Tree of Life: A Book Depicting the Life of Charles Darwin, Naturalist, Geologist, & Thinker* (Farrar, Straus and Giroux); *The Wall: Growing Up Behind the Iron Curtain* (Farrar, Straus and Giroux).

Roland Smith, *Peak* (Harcourt).

Lemony Snicket, illustrations by Brett Helquist, *The Bad Beginning* (HarperCollins).

Gary Soto, *Mercy on These Teenage Chimps* (Harcourt).

Elizabeth Speare, *The Witch of Blackbird Pond* (Houghton Mifflin).

Rebecca Stead, *When You Reach Me* (Random House).

Robert Louis Stevenson, *A Child's Garden of Verses* (Grolier); *Treasure Island* (Scribner).

Trenton Lee Stewart, illustrations by Carson Ellis, *The Mysterious Benedict Society* (Little, Brown).

Tanya Lee Stone, *Almost Astronauts: 13 Women Who Dared to Dream* (Candlewick).

Rosemary Sutcliff, *Warrior Scarlet* (Walck).

Shaun Tan, *The Arrival* (Scholastic).

Lauren Tarshis, *Emma-Jean Lazarus Fell Out of a Tree* (Dial).

Mildred D. Taylor, *Roll of Thunder, Hear My Cry* (Dial).

Peter Lane Taylor and Christos Nicola, *The Secret of Priest's Grotto: A Holocaust Survival Story* (Kar-Ben).

Catherine Thimmesh, *Lucy Long Ago: Uncovering the Mystery of Where We Came From* (Houghton Mifflin).

Kate Thompson, *The New Policeman* (Greenwillow).

J. R. R. Tolkien, *The Hobbit, or There and Back Again* (Houghton Mifflin).

P. L. Travers, illustrations by Mary Shepard, *Mary Poppins* (Harcourt).

Pamela S. Turner, photographs by Andy Comins, *The Frog Scientist* (Houghton Mifflin).

Judith Viorst, illustrations by Erik Blegvad, *The Tenth Good Thing about Barney* (Atheneum).

Sophie Webb, *My Season with Penguins: An Antarctic Journal* (Houghton Mifflin).

Elissa Brent Weissman, *The Trouble with Mark Hopper* (Dutton).

David Weitzman, *Pharaoh's Boat* (Houghton Mifflin).

Scott Westerfeld, illustrations by Keith Thompson, *Leviathan* (Simon & Schuster).

E. B. White, illustrations by Garth Williams, *Charlotte's Web* (HarperCollins).

T. H. White, *The Sword in the Stone* (Putnam).

The Whopping Great Big Bonkers Joke Book: Over 1000 Side-Splitting Jokes (Puffin).

Laura Ingalls Wilder, illustrations by Garth Williams, *Little House on the Prairie* (HarperCollins).

Rita Williams-Garcia, *One Crazy Summer* (Amistad).

Jacqueline Wilson, illustrations by Nick Sharratt, *Candyfloss* (Roaring Brook).

Judd Winick, *Pedro and Me* (Holt).

Virginia Euwer Wolff, *Make Lemonade* (Atheneum); *True Believer* (Atheneum).

Maryrose Wood, illustrations by Jon Klassen, *The Incorrigible Children of Ashton Place: The Mysterious Howling* (Balzer & Bray).

Jacqueline Woodson, *After Tupac & D Foster* (Putnam).

Tim Wynne-Jones, *Rex Zero and the End of the World* (Farrar, Straus and Giroux).

Gene Luen Yang, *American Born Chinese* (Roaring Brook).

Lisa Yee, *Millicent Min, Girl Genius* (Scholastic).

Jane Yolen, illustrations by Mark Teague, *How Do Dinosaurs Say Good Night?* (Blue Sky/Scholastic).

Part Four: Leaving Them Alone

Sherman Alexie, illustrations by Ellen Forney, *The Absolutely True Diary of a Part-Time Indian* (Little, Brown).

Laurie Halse Anderson, *Speak* (Farrar, Straus and Giroux).

Anonymous, *Go Ask Alice* (Prentice-Hall).

Judy Blume, *Forever . . .* (Atheneum).

Coe Booth, *Kendra* (Scholastic).

Robert Cormier, *The Chocolate War* (Knopf); *I Am the Cheese* (Knopf).

Sarah Dessen, *Just Listen* (Viking); *Lock and Key* (Viking); *The Truth about Forever* (Viking).

Sharon Dogar, *Annexed* (Houghton Mifflin).

S. E. Hinton, *The Outsiders* (Viking).

Hadley Irwin, *Abby, My Love* (Atheneum).

M. E. Kerr, *Dinky Hocker Shoots Smack!* (HarperCollins); *Gentlehands* (HarperCollins).

E. Lockhart, *The Disreputable History of Frankie Landau-Banks* (Hyperion).

Saci Lloyd, *The Carbon Diaries 2015* (Holiday House).

Janet McDonald, *Brother Hood* (Farrar, Straus and Giroux); *Chill Wind* (Farrar, Straus and Giroux); *Spellbound* (Farrar, Straus and Giroux).

Jaclyn Moriarty, *The Spell Book of Listen Taylor* (Scholastic).

Catherine Gilbert Murdock, *Dairy Queen* (Houghton Mifflin).

Walter Dean Myers, *Monster* (HarperCollins).

Jandy Nelson, *The Sky Is Everywhere* (Dial).

John Neufeld, *Lisa, Bright and Dark* (Phillips).

Richard Peck, *Are You in the House Alone?* (Viking); *Remembering the Good Times* (Delacorte).

Willo Davis Roberts, *Don't Hurt Laurie!* (Atheneum).

J. D. Salinger, *The Catcher in the Rye* (Little, Brown).

Sandra Scoppettone, *The Late Great Me* (Putnam).

Marcus Sedgwick, *Revolver* (Roaring Brook).

Francisco X. Stork, *Marcelo in the Real World* (Levine/Scholastic).

Nancy Werlin, *Black Mirror* (Dial); *Double Helix* (Dial); *Locked Inside* (Delacorte); *The Killer's Cousin* (Delacorte); *The Rules of Survival* (Dial).

Maia Wojciechowska, *Tuned Out* (HarperCollins).

FURTHER READING

Barbara Bader, *American Picturebooks from Noah's Ark to the Beast Within* (Macmillan, 1976).

Joan Bodger, *How the Heather Looks: A Joyous Journey to the British Sources of Children's Books* (Viking, 1965; McClelland and Stewart, 1999).

Kathleen T. Horning, *From Cover to Cover: Evaluating and Reviewing Children's Books* (HarperCollins, 2010).

Selma G. Lanes, *Through the Looking Glass: Further Adventures & Misadventures in the Realm of Children's Literature* (David R. Godine, 2006).

Leonard S. Marcus, ed., *Dear Genius: The Letters of Ursula Nordstrom* (HarperCollins, 1998).

———, *Minders of Make-Believe: Idealists, Entrepreneurs, and the Shaping of American Children's Literature* (Houghton Mifflin, 2008).

———, *The Wand in the Word: Conversations with Writers of Fantasy* (Candlewick, 2006).

———, *Ways of Telling: Conversations on the Art of the Picture Book* (Dutton, 2002).

Laura Miller, *The Magician's Book: A Skeptic's Adventures in Narnia* (Little, Brown, 2008).

Daniel Pennac, illustrations by Quentin Blake, *The Rights of the Reader* (Candlewick, 2008).

Maurice Sendak, *Caldecott & Co.: Notes on Books & Pictures* (Farrar, Straus and Giroux, 1988).

Anita Silvey, ed., *The Essential Guide to Children's Books and Their Creators* (Mariner, 2002).

Francis Spufford, *The Child That Books Built: A Life in Reading* (Holt, 2002).

NOTES ON CONTRIBUTORS

Editors

ROGER SUTTON, editor in chief of *The Horn Book*, earned a master's degree in library science from the University of Chicago and has worked as a children's librarian and a full-time book review editor. Roger Sutton has served as a judge for many children's book awards and frequently teaches and speaks about children's books.

MARTHA V. PARRAVANO, executive editor of *The Horn Book*, has worked as a children's librarian and bookseller. She has a master's degree in children's literature from Simmons College and has served on multiple children's book award committees.

Contributors

MARC ARONSON is a children's book editor and author of several acclaimed nonfiction books for young people, including *Sir Walter Ralegh and the Quest for El Dorado* and *Sugar Changed the World*.

DEIRDRE F. BAKER reviews children's books for the *Toronto Star* and teaches children's literature at the University of Toronto.

COE BOOTH is the author of the teen novels *Tyrell* and *Kendra*.

BRUCE BROOKS is the author of young adult novels including *Asylum for Nightface* and *Midnight Hour Encores*. *The Moves Make the Man* and *What Hearts* each received a Newbery Honor.

BETSY BYARS is the author of more than sixty books for young people, including the Blossom Family books, the Bingo Brown books, and the Herculeah Jones mysteries, as well as the easy readers *My Brother, Ant* and *The Golly Sisters Go West*. *The Summer of the Swans* won the Newbery Medal.

BETTY CARTER is professor emerita of children's and young adult literature at Texas Woman's University and a reviewer for *The Horn Book*.

SARAH DESSEN is the author of *That Summer*, *The Truth About Forever*, *Just Listen*, and *Along for the Ride*, among many other YA novels.

SARAH ELLIS, critic, reviewer, and author, teaches at Vermont College's MFA program in writing for children and young adults. Her latest novel, *Odd Man Out*, won the 2007 TD Canadian Children's Literature Award.

KITTY FLYNN is the online content editor and a reviewer for *The Horn Book*.

DANIELLE J. FORD is an associate professor of science education at the University of Delaware and a reviewer for *The Horn Book*.

RUSSELL FREEDMAN is the much-honored nonfiction author of more than fifty books for children, including *Lincoln: A Photobiography*, winner of a Newbery Medal; *Martha Graham: A Dancer's Life; Freedom Walkers: The Story of the Montgomery Bus Boycott*; and *Immigrant Kids*. Freedman was awarded the Laura Ingalls Wilder Medal for lifetime achievement in children's literature.

VIRGINIA HAMILTON is the author of such groundbreaking novels as *Zeely; The Planet of Junior Brown*; and *Sweet Whispers, Brother Rush*. She was the first African American writer to win the Newbery Medal, for *M. C. Higgins, the Great*, and the first children's writer to be honored with a MacArthur Fellowship. She died in 2002.

KEVIN HENKES is the creator of such beloved picture-book characters as Lilly (*Julius, the Baby of the World; Lilly's Purple Plastic Purse*), Owen, and Chrysanthemum. His novels include *Words of Stone* and *Olive's Ocean*, a Newbery Honor Book. His picture book *Kitten's First Full Moon* is the winner of a Caldecott Medal.

CHRISTINE HEPPERMANN is a freelance writer, former bookseller, and reviewer for *The Horn Book*.

DEBORAH HOPKINSON is an award-winning author of many historical fiction and nonfiction books, including *Apples to Oregon, Sky Boys*, and *Abe Lincoln Crosses a Creek*.

KATHLEEN T. HORNING is the director of the Cooperative Children's Book Center in Madison, Wisconsin. She is a former children's librarian and the author of the children's literature resource *From Cover to Cover: Evaluating and Reviewing Children's Books*.

MAEVE VISSER KNOTH, a reviewer and blogger, is also a librarian at the San Mateo County Library in California.

MEGAN LAMBERT is an instructor at the Center for the Study of Children's Literature at Simmons College, where she teaches undergraduate and graduate courses. Since 2001 she has also worked in the education department of the Eric Carle Museum of Picture Book Art.

JANE LANGTON is the author of the middle-grade fantasy novels the Hall Family Chronicles. *The Fledgling* received a Newbery Honor.

MOLLY LEACH is a book designer. Among the books she has designed are *The Stinky Cheese Man* and *Math Curse* by Jon Scieszka and Lane Smith; *Baby! Talk!* by Penny Gentieu; and the complete Puffin library of Roald Dahl books.

ROBERT LIPSYTE is the author of the young adult classic *The Contender* and its sequels.

JOANNA RUDGE LONG is a former editor of *Kirkus Reviews*, a frequent lecturer on children's literature, and a reviewer for *The Horn Book*.

LOIS LOWRY is the author of *Number the Stars* and *The Giver,* both winners of the Newbery Medal.

DIANA LUTZ is a science writer, reviewer, and the former editor of *Muse,* a nonfiction magazine for children.

ANNE SCOTT MACLEOD is a historian, a professor emerita at the University of Maryland, and the author of *American Childhood: Essays on Children's Literature of the Nineteenth and Twentieth Centuries.*

GREGORY MAGUIRE is a founding co-director of Children's Literature New England, Inc., and an author of books for children and adults, including *What-the-Dickens: The Story of a Rogue Tooth Fairy* and *Wicked,* which inspired a Broadway musical.

MARGARET MAHY is New Zealand's most highly regarded writer for children. Her picture books include *The Great White Man-Eating Shark* and *Bubble Trouble;* her novels include *The Changeover, The Tricksters, Memory,* and *24 Hours.* She is the winner of the Hans Christian Andersen Award.

JANET MCDONALD is the author of the adult memoir *Project Girl* and several young adult novels, including *Off-Color* and *Spellbound.* She died in 2007.

NAOMI SHIHAB NYE is a poet and author of picture books and novels, including *Sitti's Secrets* and *Habibi,* and is the editor of the acclaimed poetry anthologies *This Same Sky: A Collection of Poems from Around the World; 19 Varieties of Gazelle: Poems of the Middle East;* and *A Maze Me: Poems for Girls.*

KATHERINE PATERSON is the author of *Bridge to Terabithia* and *Jacob Have I Loved,* both winners of the Newbery Medal. She has also received the Hans Christian Andersen Medal and the Astrid Lindgren Memorial Award. In 2010 she was named the second National Ambassador for Young People's Literature.

MITALI PERKINS is the author of several novels set in her native India or about the Indian-American experience, including *Secret Keeper* and *Monsoon Summer.*

LOLLY ROBINSON teaches children's literature at Harvard University's department of education and works as a designer at *The Horn Book.*

ALICE SCHERTLE is a poet and the author of over forty books for children, including *We; Little Blue Truck;* and several poetry collections.

DEAN SCHNEIDER is a reviewer for *Kirkus Reviews* and teaches seventh and eighth grade in Nashville, Tennessee.

JON SCIESZKA is the author of many books, including *The Stinky Cheese Man,* a Caldecott Honor Book, and *The True Story of the 3 Little Pigs!.* In 2008 he was named the first National Ambassador for Young People's Literature.

MAURICE SENDAK is the winner of the Caldecott Medal for *Where the Wild Things Are*. He has also received the Hans Christian Andersen Medal, the Laura Ingalls Wilder Award, the National Medal of Arts, and the Astrid Lindgren Memorial Award.

GINEE SEO is a children's book editor.

LANE SMITH is the author and illustrator of *Madam President* and *John, Paul, George & Ben*. He is also the illustrator of *The Stinky Cheese Man*, a Caldecott Honor Book; *The True Story of the 3 Little Pigs!*; and *Science Verse*.

ROBIN SMITH teaches second grade in Nashville, Tennessee, and is a reviewer for *Kirkus Reviews* and *The Horn Book*.

VICKY SMITH is the children's book editor of *Kirkus Reviews* and a former public librarian and reviewer for *The Horn Book*.

DEBORAH STEVENSON is the editor of the review journal *The Bulletin of the Center for Children's Books* and an assistant professor in the library school at the University of Illinois at Urbana-Champaign.

CYNTHIA VOIGT is best known for her series of Tillerman family novels, including *Dicey's Song*, winner of the Newbery Medal. She is also the winner of the Margaret A. Edwards Award for her contributions to young adult literature.

NANCY WERLIN is the author of many young adult novels, including *Impossible, The Rules of Survival*, and *Are You Alone on Purpose?*

VIRGINIA EUWER WOLFF is the author of the young adult verse novels *Make Lemonade, True Believer*, and *This Full House*.

MARGOT ZEMACH is the illustrator of dozens of picture books, including *It Could Always Be Worse* and *The Little Red Hen*. She is the winner of the Caldecott Medal for *Duffy and the Devil*.

CHARLOTTE ZOLOTOW is a former editor of children's books and the author of many picture books, including *Over and Over, William's Doll*, and *Mr. Rabbit and the Lovely Present*, a Caldecott Honor Book.

CREDITS AND PERMISSIONS

READING TO THEM

p. 1: Illustration from *Everywhere Babies* by Susan Meyers, illustrated by Marla Frazee. Illustrations copyright © 2001 Marla Frazee. Reprinted by permission of Houghton Mifflin Harcourt Publishing Company. All rights reserved.

p. 11: Cover from *Good Night, Gorilla* by Peggy Rathmann reprinted with permission of Penguin Group USA.

p. 12: Excerpt from *Blue Hat, Green Hat* written and illustrated by Sandra Boynton, copyright © 1984. Used with permission of Little Simon, an imprint of Simon & Schuster Children's Publishing.

pp. 14, 18, 21: *Here Comes Mother Goose*. Illustration © 1999 Rosemary Wells. Text selections © 1999 Iona Opie. Reproduced by permission of Candlewick Press.

pp. 18–19: Excerpt by Leonard S. Marcus from *Mary Engelbreit's Mother Goose*. Used by permission of Harper-Collins Publishers.

p. 38: Cover illustrations and text for *First the Egg* by Laura Vaccaro Seeger, © Laura Vaccaro Seeger, used with permission of Roaring Brook Press.

p. 39: Excerpt, illustration, and cover from *Mr. Gumpy's Outing* by John Burningham. Copyright © 1970 John Burningham. Reprinted by permission of Henry Holt and Company, LLC.

pp. 45–47: Illustrations from *The Three Wishes* by Margot Zemach. Copyright © 1986 Margot Zemach. Reprinted by permission of Farrar, Straus and Giroux, LLC.

pp. 49–50: Illustration from *Baby Says* Copyright © 1988 John Steptoe. Used by permission of HarperCollins Publishers.

pp. 54–56: From *The Stinky Cheese Man and Other Fairly Stupid Tales* Jon Scieszka, illustrated by Lane Smith, designed by Molly Leach. Text © 1992 Jon Scieszka. Illustrations © 1992 Lane Smith. Used by permission of Viking Penguin, A Division of Penguin Young Readers Group. All rights reserved.

p. 58: From *Math Curse* by Jon Scieszka, illustrated by Lane Smith, designed by Molly Leach. Text © 1995 Jon Scieszka. Illustrations © 1995 Lane Smith. Used by permission of Viking Penguin, A Division of Penguin Young Readers Group. All rights reserved.

p. 60: Photograph of Maurice Sendak copyright © John Dugdale.

p. 62: Illustration from *Outside Over There* by Maurice Sendak. Copyright © 1981 Maurice Sendak. Used by permission of HarperCollins Publishers.

p. 66: Cover from *Go Away, Big Green Monster!* Ed Emberley. Copyright © Ed Emberley, reprinted with permission of Little, Brown and Company.

p. 72: Illustration by Melissa Sweet, copyright © 2009 Melissa Sweet, from *The Sleepy Little Alphabet: A Bedtime Story from Alphabet Town* by Judy Sierra and illustrated by Melissa Sweet. Used by permission of Alfred A. Knopf, an imprint of Random House Children's Books, a division of Random House, Inc.

p. 75: *Runaway Bunny* Copyright © 1942 Harper & Row Publishers. Text copyright renewed 1970 Roberta Brown Rauch. Used by permission of HarperCollins Publishers.

p. 81: Illustrations from *The Three Pigs* by David Wiesner. Copyright © 2001 David Wiesner. Reprinted by permission of Clarion Books, an imprint of Houghton Mifflin Harcourt Publishing Company. All rights reserved.

p. 84: Art from *I See Myself* by Vicki Cobb, illustrated by Julia Gorton. Text and illustration copyright © 2002, used by permission of HarperCollins Publishers.

p. 84: Excerpt from *What Is Science* by Rebecca Dotlitch. Copyright © 1999, 2006 Rebecca Kai Dotlitch. Reprinted by permission of Henry Holt and Company, LLC.

p. 85: Excerpt from *I Fall Down* by Vicki Cobb, illustrated by Julia Gorton. Text and illustration copyright © 2004, used by permission of HarperCollins Publishers.

READING WITH THEM

p. 93: Illustration from *Sweet Jasmine! Nice Jackson!* by Robie Harris, illustrated by Michael Emberley. Illustration copyright © 2004 Michael Emberley. Used with permission of Margaret K. McElderry Books, an imprint of Simon & Schuster Children's Publishing.

pp. 98–99: From *The Cat in the Hat* by Dr. Seuss, Trademark™ and copyright © Dr. Seuss Enterprises, L.P. 1957, renewed 1985. Used by permission of Random House Children's Books, a division of Random House, Inc.

pp. 99–101: Excerpt from *Little Bear* by Else Holmelund Minarik, illustrated by Maurice Sendak. Copyright © 1957 Else Holmelund Minarik. Used by permission of HarperCollins Publishers.

p. 100: Illustration from *Little Bear* by Else Holmelund Minarik, illustrated by Maurice Sendak. Copyright © 1957, 1985 Maurice Sendak. Used by permision of HarperCollins Publishers.

p. 102: "Fossil Finds" by Rebecca Kai Dotlich. Copyright © 2005 Rebecca Kai Dotlich. First appeared in *Days to Celebrate*, edited by Lee Bennett Hopkins, published by Greenwillow Books. Reprinted by permission of Curtis Brown, Ltd.

p. 112: Illustration from *Captain Underpants and the Wrath of the Wicked Wedgie Woman* by Dav Pilkey. Copyright © 2001 Dav Pilkey. Used by permission of Scholastic Inc./The Blue Sky Press.

READING ON THEIR OWN

p. 117: Illustration from *Camp Babymouse* by Jennifer L. Holm and Matthew Holm, copyright © 2007 Jennifer Holm and Matthew Holm. Used by permission of Random House Children's Books, a division of Random House, Inc.

p. 135: Illustration by Pauline Baynes. Copyright © C. S. Lewis Pte. Ltd. 1950. Reprinted by permission.

p. 161: Ilustration from *Sit on a Potato Pan, Otis!* by John Agee. Copyright © 1999 John Agee. Reprinted by permission of Farrar, Straus and Giroux, LLC.

p. 189: From *John Lennon: All I Want Is the Truth* by Elizabeth Partridge, copyright © 2005 Elizabeth Partridge, text. Used by permission of Viking Children's Books, A Division of Penguin Young Readers Group, A Member of Penguin Group (USA) Inc. All rights reserved.

p. 204: Photograph of Russell Freedman copyright © Evans Chan.

p. 211: Cover of *The Frog Scientist* by Pamela S. Turner, photographs by Andy Comins. Photographs copyright © 2009 Andy Comins. Reprinted by permission of Houghton Mifflin Harcourt Publishing Company. All rights reserved.

p. 220: Illustration from *Prehistoric, Actual Size* by Steve Jenkins. Copyright © 2005 Steve Jenkins. Reprinted by permission of Houghton Mifflin Harcourt Publishing Company. All rights reserved.

p. 232: Excerpt reprinted by permission of the publishers and the Trustees of Amherst College from *The Poems of Emily Dickinson*, Thomas H. Johnson, ed., Cambridge, Mass.: The Belknap Press of Harvard University Press, Copyright © 1951, 1955, 1979, 1983 the President and Fellows of Harvard College.

p. 263: Photograph of Jon Scieszka copyright © Marty Umans.

pp. 272, 287: *It's So Amazing!* by Robie H. Harris, illustrations by Michael Emberley. Text © 1999 Bee Productions, Inc. Illustrations © 1999 Bird Productions, Inc. Reproduced by permission of Candlewick Press.

p. 283: Photograph of Katherine Paterson copyright © Samantha Loomis Paterson.

LEAVING THEM ALONE

p. 287 From *The Absolutely True Diary of a Part-time Indian* by Sherman Alexie. Copyright © 2007 Sherman Alexie. Illustrations copyright 2007 by Ellen Forney, used by permission of Little, Brown and Company.

p. 295: Cover of *Monster* © 1999 Christopher Myers. Cover © 2001 HarperCollins Publishers, Inc. Used by permission of HarperCollins Publishers.

p. 306: Photograph of Sarah Dessen copyright © KPO Photo.

p. 310: Cover of *Just Listen* by Sarah Dessen used with permission of Penguin Group USA.

INDEX